EDEXCEL
A LEVEL
HISTORY

Active Book included

CW00536272

Paper 3:
The witch craze in Britain, Europe and North America, c1580–c1750

Oliver Bullock
Series editor: Rosemary Rees

ALWAYS LEARNING

PEARSON

Published by Pearson Education Limited, 80 Strand, London, WC2R 0RL

www.pearsonschoolsandfecolleges.co.uk

Copies of official specifications for all Edexcel qualifications may be found on the website:
www.edexcel.com

Text © Pearson Education Limited 2016

Designed by Elizabeth Arnoux for Pearson

Typeset and illustrated by Phoenix Photosetting, Chatham, Kent

Produced by Out of House Publishing

Original illustrations © Pearson Education Limited 2016

Cover design by Malena Wilson-Max for Pearson

Cover photo/illustration © Corbis/Bettmann

The rights of Oliver Bullock to be identified as author of this work have been asserted by him in
accordance with the Copyright, Designs and Patents Act 1988

First published 2016

21

10

British Library Cataloguing in Publication Data
A catalogue record for this book is available from the British Library

ISBN 978 1 447 985501

Printed in Great Britain by Bell and Bain Ltd, Glasgow

Websites

Pearson Education Limited is not responsible for the content of any external internet sites. It is essential
for tutors to preview each website before using it in class so as to ensure that the URL is still accurate,
relevant and appropriate. We suggest that tutors bookmark useful websites and consider enabling
students to access them through the school/college intranet.

A note from the publisher

In order to ensure that this resource offers high-quality support for the associated Pearson
qualification, it has been through a review process by the awarding body. This process confirms
that this resource fully covers the teaching and learning content of the specification or part of
a specification at which it is aimed. It also confirms that it demonstrates an appropriate balance
between the development of subject skills, knowledge and understanding, in addition to preparation
for assessment.

Endorsement does not cover any guidance on assessment activities or processes (e.g. practice
questions or advice on how to answer assessment questions) included in the resource nor does it
prescribe any particular approach to the teaching or delivery of a related course.

While the publishers have made every attempt to ensure that advice on the qualification and its
assessment is accurate, the official specification and associated assessment guidance materials are
the only authoritative source of information and should always be referred to for definitive guidance.

Pearson examiners have not contributed to any sections in this resource relevant to examination
papers for which they have responsibility.

Examiners will not use endorsed resources as a source of material for any assessment set by Pearson.

Endorsement of a resource does not mean that the resource is required to achieve this Pearson
qualification, nor does it mean that it is the only suitable material available to support the qualification,
and any resource lists produced by the awarding body shall include this and other appropriate
resources.

Contents

Paper 3

How to use this book

STRUCTURE

This book covers Paper 3, Option 33: The witch craze in Britain, Europe and North America, c1580–c1750 of the Edexcel A Level qualification.

You will also need to study a Paper 1 and a Paper 2 option and produce coursework in order to complete your qualification. All Paper 1/2 options are covered by other textbooks in this series.

EXAM SUPPORT

The examined assessment for Paper 3 requires you to answer questions from three sections. Throughout this book there are exam-style questions in all three section styles for you to practise your examination skills.

Section A contains a compulsory question that will assess your source analysis and evaluation skills.

> **A Level Exam-Style Question Section A**
>
> **Read Source 5 before you answer this question.**
>
> Assess the value of the source for revealing popular attitudes to witches and sceptical opinion in late 16th- and early 17th-century England.
>
> Explain your answer, using the source, the information given about its origin and your own knowledge about the historical context. (20 marks)
>
> **Tip**
> *Ensure you tackle both popular attitudes and sceptical opinion, as well as providing context to the source.*

Section B contains a choice of essay questions that will look at your understanding of the studied period in depth.

> **A Level Exam-Style Question Section B**
>
> To what extent was the North Berwick witch-hunt in the years 1590–91 influenced by Gilly Duncan's confession? (20 marks)
>
> **Tip**
> *You should discuss Gilly Duncan's confession, as well as other factors such as the influence of events in Denmark, and weigh up their respective influence.*

Section C will again give you a choice of essay questions but these will assess your understanding of the period in breadth.

> **A Level Exam-Style Question Section C**
>
> To what extent did the coming of the age of science and reason result in the end of a belief in magic and witchcraft in the years c1580–c1750? (20 marks)
>
> **Tip**
> *The decline of witchcraft was not steady, and it should be noted that the speed of decline was faster in the second half of the period.*

The Preparing for your exams sections at the end of this book contains sample answers of different standards, with comments on how they could be improved.

FEATURES
Extend your knowledge

These features contain additional information that will help you gain a deeper understanding to the topic. This could be a short biography of an important person, extra background information about an event, an alternative interpretation, or even a research idea that you could follow up. Information in these boxes is not essential to your exam success, but still provides insights of value.

> **EXTEND YOUR KNOWLEDGE**
>
> **The writings of Frederick Förner**
> Förner was well known as an author on theology and witchcraft, and his works all point towards his obsession with suppressing Protestant heresy.
>
> He is especially remembered for his 1626 work on witchcraft, *Panoplia Armaturae Dei* (Armour of God), but he wrote widely on a number of subjects. He was especially interested in history, and in *Relatio Historico-Parenetica* he shows himself to be a strong supporter of the Counter-Reformation by describing church properties converted to secular use after the Reformation. This work was intended to encourage Ferdinand II to enforce the Edict of Restitution, authorising the forced conversion of Protestants, in the city of Nuremberg.

Knowledge check activities

These activities are designed to check that you have understood the material that you have just studied. They might also ask you questions about the sources and extracts in the section to check that you have studied and analysed them thoroughly.

ACTIVITY
KNOWLEDGE CHECK

The impact of revolution and revolt

1 Why was Sir Edmund Andros resented by the people of Massachusetts? Why did he cause the revolt of 1689?

2 Why did the Glorious Revolution in England cause problems in New England?

3 Why did weakened authority make a witch-hunt more likely?

Summary activities

At the end of each chapter, you will find summary activities. These are tasks designed to help you think about the key topic you have just studied as a whole. They may involve selecting and organising key information or analysing how things changed over time. You might want to keep your answers to these questions safe – they are handy for revision.

ACTIVITY
SUMMARY

Society in the 17th century

1 Create a graph showing the major changes in human understanding and the universe between c1580 and c1750. The x-axis should denote time, and the y-axis should represent periods of significant change. From this you should be able to establish when the most significant changes took place.

2 Choose three changes that you feel are the most noteworthy, and explain why they are important.

3 Does your graph support the view that the Scientific Revolution and an increased understanding of human knowledge contributed to the decline of magic and witchcraft? Explain your answer.

Thinking Historically activities

These activities are found throughout the book, and are designed to develop your understanding of history, especially around the key concepts of evidence, interpretations, causation and change. Each activity is designed to challenge a conceptual barrier that might be holding you back. This is linked to a map of conceptual barriers developed by experts. You can look up the map and find out which barrier each activity challenges by downloading the progression map from this website: www.pearsonschools.co.uk/historyprogressionsapproach.

progression map reference

THINKING HISTORICALLY Evidence (6b)

Reading secondary sources

1 Read Extract 1.

  a) What is weak about this claim?

  b) What could be added to it to make it stronger?

2 Read Extract 2.

  a) Is this an argument? If yes, what makes it one?

  b) How might this argument be strengthened?

3 Read Extract 3.

  a) How have they expanded their explanation to make the claim stronger?

  b) Can you explain why this is the strongest claim of the three extracts?

4 What elements make a historian's claims strong?

Getting the most from your online ActiveBook

This book comes with three years' access to ActiveBook* – an online, digital version of your textbook. Follow the instructions printed on the inside front cover to start using your ActiveBook.

Your ActiveBook is the perfect way to personalise your learning as you progress through your A Level History course. You can:

- access your content online, anytime, anywhere

- use the inbuilt highlighting and annotation tools to personalise the content and make it really relevant to you.

Highlight tool – use this to pick out key terms or topics so you are ready and prepared for revision.

Annotations tool – use this to add your own notes, for example links to your wider reading, such as websites or other files. Or, make a note to remind yourself about work that you need to do.

*For new purchases only. If the access code has already been revealed, it may no longer be valid. If you have bought this textbook secondhand, the code may already have been used by the first owner of the book.

Introduction
A Level History

WHY HISTORY MATTERS

History is about people and people are complex, fascinating, frustrating and a whole lot of other things besides. This is why history is probably the most comprehensive and certainly one of the most intriguing subjects there is. History can also be inspiring and alarming, heartening and disturbing, a story of progress and civilisation and of catastrophe and inhumanity.

History's importance goes beyond the subject's intrinsic interest and appeal. Our beliefs and actions, our cultures, institutions and ways of living, our languages and means of making sense of ourselves are all shaped by the past. If we want to fully understand ourselves now, and to understand our possible futures, we have no alternative but to think about history.

History is a discipline as well as a subject matter. Making sense of the past develops qualities of mind that are valuable to anyone who wants to seek the truth and think clearly and intelligently about the most interesting and challenging intellectual problem of all: other people. Learning history is learning a powerful way of knowing.

WHAT IS HISTORY?

History is a way of constructing knowledge about the world through research, interpretation, argument and debate.

Building historical knowledge involves identifying the traces of the past that exist in the present – in people's memories, in old documents, photographs and other remains, and in objects and artefacts ranging from bullets and lipsticks, to field systems and cities. Historians interrogate these traces and *ask questions* that transform traces into *sources of evidence* for knowledge claims about the past.

Historians aim to understand what happened in the past by *explaining why* things happened as they did. Explaining why involves trying to understand past people and their beliefs, intentions and actions. It also involves explaining the causes and evaluating the effects of large-scale changes in the past and exploring relationships between what people aimed to do, the contexts that shaped what was possible and the outcomes and consequences of actions.

Historians also aim to *understand change* in the past. People, states of affairs, ideas, movements and civilisations come into being in time, grow, develop, and ultimately decline and disappear. Historians aim to identify and compare change and continuity in the past, to measure the rate at which things change and to identify the types of change that take place. Change can be slow or sudden. It can also be understood as progressive or regressive – leading to the improvement or worsening of a situation or state of affairs. How things change and whether changes are changes for the better are two key issues that historians frequently debate.

Figure 1 Fragment of a black granite statue possibly portraying the Roman politician Mark Antony.

Debate is the essence of history. Historians write arguments to support their knowledge claims and historians argue with each other to test and evaluate interpretations of the past. Historical knowledge itself changes and develops. On the one hand, new sources of knowledge and new methods of research cause *historical interpretations* to change. On the other hand, the questions that historians ask change with time and new questions produce new answers. Although the past is dead and gone, the interpretation of the past has a past, present and future.

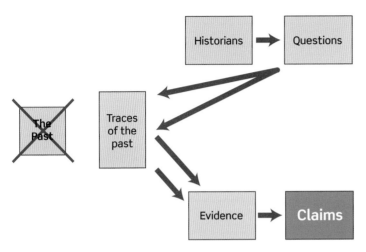

Figure 2 Constructing knowledge about the past.

THE CHALLENGES OF LEARNING HISTORY

Like all other Advanced Level subjects, A Level history is difficult – that is why it is called 'advanced'. Your Advanced Level studies will build on knowledge and understanding of history that you developed at GCSE and at Key Stage 3 – ideas like 'historical sources', 'historical evidence' and 'cause', for example. You will need to do a lot of reading and writing to progress in history. Most importantly, you will need to do a lot of thinking, and thinking about your thinking. This book aims to support you in developing both your knowledge and your understanding.

History is challenging in many ways. On the one hand, it is challenging to build up the range and depth of knowledge that you need to understand the past at an advanced level. Learning

about the past involves mastering new and unfamiliar concepts arising from the past itself (such as the Inquisition, Laudianism, *Volksgemeinschaft*) and building up levels of knowledge that are both detailed and well organised. This book covers the key content of the topics that you are studying for your examination and provides a number of features to help you build and organise what you know – for example, diagrams, timelines and definitions of key terms. You will need to help yourself too, of course, adding to your knowledge through further reading, building on the foundations provided by this book.

Another challenge is to develop understandings of the discipline of history. You will have to learn to think historically about evidence, cause, change and interpretations and also to write historically, in a way that develops clear and supported argument.

Historians think with evidence in ways that differ from how we often think in everyday life. In history, as Figure 2 shows, we cannot go and 'see for ourselves' because the past no longer exists. Neither can we normally rely on 'credible witnesses' to tell us 'the truth' about 'what happened'. People in the past did not write down 'the truth' for our benefit. They often had clear agendas when creating the traces that remain and, as often as not, did not themselves know 'the truth' about complex historical events.

A root of the word 'history' is the Latin word *historia*, one of whose meanings is 'enquiry' or 'finding out'. Learning history means learning to ask questions and interrogate traces, and then to reason about what the new knowledge you have gained means. This book draws on historical scholarship for its narrative and contents. It also draws on research on the nature of historical thinking and on the challenges that learning history can present for students. Throughout the book you will find 'Thinking Historically' activities designed to support the development of your thinking.

You will also find – as you would expect given the nature of history – that the book is full of questions. This book aims to help you build your understandings of the content, contexts and concepts that you will need to advance both your historical knowledge and your historical understanding, and to lay strong foundations for the future development of both.

Dr Arthur Chapman
Institute of Education
University College London

The witch craze in Britain, Europe and North America, c1580–c1750

The witch craze in Britain, Europe and North America, c1580–c1750

SOURCE 1

Two witches conspire to conjure up storms. From *Tractatus von den boesen weiben, die man nennet die hexen* (Tract on the evil women called witches), published in Germany in 1508.

Source 1 depicts a well-entrenched image in the minds of Europeans in the 16th and 17th centuries. Two witches use their magical powers, together with some select ingredients placed into a cauldron, to cause damage, in this case by conjuring up storms. Fear of witches and witchcraft had existed since the days of the Old Testament, and probably even earlier, but in the Early Modern period this fear peaked. For many years, witches had been accused of causing damage to property, livestock and people, but across the European continent in the Middle Ages, a new fear began to emerge: that of the **diabolical pact.** This soon spread to England's colonies in North America.

1590	1590 – The North Berwick witch craze begins
1599	1599 – Samuel Harsnett publishes *A Discovery of the Fraudulent Practises of John Darrel*
1609	1609 – Johannes Kepler publishes *Astronomia Nova*
1623	1623 – John George Fuchs von Dornheim becomes Prince-Bishop of Bamberg, triggering a witch craze
1656	1656 – Thomas Ady's sceptical work, *A Candle in the Dark*, is published
1662	1662 – The Demon Drummer of Tedworth case
1687	1687 – Isaac Newton publishes *Principia Mathematica*
1712	1712 – The case of Jane Wenham

1584

1584 – Reginald Scot publishes his sceptical work, *The Discoverie of Witchcraft*

1597

1597 – James I publishes *Daemonologie*

1597 – Thomas Darling accuses Alice Goodridge in the fraudulent 'Boy of Burton' case

1604

1604 – The Witchcraft Act is passed in England

1612

1612 – The Lancashire witch trials take place

1645

1645 – The East Anglian witch craze begins

1660

1660 – The Royal Society is founded

1677

1677 – John Webster's *The Displaying of Supposed Witchcraft* is published

1692

1692 – The Salem witch trials take place

Diabolical pact
A pact made with the Devil. According to tradition, a witch who enters into the pact usually offers their soul in exchange for wealth or power.

This book explores both why the fear of witchcraft was so widespread, and also why it fell into decline. The 16th and 17th centuries were volatile, and religious clashes, as well as social and economic changes, lay behind many accusations of witchcraft. In these centuries, however, two factors triggered a change in attitudes towards magic.

- Understanding of the natural world, and in particular man's place within it, was changing. The Scientific Revolution gained pace in these centuries, and figures such as Copernicus, Galileo, Kepler and Newton made breakthroughs that proved that God did not necessarily control events on Earth on a day-to-day basis. Human understanding and knowledge more generally was enhanced by Bacon, Hobbes, Locke and the founding members of the Royal Society. These issues are explored more widely in Chapter 2.

- With an increased number of witchcraft cases reported, it was inevitable that more fraudulent cases would be discovered. People desperate for money, fame or those who were simply bored claimed to be possessed or to have witnessed the work of witches. A number of sceptical publications were also produced that questioned the reality of witchcraft. These are detailed in Chapter 1.

Chapters 3–7 are dedicated to five case studies from Britain, Germany and North America. Each of the witch-hunts featured had complex causes and took place in unique circumstances, but all ended relatively abruptly, often when outside forces became involved.

The extent of witchcraft in Britain, Europe and North America

Historians have estimated that as many as 100,000 people were executed for witchcraft across Europe with around 200,000 facing charges, although executions were much more common on the continent than in Britain. By 1700, the practice of witch-hunting had virtually died out in Britain, and only a few isolated cases are documented from the late 17th century, before the repeal of witchcraft legislation in Britain in 1736. However, in other parts of Europe, witch trials continued well into the late 18th century.

Witch-hunts took place in most parts of Europe, and a large proportion took place in German-speaking territories. There is evidence of witch-hunts in areas as diverse as Sweden, Iceland and southern Spain, although some regions, such as southern Italy, were barely affected. Despite the large number of persecutions in Europe, no more than 1,000 executions took place in England, with several hundred more in Scotland. In Scotland, 84 percent of those accused in witchcraft trials were women, and in some countries this proportion was even higher. Outside Europe, the executions of 20 people accused of witchcraft in Salem, Massachusetts, in 1692–93 stand out as unusual, as the craze had already diminished considerably in Europe and the North American colonies and the people of Salem were exposed to some of the same rational and scientific ideas as Europeans. The peak of witch-hunting in the 16th and 17th centuries also coincided with the so-called 'Little Ice Age', a period of distinct cooling that caused widespread agricultural catastrophe. Many of the witch-hunts explored in this book took place in the context of poor weather and difficult harvests.

The majority of witches, particularly in England, were hanged rather than burned, and the idea that witches could fly or transform themselves into other beings was rarely put forward. The broomstick, made famous in later fiction, is only mentioned in one English witch trial.

3.1

Changing attitudes to witchcraft in Britain

KEY QUESTIONS

- Why did sceptical attitudes towards witchcraft grow and develop in the years c1580–c1750?
- What was the impact of notable sceptical publications on attitudes to witchcraft?

INTRODUCTION

Types of witchcraft

By 1580, a distinction could be made between two different types of witchcraft in Britain.

- The well-established view was that witches were capable of committing evil acts against people, farm animals or crops by using supernatural powers or interfering with nature. This power was commonly referred to as **maleficium**. It was believed that the victims of *maleficium* had been caught by the gaze of a witch, or more often than not cursed by them.

- With the publication of the influential *Malleus Maleficarum* (Hammer of Witches) by two German Dominican friars in 1486, a belief that witches held a covenant with the Devil became an obsession for witch-hunters. The *Malleus* acted as a guidebook for witch-hunters, and set out the precise steps that were required in order to secure the conviction of a witch (see Source 1). The idea that witches held a pact with the Devil spread quickly throughout Europe, and the English were relatively late in adopting the idea, although by 1580 the belief was well established. The book was indirectly responsible for the deaths of thousands of people accused of witchcraft in Europe.

SOURCE

From the *Malleus Maleficarum* (1486).

Now the method of profession [becoming a witch] is twofold. One is a solemn ceremony, like a solemn vow. The other is private, and can be made to the devil at any hour alone. The first method is when witches meet together in the conclave on a set day, and the devil appears to them in the assumed body of a man, and urges them to keep faith with him, promising them worldly prosperity and length of life; and they recommend a novice to his acceptance. And the devil asks whether she will abjure the Faith, and forsake the holy Christian religion and the worship of the Anomalous Woman (for so they call the Most Blessed Virgin Mary), and never venerate the Sacraments; and if he finds the novice or disciple willing, then the devil stretches out his hand, and so does the novice, and she swears with upraised hand to keep that covenant. And when this is done, the devil at once adds that this is not enough; and when the disciple asks what more must be done, the devil demands the following oath of homage to himself: that she give herself to him, body and soul, for ever, and do her utmost to bring others of both sexes into his power. He adds, finally, that she is to make certain unguents [ointments] from the bones and limbs of children, especially those who have been baptized; by all which means she will be able to fulfil all her wishes with his help.

1486 – *Malleus Maleficarum* published

1563 – Second Witchcraft Act

1597 – The Boy of Burton case

1604 – Third Witchcraft Act

| 1480 | 1490 | 1540 | 1550 | 1560 | 1570 | 1580 | 1590 | 1600 | 1620 | 1630 |

1542 – First Witchcraft Act

1584 – Reginald Scot's *The Discoverie of Witchcraft* published

1599 – Samuel Harsnett's *A Discovery of the Fraudulent Practises of John Darrel* published

1634 – The Pendle Swindle

EXTEND YOUR KNOWLEDGE

Malleus Maleficarum

Fear of witchcraft had been commonplace in the medieval Catholic Church, and in 1484, Pope Innocent VIII issued a proclamation that vigorously denounced the work of witches, and called for measures against witchcraft, particularly in Germany. Unpredictable weather, resulting in poor harvests and starvation, led to increasing accusations in Germany that witches were to blame.

Two members of the Inquisition – the Catholic judicial institution designed to clamp down on heretics – Heinrich Kramer and Jacob Sprenger, followed the pope's instructions and produced the *Malleus Maleficarum* in 1486. It immediately became the chief source of information about the activities of witches, and all future handbooks on the matter looked back to the *Malleus* for inspiration.

The *Malleus* is divided into three parts. The first part explains the effects of witchcraft, and goes to great lengths to explain why women are much more likely to be witches than men, justified by the fact that women are more impressionable, have 'slippery tongues' and feeble minds. The second part explains the different types of witchcraft and types of investigation that can be carried out. The third part uses carefully chosen references to Scripture to justify the unusual legal proceedings that were deemed to be necessary in cases of witchcraft.

Witchcraft and the Reformation

The *Malleus* was a document clearly intended to counter what had been seen as a long-standing threat to the Catholic Church. With the coming of the Reformation, suspicion between Catholics and Protestants led to further distrust and accusations from both sides that the other fostered witches. Born in Germany, Martin Luther (1483–1546) was instrumental in starting the Protestant Reformation in Europe in 1517 when he openly criticised the Catholic Church's focus on salvation through good works and rituals rather than through faith alone. A Protestant Reformation took hold in England in the 16th century, when Henry VIII broke away from the Church in Rome and his daughter, Elizabeth, established a Protestant Church settlement in 1559 that held that an individual relationship with God through prayer was more important than the **sacraments** of the Catholic Church. Although Luther and other early Protestants had rejected Catholic theology, a belief in the Devil and witchcraft was still central to Protestant faith. In the 16th and 17th centuries, a more extreme form of Protestantism emerged in the British Isles, known as Puritanism. Puritans believed in a basic, stripped down version of the Protestant religion, as they viewed certain outward celebrations of faith, such as excessive singing in church, as ungodly and distracting. A number of the leading witch-hunters of the period were Puritans.

KEY TERMS

Sacrament
A ceremony carried out in order to attain spiritual grace, such as baptism and Holy Communion.

Devil's mark
A mark, usually a scar, mole or blemish on the body of a person who had entered into a covenant with the Devil.

Witches and familiars

A theme present in many witch-hunts and accusations is the presence of so-called familiars. Familiars (sometimes referred to as imps) were supernatural creatures associated with witches as representatives of the Devil. They would often take the form of animals such as dogs, cats, toads, mice, and even flies and wasps, but could sometimes take the shape of a man. In England, they were believed to have used the **Devil's mark** on the witch to feed and suckle blood, and would assist the witch by carrying out acts on their behalf. Many accused witches were alleged to have received their familiar after a meeting with the Devil (see Source 2 on page 12).

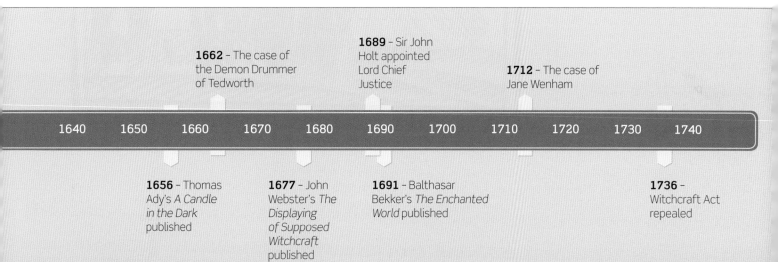

1662 – The case of the Demon Drummer of Tedworth

1689 – Sir John Holt appointed Lord Chief Justice

1712 – The case of Jane Wenham

1640   1650   1660   1670   1680   1690   1700   1710   1720   1730   1740

1656 – Thomas Ady's *A Candle in the Dark* published

1677 – John Webster's *The Displaying of Supposed Witchcraft* published

1691 – Balthasar Bekker's *The Enchanted World* published

1736 – Witchcraft Act repealed

Familiars had long been associated with **cunning-folk** as harmless fairies rather than demons, but the purpose of a witch's familiar was quite different. Witches were thought to have been protected by their familiars after they had been initiated. Sometimes familiars were thought to have shape-shifting qualities, and were often given affectionate names. Stories recounted at witch trials and interrogations of the initial meeting between witch and familiar usually conformed to one of the following.

- A spirit or familiar would suddenly appear when the witch was alone, urging them to make a pact with the Devil or cause harm.

- The familiar could be given by someone else. Often a mother charged with witchcraft would be accused of passing a familiar to her daughter. Two women, a Widow Bridge and her sister, Margaret Ley, were accused of witchcraft in Liverpool in 1667. They claimed that they had both been given 'spirits' by their mother 30 years before.

- Many accused witches were in personal or financial difficulties, and would confess that the Devil gave them a familiar with promises to make them rich or take revenge on their enemies.

Familiars were used to cause harm to others or damage property, and were rewarded for their work with the blood of the witch. The familiar did not necessarily have to belong to the witch; at the trial of the Bideford witches in 1682, one witness recounted seeing an unknown cat jumping through the window of one of the accused.

SOURCE

The Devil presents a newly initiated witch with a familiar, in this case a black dog. From an anonymous ballad of c1600.

SOURCE 3

From the Witchcraft Act (1604).

1. These Witches have ordinarily a familiar, or spirit, which appeareth to them; sometimes in one shape, sometimes in another, as in the shape of a Man, Woman, Boy, Dogge, Cat, Foale, Fowle, Hare, Rat, Toad, etc. And to these their spirits they give names, and they meet together to christen them.

2. Their said Familiar hath some big or little teat upon their body, where he sucketh them; and besides their sucking, the Devil leaveth other marks upon their bodies, sometimes like a Blew-spot, or Red-spot, like a flea-biting, sometimes the flesh sunk in and hollow, all which, for a time, may be covered, yea, taken away, but will come againe to their old forme; and these the Devil's markes be insensible, and being pricked will not bleed; and be often in their secret parts, and therefore require diligent and carefull search....

So likewise, if the suspected be proved to have been heard to call upon their Spirit, or to talk to them, or of them, or have offered them to others.

So, if they have been seen with their Spirits, or seen to feed something secretly, these are proofes that they have a familiar.

ACTIVITY
KNOWLEDGE CHECK

Witches and familiars

Read Source 3. What can be learned from this Act about contemporary beliefs in familiars and their role in witchcraft?

Witchcraft and the law

Prosecutions for witchcraft were relatively rare in Europe before 1550. Evidence of scattered trials exists, with most focusing on individuals accused of causing harm through magic and occasional mass trials. In England, three Acts of Parliament made witchcraft an offence. The first, in 1542, during the reign of Henry VIII (repealed in 1547 under his son, Edward VI) made the conjuring of spirits, witchcraft and sorcery in order to find treasure, cause harm to a person or their goods, or to discover what had happened to stolen goods, a **capital offence**. This Act clearly focused on the crime of witchcraft consisting of acts of hostility against the community, rather than through a pact with the Devil.

KEY TERM

Capital offence
Any crime which is punishable by the death penalty.

The second Act, passed in the reign of Elizabeth I in 1563 (repealed in 1604), was more severe, as it made it a crime to invoke evil spirits for any purpose, whether *maleficium* was involved or not. It was, however, more lenient, because the death penalty was only imposed if the act of witchcraft resulted in the death of a person. If injury or the death of an animal occurred, the guilty witch was given the lesser sentence of imprisonment for one year. Importantly, the continental notion of the diabolical pact had not entered English consciousness and the focus of this Act was still very much on harm caused by witches.

The third Act, passed in 1604 and finally repealed in 1736, was more severe than the 1563 Act. The new king, James I (1603–25) had a personal interest in witchcraft and even wrote a book on witch-hunting called *Daemonologie*. The death penalty was retained for the killing of a person, and it was reintroduced for a second offence in lesser kinds of magic, such as the destroying of livestock and goods, or attempting unsuccessfully to kill a person. The Act also made it an offence to consult with or feed any evil spirit. Different Acts were passed in Scotland, and the difference between English and Scottish witch-hunting is discussed further on page 65.

Evidence exists of hundreds of witch trials carried out under these laws, many on the **assize circuits**. The law was used most often in relation to accusations of damage caused to neighbours and their goods. Two hundred people are known to have been convicted of witchcraft on the Home Circuit (which covered Essex, Hertfordshire, Kent, Surrey and Sussex) between 1558 and 1736. If the prosecutions in the mass witch-hunt associated with Matthew Hopkins (1645–47) are discounted, only seven were found not guilty of causing damage to people or their property on the Home Circuit.

KEY TERM

Assize circuit
Assize courts were courts that travelled in six 'circuits' around the country, hearing the most serious cases.

Identifying witches

The identification of witches was not always straightforward. If a mystery illness or misfortune struck a community and there was a known witch in the vicinity, he or she would usually be the first suspect. However, more often than not, obvious suspects were lacking, and neighbours would cast their eye around their locality in order to discover a hidden witch. People who were physically deformed or stood out in some way were more likely to be accused, and those who were withdrawn or socially awkward were also common targets. It is true that women, particularly older women, were most often accused of witchcraft, although men were not free from suspicion. In order to confirm whether someone was a witch, a number of tests were employed in witch-hunts.

- A suspected witch could be scratched in order to break a spell by drawing blood.

- The infamous swimming test involved binding the suspect's right thumb to their left big toe and left thumb to their right big toe. They would then be secured with ropes and thrown in a pond or river three times. If they floated, they were guilty, as it was believed that the water would reject a witch, and if they sank, there was usually a scramble to rescue them from the water before they drowned.

- A suspected witch might be asked to recite the Lord's Prayer, as it was believed that no witch could recite it to the end.

- Marks of various forms were taken as a sign of guilt, and the body of a suspected witch could be searched in order to find them (female suspects were normally only searched by women). These marks were probably warts, moles or extra nipples.

- Suspects would sometimes be 'watched' for several days and nights. This was a favoured method of the most famous witch-hunter, Matthew Hopkins, who would deprive suspects of sleep or rest and force them to go hungry. It was through this method that he was able to acquire a large number of remarkable confessions.

ACTIVITY
KNOWLEDGE CHECK

The extent of witchcraft

1 Under what circumstances did people become witches, according to claims made at witch trials?

2 Why was the 1604 Witchcraft Act so severe?

3 Why do you think older women were particularly vulnerable to accusations of witchcraft?

WHY DID SCEPTICAL ATTITUDES TOWARDS WITCHCRAFT GROW AND DEVELOP IN THE YEARS c1580–c1750?

A belief in witchcraft was well entrenched in the mindset of the British people in the 16th and 17th centuries, but an increasing number of dubious cases led to the development of more sceptical attitudes. This, combined with the development of more scientific and rational thought (see Chapter 2), led to the repealing of witchcraft legislation in 1736.

The Boy of Burton, 1596–97

The case of the Boy of Burton was a sensational one in which an alleged witch was held responsible for bewitching a youth and making him ill. Both the boy's symptoms and the celebrated exorcism by which he was supposed to have been healed were later proven false, greatly increasing scepticism about witchcraft and also about those who purported to be able to 'cure' it.

Thomas Darling's story

In 1599, a 17-year-old boy named Thomas Darling confessed to a lie he had told three years previously.

In February 1596, Darling had gone hare-hunting with his uncle, Robert Toone. When Darling returned he fell ill, and the next day he began having fits. He also started to have hallucinations, and claimed that he saw green angels and a green cat. His fits became worse when passages from the New Testament were read out to him, confirming the doctor's suspicions that he had become bewitched. Darling's version of events is recounted in Source 4; he claimed that when he lost his uncle in a wood, he met a strange woman with whom he had a disagreement.

SOURCE 4

Words attributed to Thomas Darling, in *A true report of the strange torments of Thomas Darling, a boy of thirteene years of age, that was possessed of the Devil, with his horrible fittes and terrible Apparitions by him uttered at Burton upon Trent in the County of Stafford, and of his marvellous deliverance* (1597).

I heard my aunt tell Jesse Bee that I was bewitched. The same Saturday that my sickness took me, I lost my uncle in the wood. And in the coppice I met a little old woman. She had a gray gown with a black fringe about the cape, a broad thrummed [rough, shaggy] hat, and three warts on her face. I have seen her begging at our door. As for her name I know it not, but by sight I can know her again. As I passed by her in the coppice I chanced (against my will) to let a scape [break wind]. Which she, taking in anger, said, *Gyp with a mischief and fart with a bell: I will go to heaven and thou shalt go to hell.* And forthwith she stooped to the ground. I stood still and looked at her, viewing every part of her, marveling what she stooped for. So I came home and she went to Winsell.

From the boy's description, his neighbours immediately identified the woman as one of the witches of Stapenhill, either 60-year-old Alice Gooderidge or her mother, 80-year-old Elizabeth Wright. It seems likely that Darling knew who the woman was, and may have blamed her for his fits as he was already aware of her reputation. The fits continued, and in April, Alice Gooderidge was brought to the Darling house in order to confront her victim. Darling immediately began to fit, and scratched her face in an effort to break the spell. This was unsuccessful, and Gooderidge claimed that although she did meet the boy in the woods, she had never practised witchcraft, and was only stern with him because she mistook him for another boy who had once played a trick on her.

The arrest of Alice Gooderidge

Two days after her visit to the house, Gooderidge was arrested with her mother, and they were both searched for witch-marks, which were apparently found. Gooderidge was detained at Derby prison, and there changed her story and admitted that she had bewitched Darling (most likely after a long period of sleep deprivation and starvation). She explained that she had a familiar in the shape of a red and white dog called Minny, which had been given to her by her mother. She claimed that she had sent this familiar to harm the boy after their encounter in the woods. Before her trial began, she was once again put in front of Darling, and he once again fell ill, resulting in a total of 37 fits in succession. She explained to the local **Justices of the Peace** (JPs) that it was possible to break the spell, but before she could explain, she had a choking fit which prevented her from speaking. She was later put on trial and found guilty, but before a date could be fixed for her execution she died in custody.

KEY TERM

Justice of the Peace
A public official appointed to preserve peace and administer the law at a local level.

The role of John Darrell

Despite the death of Gooderidge, Darling's fits continued, and a well-known exorcist called John Darrell was called in. Ten years earlier, Darrell had been given a warning by a judge at a witch trial for falsely accusing a woman, Margaret Roper, of witchcraft in Mansfield, but he continued to carry out exorcisms. Darrell recommended a combination of prayer, fasting and reading particular Bible extracts in order to cast out the Devil.

Darrell used his exorcism techniques on Thomas Darling in May 1596 with apparent success, and went on to exorcise an apprentice called William Somers in Nottingham in 1597. Somers claimed that he had been bewitched by 13 women headed by Alice Freeman. All were arrested, but only two were sent for trial. Darrell supported Somers, but was already attracting suspicion. Somers was questioned, and confessed that his possession by the Devil was fraudulent, and that he and Darrell had worked together. As Darrell was a minister, the matter was reported to the Archbishop of York, who set up a commission to investigate the case. When Somers was questioned at the commission, he took back his confession and fell into violent fits that were so convincing that the commissioners believed he was possessed.

Alice Freeman was then brought to trial in front of Judge Edward Anderson, who had already been involved in the trial of Alice Gooderidge. Edwards pressed Somers to state whether or not his accusation was truthful, and Somers once again confessed. Alice Freeman was immediately released.

Thomas Darling's confession

Edward Anderson wrote to the Archbishop of Canterbury, the most senior bishop in the Church of England, about Darrell's case. Darrell was summoned, together with another minister he had worked with on exorcisms, George More, to be examined by the Archbishop and the Bishop of London, Richard Bancroft. Also present at the examination was Samuel Harsnett, chaplain to Bishop Bancroft, who would become famous for writing sceptical publications. Among the witnesses were Thomas Darling and William Somers, who both confessed that their stories were untrue. Somers even added that he had been told by Darrell to fake his symptoms and exorcism. Darling's confession was tainted by the fact that he had undergone physical and verbal abuse in jail for seven weeks beforehand. George More spoke in Darrell's defence, but both were imprisoned for a year, where they both wrote passionate defences of their techniques and vigorously claimed they were innocent.

Although he never admitted to being a fraud, Darrell was unable to resume a career as a minister. There can be little doubt that he intended to boost his reputation and perhaps profit from faking exorcisms. Upon his release, he lived a quiet life and disappears from the public record, apart from an incident where he insulted the rector of Cambridge and had his ears clipped as a punishment. His lasting legacy was a **canon** drawn up by Bishop Bancroft in 1604 that forbade any clergymen to practise exorcism without a licence.

KEY TERM

Canon
A code of laws established by the Church.

Samuel Harsnett, who had been present at the examinations of Darrell and Darling, issued a pamphlet entitled *A Discovery of the Fraudulent Practises of John Darrel* in 1599 (Source 5), and later published *A Declaration of Egregious Popish Impostures* in 1603, where he blamed the usual English scapegoat of the age for the fraudulent claims: the Catholic Church.

SOURCE

5 From Samuel Harsnett's *A Discovery of the Fraudulent Practises of John Darrel* (1599). Harsnett was a clergyman who was serving as chaplain to the Bishop of London in 1599, and later became Archbishop of York.

Thomas Darling being sent for by virtue of her Majesties Commission for causes ecclesiastical: was examined, concerning his pretended possession, and dispossession, and afterwards again was dismissed...

When they perceived that the power of God in the boy, was stronger than the malice of Satan, they let him go. His meaning is, that the boy could not be removed from justifying his own, and Master Darrel's proceedings with him. It may please you therefore to consider, what the boy deposed, before he went... (sayeth he) 'I do voluntarily of myself confess, that whatsoever Master Darrel did say about my supposed possession, or about prayer for my dispossession, or about my fits before or after my dispossession: I did all either of ignorance, or to get my self a glory thereby... I confess that I verily think, that if I may speak with M. Darrell, I can persuade him never to take any more such courses, nor to take upon him any such power, to be able to cast out a devil. I confess, as that I think, if my Lord will deal favourably with Master Darrell, and bee good Lord unto him, he will of himself confess the truth... that he did think me never to have been possessed, and that he will promise never to enter into any such practise again. I confess, that I felt indeed at first some pricklings in my legges: and that at the first I vomited, and was somewhat ill at ease: but as for all and singular the fits mentioned in the Book, and the dialogues with Satan... my saying of sentences out of the scriptures to Satan, his supposed saying to me, as also all those supposed apparitions of a Cat, a Dragon, a Bear, Lightnings, Thundering, a Lamb, a Doe, a Woman, and so of all the several visions and torments set down in the printed book, I confess they bee all untruths, and no credit to be given to them, or any of them.'

And again: the special occasion he sayeth, that first drew him on more apparently to the said fictions, was this conceit put into his head: that the Devil could not abide the word of God: that therefore when the word of God was read, he did willingly at the hearing of some especial points, cast himself into many fits: that in the same he used sundry godly speeches: that the Standers-by thereupon observed the power of the word...

Being then further asked, why after his pretended dispossession, he fell again to his former course: his answer is: that having heard of Master Darrel, that Satan was accustomed to seek to reenter into those, out of whom he had been cast: he thought... for the better crediting of his former dealing, to take upon him, as though Satan had sought to have again repossessed him.

ACTIVITY
KNOWLEDGE CHECK

The Boy of Burton

1 Why do you think Thomas Darling's family and neighbours were so quick to believe his story?

2 How were Darling and Darrell discovered to be acting fraudulently?

3 What rational explanations can account for Thomas Darling's behaviour?

4 Why was the Boy of Burton case a key development in the growth of sceptical opinion?

The Pendle Swindle, 1634

The Pendle Forest of Lancashire was the setting of one of the most famous witch-hunts in British history in 1612, which is discussed in detail in Chapter 4. In 1633–34, another hunt took place in the same area. The king at the time of the first hunt, James I, had died in 1625, and the crown had now passed to his son, Charles I, who took a personal interest in the latest Pendle case.

Edmund Robinson's claims

This hunt was triggered by the actions of a ten-year-old boy named Edmund Robinson. Robinson was well aware of the local reputation of Jennet Device, who had given evidence against her own mother as a nine-year-old at the original trials, and who would be accused in the latest case. Robinson originally brought up the issue of witchcraft in order to avoid punishment for not looking after his father's cattle when he was asked to, and, as a diversion tactic, claimed that when he was looking for plums in the woods one night in November 1633, he was approached by two greyhounds, one black and one brown. Both dogs had a string around their necks, and he took hold of them. When a hare ran past and the dogs made no movement, he immediately became suspicious. He claimed that the black greyhound then changed into Frances Dickinson, the wife of a local man he knew, and the other into an unknown boy.

Robinson claimed that the woman offered him a shilling to keep quiet, but he refused the money and made it clear that he intended to report her as a witch. The unknown boy then changed into a white horse, and the woman forced Robinson to ride with her to a house called Hoarstones. Here, he found a gathering of witches, both men and women, who were feasting, and he was able to escape.

Accusations and trial

Robinson's father, also called Edmund, found his son in a distressed state, and was told the story. After an unusually long break of three months, the local magistrates, Richard Shuttleworth and John Starkie, were informed and the younger Edmund recounted his story once again. The magistrates were led to a number of churches, where Robinson identified witches to be brought to trial, numbering around 25 in all. They were taken to Lancaster for trial, and 17 were found guilty. The sceptical attitude of the presiding magistrates is evident in the fact that a report of the trial was immediately sent to the **Privy Council** in London. They stated that although they had followed the letter of the law and found the witches guilty based on the evidence presented in court, they were beginning to have doubts about both written evidence and spoken testimony. They instructed the Bishop of Chester, Henry Bridgeman, to investigate some of the women.

KEY TERM

Privy Council
The private council of the monarch, made up of advisers handpicked by the king.

Fraud discovered

As a result of his investigation, Bridgeman concluded that Robinson's motive for the accusations was not founded in magic, and father and son were sent to London to be interrogated, along with four of the accused women. The women were examined by a number of surgeons and midwives for the Devil's mark, and later questioned by King Charles himself. One of the surgeons was William Harvey, who became famous for discovering the circulation of blood. The group that examined the women issued a certificate stating their conclusions (Source 6).

SOURCE 6

The certificate issued by the medical jury of accused witches Jennet Hargreaves, Frances Dickinson, Mary Spencer and Margaret Johnson, 2 July 1635.

We have inspected the bodies of Jennet Hargreaves, Frances Dickinson, and Mary Spencer, and have found nothing unnatural, nor anything like a teat or a mark. There was nothing on the body of Margaret Johnson inconsistent with a well known disease [the letter did not specify what disease this was].

Despite this lack of evidence, Margaret Johnson did confess to witchcraft, and told a tale of when she sold her soul to the Devil, who had called himself Mamilion and who promised to give her all she desired. She also claimed that she met with other witches, although her descriptions did not match Robinson's story of the gathering he had witnessed. The 1630s saw very few prosecutions for witchcraft, and it may be that the king had a hand in reprieving the accused, although a number of the original suspects were still being held in custody at Lancaster three years later.

After the trial, Edmund Robinson became known as a witchfinder for a time. Encouraged by his father and uncle, he would visit church services in Lancashire where he would apparently identify witches in the congregation. Although it is difficult to ascertain exactly how this became a profitable endeavour for the family, the elder Edmund gained enough money to purchase two cows. However, when they were summoned to London, the boy was separated from his father and admitted that his story was entirely fictitious. He said that his father had forced him to tell the story, motivated by a desire for revenge against Frances Dickinson, with whom he had entered into a dispute over the payment for a cow. Once again, accusations of witchcraft proved to be motivated by reasons that had nothing to do with the supernatural, and the case increased scepticism about the existence of witchcraft and witches.

ACTIVITY
KNOWLEDGE CHECK

The Pendle Swindle

1 Why were the authorities sceptical about Edmund Robinson's claims?

2 Why do you think some of the accused were kept in jail by the authorities in Lancaster, despite being given a pardon by the king?

3 Why was the Pendle Swindle a key development in the growth of scepticism?

The Demon Drummer of Tedworth, 1662

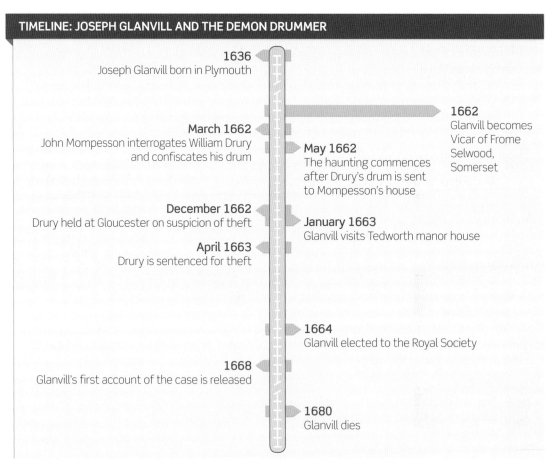

TIMELINE: JOSEPH GLANVILL AND THE DEMON DRUMMER

1636
Joseph Glanvill born in Plymouth

1662
Glanvill becomes Vicar of Frome Selwood, Somerset

March 1662
John Mompesson interrogates William Drury and confiscates his drum

May 1662
The haunting commences after Drury's drum is sent to Mompesson's house

December 1662
Drury held at Gloucester on suspicion of theft

January 1663
Glanvill visits Tedworth manor house

April 1663
Drury is sentenced for theft

1664
Glanvill elected to the Royal Society

1668
Glanvill's first account of the case is released

1680
Glanvill dies

The haunting at Tedworth

John Mompesson was a landowner and JP who lived at Tedworth on the Wiltshire-Hampshire border. In March 1662, Mompesson, who also acted as a commissioned officer in the **county militia**, intervened in the case of a drummer and ex-soldier, William Drury, who was fraudulently attempting to raise **alms** for the poor with a forged pass, and attempting to draw attention to his cause by repeatedly banging his drum. The fraud was discovered when he demanded money from a constable, who became suspicious. When Mompesson reviewed the pass presented by Drury, apparently signed by two JPs known to Mompesson, he could see immediately that the signatures were forgeries.

Under the law, such passes were essential for people travelling from parish to parish (such as entertainer Drury, who was also a juggler, conjurer and hoop-dancer) in order to avoid punishment as a **vagrant**. Drury was arrested on the orders of Mompesson and his drum was confiscated, although he was later released. The drum was then sent to Mompesson's house in April, and the next month Mompesson's family experienced a series of unexplained disturbances.

- Thumpings were heard in Mompesson's house, as well as the sound of the drum playing military marches.

- The family heard the sound of scratching and what sounded like a dog panting.

- Strange lights were seen and sulphurous smells detected. The smell was linked with the brimstone associated with the Devil.

- Objects were thrown around rooms, beds were raised in the air and the family's horses mysteriously injured.

- On Christmas Day, a Bible belonging to Mompesson's mother was found buried beneath the hearth ashes.

These strange occurrences continued for a number of months, even when Drury was jailed in Gloucester on a charge of pig stealing. The house became a local attraction, and many people visited in order to witness the disturbances for themselves. Even representatives of King Charles II were sent to investigate. Interest became even more intense when it was rumoured that Drury had confessed to a fellow inmate that he had bewitched Mompesson.

SOURCE

7 The frontispiece of Joseph Glanvill's *Saducismus Triumphatus* (Sadducism Triumphed Over)* (1681) showing various cases of possession and witchcraft. The upper-left image depicts the Demon Drummer of Tedworth.

*The title is a reference to the ancient Jewish sect of Sadducism, which rejected many of the core beliefs of Christianity, including a belief in the Devil.

Joseph Glanvill's involvement

The case appeared in two newspapers at the time, *Mercurius Publicus* and *The Kingdom's Intelligencer*, which were both widely read in London and accessed by many of the gentry in the counties and some educated tradesmen and farmers. Interestingly, Mompesson's name is only found in these newspaper reports, and not in Joseph Glanvill's more detailed *A Blow at Modern Sadducism, In Some Philosophical Considerations about Witchcraft* (1668). The case was brought to Glanvill's attention after it had become notorious, and he visited the house in January 1663 in order to investigate the spirit. Glanvill claimed to have heard noises himself, and spent time speaking to eyewitnesses. Many of the eyewitnesses he spoke to claimed that William Drury was somehow responsible and was using witchcraft to control events from afar.

Drury was found guilty of theft in April 1663, and was sentenced to deportation. Glanvill wrote that the disturbances stopped immediately, but that Drury was able to escape while being transported to the English colony of Virginia because he was able to use his supernatural powers to raise storms at sea. He escaped while his ship was still on the Severn Estuary but was recaptured, and tried for witchcraft at Salisbury. He was acquitted, but was once again sentenced to deportation for theft. The disturbances began again and apparently continued for several years.

Scepticism about Glanvill's account

A long history of scepticism about the case began almost immediately, despite Glanvill's account. Glanvill attempted to persuade the **Royal Society** that the study of witchcraft could be carried out and cases proved to be true by approaching them in a rational, scientific way, and many within the Society favoured his approach. The first substantial sceptical response to Glanvill came from John Webster, a preacher and doctor, who published *The Displaying of Supposed Witchcraft* in 1677 (detailed later in the chapter). Webster hoped that his book would impress the Royal Society, and the publication was approved by Sir Jonas Moore, the Vice-President of the Society, much to the annoyance of Glanvill. Webster claimed that he had been informed by reliable sources that the entire case was fraudulent, and that Mompesson was responsible for the noises heard in the house.

KEY TERM

Royal Society
A society founded in 1660 in order to promote the advancement of science and rational thought.

The case was attacked again in Balthasar Bekker's *The World Bewitched* (1692–94), which inspired further criticism in John Beaumont's *Historical, Physiological and Theological Treatise of Spirits, Apparitions, Witchcrafts, and other Magical Practices* (1705). Beaumont's view was that Mompesson's servants may have been responsible, and he recounts a rumour that two young women who worked in the house carried out the disturbances in order to scare Mompesson's mother. Indeed, Mompesson's letters reveal his anxious state of mind after his servants had claimed that if they left their employment, no one else would want to take their place, thus making them his masters.

Intriguingly, Mompesson's dislike for Drury may have been exacerbated by Drury's career as a Parliamentarian soldier in the Civil War (1642–46). When he was first interrogated by Mompesson (who fought for the Royalists in the war), Drury presented a forged warrant claiming he was seeking alms for disabled soldiers. After the Restoration of the monarchy in 1660, only Royalist soldiers were eligible for financial aid, and Drury claimed to have been a military drummer in a Royalist regiment commanded by Mompesson's friend. It later turned out that Drury had served four years in the Parliamentary army, and it is very likely that Mompesson knew this.

As well as this, it is clear from letters sent by Mompesson that his explanation for the events was shaped by neighbours and visitors and not necessarily by his own experiences. To begin with, his letters show that he was mystified, and originally suspected burglary. When a minister visited the house and suggested the Devil may have been responsible, Mompesson's tone changed, and a spiritual explanation was put forward. After a neighbour came to the house and explained that they had heard stories of fairies leaving money in people's shoes, a letter from Mompesson revealed that the sound of jingling money was heard in the house.

Overall, the importance of the Tedworth case lies not in the fact that doubts were raised at the time of the disturbances; indeed, there appeared to be a national consensus that supernatural forces were to blame. Instead, its importance lies in the fact that the case was revisited in a number of works over the ensuing decades, and as the great thinkers of the age began to approach witchcraft with a more critical eye, they became suspicious of Mompesson.

EXTEND YOUR KNOWLEDGE

Joseph Glanvill (1636–80)
Glanvill was raised a Puritan and, after being educated at Oxford University, became a clergyman. Despite his deep-rooted religious beliefs, he also recognised the need to approach the study of the world in a rational, scientific way, and he became a member of the Royal Society in 1664.

Despite the fact that he wrote the *Scepsis Scientifica* (Scientific Scepticism) in 1665, where he advocated the scientific method, he was fascinated by witchcraft. His *A Blow at Modern Sadducism* (1668) is a valuable source for information on the Demon Drummer of Tedworth, and a collection of his writings was released after his death, known as *Saducismus Triumphatus*, published in 1688–89.

Despite being a member of the Royal Society, Glanvill had little understanding of science, and was prepared to believe that magic was entirely plausible. By the time the *Saducismus* was published, however, the peak of English witch-hunting had passed, and his book was not taken seriously.

ACTIVITY
KNOWLEDGE CHECK

The Demon Drummer of Tedworth

1 Why does Mompesson's account of the events seem suspicious?

2 Why do you think sceptical accounts only emerged decades after the events in question?

3 Why is the case an important development in the growth of scepticism?

The case of Jane Wenham, 1712

The last formal witch trial in England

One case that stands out as doubtful in the early 18th century is that of Jane Wenham. It has become famous as the last formal trial of a suspected witch in England. Wenham was from Walkern, near Stevenage, and had a long-held reputation as a witch. Her nickname was the 'Wise Woman of Walkern', and at over 70 years old a number of stories had been circulating about her in the years before her March 1712 trial. A typical story relates to the accusation that she bewitched a farm labourer, Matthew Gilson, who refused to give her a small amount of straw. Wenham was said to have cursed Gilson, who proceeded to run down the road begging people for straw and stuffing his shirt with manure. When Gilson's employer publicly voiced the allegation, Wenham reported him to the local JP, Sir Henry Chaucey, and the farmer was fined one shilling. Wenham was not satisfied with this outcome, and was alleged to have promised to get justice in another way. The farmer's daughter and livestock then fell ill.

The case that would result in her eventual acquittal stemmed from a complaint made by Anne Thorne, a 16-year-old servant who worked in the house of a local clergyman, Godfrey Gardiner. Thorne complained that Wenham had bewitched her, and caused her to suffer from fits and hallucinations of demons with faces of cats, as well as causing her to vomit pins. The case was brought to the attention of Gardiner and his wife when they left Thorne alone for a few minutes, only to return to find that she had run almost a mile in order to collect sticks. Gardiner's wife immediately suspected witchcraft, and as she placed the sticks on the fire she saw the figure of Jane Wenham emerge in the doorway.

The allegations against Wenham were verified by a number of locals, including James Burville, who stated that he had seen a cat with Jane Wenham's face at Anne Thorne's door. Wenham was arrested and searchers were tasked with finding the Devil's mark on her. Nothing unusual was found, but Wenham apparently gave a full confession. She claimed that she was a witch but only practised harmless magic.

Despite the confession, the only charge the accusers could agree on was that of conversing with the Devil in the shape of a cat. A total of 16 witnesses were called to give evidence, including three local clergymen, and an ointment found under Wenham's pillow was presented as evidence. This ointment was said to have been made from human fat. When she was asked to recite the Lord's Prayer, she stumbled over some of the words. The judge, Sir John Powell, was sceptical of the evidence from the beginning. When a witness stated that they had seen Wenham soaring through the air, he remarked that there was no law against flying.

Despite the objections of Powell, the jury found Wenham guilty. In order to prevent the inevitable hanging, Powell secured a royal pardon and, although she was unable to return to Walkern, Wenham was offered a cottage by the sympathetic **Whig politician** William Cowper, where she lived until her death in 1730. Anne Thorne, the servant who originally made the accusations against Wenham, was ordered to be watched over until she recovered from her hysteria.

Why was Wenham found guilty and then acquitted?

The case of Jane Wenham took place at a time when witchcraft convictions were extremely rare, so it is surprising that the jury found her guilty. The answer seems to lie in the local context. Walkern was a village of approximately 500 people, including a number of upwardly mobile farmers, such as the Chapman and Adams families (who both accused Wenham), and a large number of **Dissenters**, accounting for around 20 percent of the population. It seems likely that Wenham was a Dissenter, as her accusers mentioned this at her trial, and the involvement of local clergymen may represent their desire to demonstrate the power of the Church of England. She was also very poor, as evidenced by her stealing of turnips and straw. Walkern did not appear to have adequate provisions for the poor, and in a time when the gap between rich and poor was widening, it is no coincidence that most of her accusers were relatively wealthy.

Sir John Powell, the judge in the case, was clearly unimpressed with the witnesses and the evidence put before him. No doubt influenced by recent sceptical cases and publications, he went as far as to acquire a royal pardon for Wenham. Crucially, Powell was an outsider (he was originally from Gloucester) who was able to approach the case in a rational and objective way, realising that many of the witnesses had personal grudges against Wenham.

Wenham's case, like the career of Lord Chief Justice Holt (see page 23), is mentioned in Hutchinson's *An Historical Essay Concerning Witchcraft* (1718). Hutchinson met Wenham after her trial, and reported that she was not guilty. Hutchinson did, however, state that supernatural phenomena were plausible, but that the most far-fetched accusations could only be thought up by fools.

KEY TERMS

Whig politician
A member of the faction within parliament that favoured restraints on the power of the monarch. They were opposed by the Tories, who were more sympathetic to the Crown.

Dissenter
A member of a non-established church outside the Church of England.

ACTIVITY
KNOWLEDGE CHECK

The case of Jane Wenham

1 Why was Jane Wenham suspected of witchcraft?

2 Why do you think the jury found her guilty?

3 Why do you think the judge subsequently sought a reprieve?

The influence of Lord Chief Justice Sir John Holt, 1689–1710

EXTRACT

1 From Montague Summers, *A Popular History of Witchcraft* (2011).

Towards the end of the seventeenth century and during the first decade of the eighteenth cases of witchcraft still came before the English courts, but the judges for the most part refused to convict. Sir John Holt, Chief Justice of the King's Bench (1689–1710), showed himself a notorious sceptic in these matters and secured acquittal after acquittal.

Legal scepticism before Holt: Sir George Mackenzie

Sir John Holt, who served as Lord Chief Justice from 1689 to 1710, acquitted almost a dozen witches as a result of his critical approach to evidence and his suspicion of supernatural events. As Extract 1 shows, he made a name for himself as a rational and sympathetic judge. Holt was not, however, the first judge to become renowned for his scepticism. Sir George Mackenzie, a Scottish lawyer and Lord Advocate (the chief legal officer in Scotland) from 1677 to 1686, became concerned at the legitimacy of witchcraft trials after the Scottish witch-hunt of 1661–62. He recorded in 1672 that he even represented an accused witch named Maevia in court. Maevia was accused of shape-shifting and using *maleficium* against a woman.

In 1678, Mackenzie published *Laws and Customs of Scotland in Matters Criminal,* where he conceded that although he believed that witchcraft was possible, most of the people accused were not genuine witches. Mackenzie put forward a number of arguments against continued witch-hunts.

- He accepted that true witches deserved punishment, but also laid blame on the careless judges who found innocent people guilty and sent them to their deaths.

- He stated that he believed in the traditional view that witches were people who had been deceived, but were not necessarily evil and deserving of harsh punishments.

- He doubted that the Devil would offer riches to people, as most accused witches were destitute.

- Normal legal procedures were not followed in witchcraft cases, as the crime was seen as exceptionally evil. Mackenzie disagreed with this, and pointed out the fact that suspected witches often gave false confessions as a result of torture or sleep deprivation.

When Mackenzie was promoted to Lord Advocate in 1677, he used his powers to free a number of suspected witches. He paid particular attention to the way in which investigations had been carried out. If he found evidence of foul play or torture, he usually threw out the case. A number of leading bishops and theologians accused Mackenzie of atheism; however, his work contributed to a steep decline in witchcraft cases being heard at court.

EXTEND YOUR KNOWLEDGE

The Scottish witch-hunt (1661–62)

Starting in April 1661, a large number of witch trials took place across Scotland. Court records show that at least 660 individuals were named as witches. After an initial set of trials in Midlothian, the Privy Council of Scotland hastily issued commissions to local authorities to try suspected witches.

It is difficult to ascertain exactly how many people were executed in the 16 months of the witch-hunt. The English naturalist, John Ray, wrote that during his brief visit to Scotland, 120 were burned. It is one of the few witch-hunts in Britain that is comparable in size with the great hunts of mainland Europe, and four times more people were involved in this hunt than the Salem trials in North America.

The causes of the hunt remain a historical controversy. Most historians agree that the Restoration of the monarchy in 1660 played an important part. During the Protectorate of Oliver Cromwell and his son, Richard (1653–59), many affairs relating to English and Scottish justice were managed jointly. At the Restoration, Scotland regained complete control of its own legal affairs, and Scottish judges were far more prepared to persecute suspected witches. The hunt could not have taken place without the approval of Charles II's government, and as soon as judges like Mackenzie began to question the judgements, the hunt could not be sustained any longer.

The career of John Holt

Holt was born in Oxfordshire in 1642, and although he entered Oxford University, he left without achieving a degree. He began training as a lawyer in 1660, and was **called to the bar** in 1663. He seems to have been well liked by James II (1685–88) and became Recorder of London, in effect the chief judge in the City, in 1685. He was knighted around the same time. He played an important part in the negotiations over the transition of power from the Catholic James II to the Protestant William III in 1688–89, and was appointed Lord Chief Justice by William in 1689.

A record of Holt's career is preserved in Francis Hutchinson's *An Historical Essay Concerning Witchcraft* (1718). As Lord Chief Justice, he oversaw at least 11, and possibly 12, trials concerning witchcraft and each one resulted in the acquittal of the accused.

- In 1691, Holt acquitted two women who had been accused in Frome, Somerset, of bewitching a girl who had fallen ill. The girl recovered despite the acquittals.

- In 1694, Holt reviewed the case of a witch known as Mother Munnings, who was accused of causing death by witchcraft in Bury St Edmunds. Holt refused to accept charges that related to events that took place 17 years earlier, and refused to accept the evidence of a man who had been returning from an alehouse when he claimed to have seen Munnings' familiar in the form of a polecat.

- At Ipswich in 1694, Margaret Elnore, who was from a family of convicted witches (both her aunt and her grandmother were hanged for the crime), was accused of possessing familiars given to her by her grandmother. A midwife testified that the Devil's mark had been found on her body. Holt dismissed the case immediately.

- In 1695, at Launceston in Cornwall, Holt freed Mary Guy, who was alleged to have caused the possession of a local girl.

- In 1696, Elizabeth Horner of Exeter was accused of causing the possession of three children. Witnesses claimed that one of the children was seen walking nine feet up a wall. She was acquitted by Holt.

The case of Sarah Murdock (1701) in Extract 3 (on page 24) is perhaps his most famous, and although Holt acquitted the suspected witch, he was met with fierce opposition from her neighbours. Before the case reached Holt, it was dismissed by an assize judge, which resulted in an angry mob surrounding Murdock's house. When the case was put before Holt, a number of neighbours testified in defence of the accuser, Richard Hathaway, claiming that he had been unable to eat and went temporarily blind after Murdock bewitched him.

The fact that Holt was prepared to put the accuser on trial in the Murdock case for fraudulently claiming witchcraft shows how serious his scepticism was. He was inevitably influenced by the changing intellectual climate, and although there is no evidence that he read sceptical works, the works of Webster, Beaumont and Bekker would surely have been known to him. Despite Holt's efforts, there was still a widespread belief in witchcraft, and his predecessor, Matthew Hale (1671–76), was willing to accept dubious testimonies in order to secure convictions for witchcraft.

EXTRACT

2 From Christina Hole, *Witchcraft in England* (1977).

In the story of English witchcraft, Sir John Holt bears a justly honoured name. He brought to every trial a mind unclouded by prejudice, and a single-hearted desire to give the prisoner every chance. Throughout his career, he showed to all accused persons, whatever their crimes, a wide humanity that was all too uncommon in his day, and Sir Richard Steele tells us in *The Tatler* [1709] that every prisoner brought before him knew, 'though his spirit was broken with guilt and incapable of language to defend itself, all would be gathered from him which could conduce to his safety, and that his judge would wrest no law to destroy him, nor conceal anything to save him'... In the eleven sorcery trials over which he presided, he never failed to secure the discharge of the accused person, and his impartial common sense did much to hasten the decline of the witch-belief throughout the country.

EXTRACT

3 From Brian A. Pavlac, *Witch Hunts in the Western World* (2009).

Sir John Holt... acquitted almost a dozen witches through his serious questioning and scepticism of supernatural events and evidence. Spitting up pins, having a Witch's Mark, or accepting the word of a bitter neighbour were insufficient for Holt to condemn a person to death, much less convict them of any real crime. Holt even exposed fraud. Richard Hathaway of Southwark, for example, had long accused Sarah Murdock of making him suffer pains and fits; spit up pins, pieces of metal, and stones; foam at the mouth; and bark like a dog. His accusations had led to her arrest in 1700 and an expected trial for witchcraft. Instead, Holt put Hathaway himself on trial, exposed his fakery, and sentenced him to a year in prison and three sessions in the pillory.

EXTEND YOUR KNOWLEDGE

John Holt's remarkable cure: myth or reality?
A story is recorded in Thomas Pettigrew's *Medical Superstitions* (1844) that, as a young man, Holt was staying at an inn and found himself unable to pay his bill. He noticed that the landlady's 13-year-old daughter was suffering from ague, a malarial-like fever, and he offered to cure her in exchange for clearing his bill.

Holt wrote a few words of Latin on a piece of parchment, and ordered that it be tied around her wrist until she regained her health. She became well, and Holt was able to leave. Many years later, the case of a woman who was accused of witchcraft was presented to Holt. She was charged with curing illnesses with a written parchment. When the parchment was produced and handed to Holt, he could see that it was the same one he had written in his youth.

Holt recognised the woman as the landlady he had originally given the parchment to, and the charge was dismissed. Holt admitted that he did not believe in the cure that he offered. Although the story appeared over a century after the events in question, it has been recounted many times, and acts as a fair reflection of Holt's attitude and temperament.

THINKING HISTORICALLY Evidence (6b)

The strength of argument

1 Read Extract 1.

   a) What is weak about this claim?

   b) What could be added to it to make it stronger?

2 Read Extract 2.

   a) Is this an argument? If yes, what makes it one?

   b) How might this argument be strengthened?

3 Read Extract 3.

   a) How have they expanded their explanation to make the claim stronger?

   b) Can you explain why this is the strongest claim of the three extracts?

4 What elements make a historian's claims strong?

ACTIVITY
KNOWLEDGE CHECK

The influence of Sir John Holt

1 Why is the career of Sir George Mackenzie significant? Why do you think he had a different approach to previous Scottish judges?

2 Why do you think Holt's cases resulted in so many acquittals? What do his influences seem to be?

3 Why do you think, despite the actions of Holt, belief in witchcraft was still widespread at the turn of the 18th century?

The last executions and the end of witchcraft legislation

The last witch to be executed in England was Alice Molland of Exeter. She had been accused of murdering three people in 1682, and was hanged in 1684. In Scotland, ten people – seven men and three women – were executed at Paisley in 1697. One final execution in Scotland involved the burning of Janet Horne in a tar barrel in 1727. Horne had been accused of changing her daughter into a flying horse in order to travel. Her daughter had a deformity that affected her hands and feet, and neighbours began to suggest that this was as a result of the transformation. The final trials had ended, but more than 1,500 people had been executed for witchcraft in Britain.

A final attempt was made to bring a suspected witch to trial in Leicester in 1717, but this was rejected by the court. In 1736, the government finally repealed the 1604 Witchcraft Act in both England and Scotland. There was little opposition to this decision in England, but in Scotland, where belief in witchcraft was still relatively widespread, a number of clergy protested. A new Witchcraft Act was passed, specifically aimed at punishing fraudulent cases, with a maximum penalty of one year's imprisonment. Importantly, this Act declared that magic and witchcraft were not real.

Despite the repealing of witchcraft legislation, many ordinary people continued to believe in witches. Accusations against neighbours continued, and crowds would occasionally gather to confront a suspected witch. In 1751 in Long Marston, Hertfordshire, John and Ruth Osborne were attacked by an angry mob who accused them of harming cattle and people. Determined to put them to the swimming test, a 4,000-strong group dragged them to a pond, and Ruth Osborne drowned after she was thrown in. Her husband was beaten to death. One of the ringleaders, a chimney-sweep named Thomas Colley, was arrested and executed for the murder of Ruth Osborne.

> **A Level Exam-Style Question Section C**
>
> How far do you agree that the actions of Lord Chief Justice Holt were more significant than the discovery of fraudulent cases in the development of sceptical opinion towards witchcraft in the years c1580 to c1750? (20 marks)
>
> **Tip**
> *Ensure that you provide chronological balance across the period by including examples from the beginning, middle and end.*

WHAT WAS THE IMPACT OF NOTABLE SCEPTICAL PUBLICATIONS ON ATTITUDES TO WITCHCRAFT?

Reginald Scot's *The Discoverie of Witchcraft*, 1584

Scot's influences: Johann Weyer

Scot's *The Discoverie of Witchcraft* is recognised as the first major work of English scepticism, although his rationalist style of criticism was already in fashion in other areas of study. Scot (c1538–1599), who came from a Kent gentry family, was extremely well read, and took a particular interest in magic and witchcraft. He gave great attention to the Dutch physician Johann Weyer's *De Praestigiis Daemonum* (On the Illusions of Demons), published in 1563. Weyer argued that the majority of supposed witches were in fact suffering from a kind of **melancholia** and that those who were guilty were unable to cause harm themselves because they were the mere tools of the Devil.

> **KEY TERM**
>
> Melancholia
> Depression or sorrowfulness.

Scot's publication of *The Discoverie of Witchcraft*

Scot was a member of the Family of Love, a radical Protestant sect that rejected many traditional Protestant and Catholic practices, such as infant baptism. Their core belief was that nature controlled events on Earth on a daily basis, rather than God, and they showed particular contempt for the Catholic Church. Many members of the Family of Love were wealthy and high-profile figures and they usually remained members of the Church of England in order to avoid prosecution. Scot made a clear connection between fraudulent witch-hunts and the Catholic Church, as Source 8 demonstrates.

SOURCE 8 From Reginald Scot, *The Discoverie of Witchcraft* (1584).

And it is worth my labour, to show you how papists define superstition, and how they expound the definition thereof... Superstition (say they) is a religion observed beyond measure, a religion practised with evil and unperfect circumstances. Also, whatsoever usurpeth the name of religion, through humane tradition, without the pope's authority...

These popish exorcists do many times forget their own rules. For they should not directly in their conjurations call upon the devil (as they doo) with entreaty, but with authority and commandment. Neither should they have in their charmes and conjurations any unknown names. Neither should there be (as always there is) any falsehood contained in the matter of the charm of conjuration.

EXTRACT 4 From Bengt Ankerloo, Stuart Clark and William Monter, *Witchcraft and Magic in Europe* (2002).

It is frequently claimed that witch trials multiplied across much of Central and Western Europe because of the religious fanaticism engendered by both Protestant and Catholic Reformations, which disastrously exacerbated the fears of an ignorant and suspicious peasantry. While it is difficult to deny some kind of connection between these movements which had such profound effects on all layers of European society and the concurrent wave of witch trials across much of Western and Central Europe, the exact relationship between these phenomena remains elusive.

SOURCE 9 Protestants burning Catholic crucifixes and images of the Virgin Mary in Germany. From an anonymous pamphlet of c1525.

THINKING HISTORICALLY Cause and consequence (6c)

Connections

Sources 8 and 9 and Extract 4 provide information on witchcraft and the Reformation, and give an impression of why Scot disliked the Catholic Church.

1 Read Source 8. How might this be seen as being influenced by the Protestant Reformation?

2 Read Extract 4.

   a) What is suggested about the connection between the Reformation and increased witch-hunts?

   b) How is this source similar to Source 8?

3 Look at Source 9. What does this suggest about the relationship between Catholics and Protestants in the 16th and 17th centuries?

4 Make a list of other ways in which the Reformation increased dislike for Catholics.

5 Why is it important for historians to see these links across time and be able to explain how causal factors can influence situations much later in time?

Prior to Scot's work being published, a number of high-profile witch trials took place at Chelmsford in Essex. One of the suspected witches, a beer brewer named John Samon, was accused and acquitted in 1561, 1570 and 1572, before he was convicted in 1587 of using witchcraft to commit murder and kill a cow. In 1566 three women were charged, with one being sentenced to hanging, one to a year in prison and one acquitted. Another hunt in Chelmsford occurred in 1582 and was driven by the JP, Brian Darcy, who favoured harsh continental-style punishments. This hunt resulted in 14 arrests and two executions. Scot was clearly influenced by these trials, in an area he knew well, and although he ultimately believed that witches existed, he disapproved of the terrible effects of the hunts.

Scot had to self-publish his book because it was so controversial, and he begins it by claiming that disturbances are all too often attributed to witches where there is no evidence, and other explanations are possible. Throughout his work, he made a number of key points about suspected witches.

- He doubted the more far-fetched charges brought against suspected witches, such as cannibalism.

- Taking direct influence from Johan Weyer, he claimed that women who genuinely believed they were witches could have been suffering from melancholia or delusions.

- Witches who did harm to animals or people did so through natural means, such as administering poison.

He devotes a significant proportion of the text to discounting magic tricks disguised as supernatural phenomena, and the fraudulent individuals who carried them out. He includes the sacraments of the Catholic Church in his list of magic tricks, which he believed heightened fear of witches. The Inquisition of the Catholic Church is given much of the blame for the cruelty handed out to suspected witches.

In the short term, the book did more harm than good. King James VI of Scotland, who would become James I of England on the death of Elizabeth in 1603, ordered all copies of the book to be burnt. He wrote a response, *Daemonologie* (1597), which stated his clear and unwavering belief in witches. In the introduction, he even mentions Scot by name, and denounces him as unchristian.

Why was Scot sceptical about witchcraft?

Scot was sceptical because he was so devoted to a belief in the 'supernatural unknown'. A commonly held belief in intellectual circles (and in the Family of Love of which he was a member) was the idea that undiscovered elements of nature contained many mysteries that could explain unknown phenomena. For example, it was accepted that healing could be done at a distance, or that plants and stones could have hidden properties that had not yet been discovered. Because Scot was so committed to this belief in a wide range of apparent natural phenomena that would be seen as ridiculous today, he was able to discount witchcraft as an explanation for mysterious events.

Again influenced by Weyer, Scot argued that a belief in witchcraft was not compatible with views put forward in the *Canon Episcopi*, a medieval text that informed religious law in Europe. The text acknowledged that witchcraft was not real, and cases of witchcraft were simply cases of deception.

Finally, it seems that for most of his life, other than a short stint at Oxford University, Scot lived on his family estate in Kent. Most social contact in his daily life was with his tenants, who would have been strong believers in witchcraft. As a learned man, he found it difficult to rationalise their beliefs, and when he saw children being used as witnesses at the Chelmsford trials, his view that most trials were held on very dubious foundations was affirmed.

SOURCE 10 Although it was published in 1584, Scot's work was reprinted several times. The image shows the front page of the popular 1651 edition.

SCOTS

Diſcovery of VVitchcraft:

PROVING

The common opinions of Witches contracting with Divels, Spirits, or Familiars; and their power to kill, torment, and conſume the bodies of men women, and children, or other creatures by diſeaſes or otherwiſe; their flying in the Air, &c. To be but imaginary Erronious conceptions and novelties;

WHEREIN ALSO,

The lewde unchriſtian practiſes of Witchmongers, upon aged, melancholy, ignorant, and ſuperſtious people in extorting confeſſions, by inhumane terrors and tortures is notably detected.

ALSO
- The knavery and confederacy of Conjurors.
- The impious blaſphemy of Inchanters.
- The impoſture of Soothſayers, and Infidelity of Atheiſts.
- The deluſion of Pythoniſts, Figure-caſters, Aſtrologers, and vanity of Dreamers.
- The fruitleſſe beggerly art of Alchimiſtry.
- The horrible art of Poiſoning and all the tricks and conveyances of juggling and Liegerdemain are fully deciphered.

With many other things opened that have long lain hidden: though very neceſſary to be known for the undeceiving of Judges, Juſtices, and Juries, and for the preſervation of poor, aged, deformed, ignorant people; frequently taken, arraigned, condemned and executed for Witches, when according to a right underſtanding, and a good conſcience, Phyſick, Food, and neceſſaries ſhould be adminiſtred to them.

Whereunto is added, a treatiſe upon the nature, and ſubſtance of Spirits and Divels, &c. all written and publiſhed in *Anno* 1584. by *Reginald Scot*, Eſquire.

LONDON,
Printed by *Richard Cotes*. 1651.

ACTIVITY
KNOWLEDGE CHECK

Reginald Scot

1 Make a list of the publications, ideas and legal cases that influenced Scot. Rank them in order of importance and explain your top choice.

2 How does Scot explain the popularity of witchcraft beliefs?

Samuel Harsnett's *A Discovery of the Fraudulent Practises of John Darrel*, 1599

Harsnett's career

As we saw in Source 5 (on page 16), Samuel Harsnett was deeply suspicious of the Boy of Burton case and the work of the supposed exorcist John Darrell. Harsnett had first-hand experience of the case and was present at the examination of Darrell and George More. His book started an important debate about the nature of witchcraft.

Harsnett was born in Essex in 1561, into a relatively humble family, and gained a degree from Cambridge. Like Reginald Scot, Harsnett was probably all too aware of the dubious Chelmsford trials that took place when he was growing up, and became deeply religious as a young man. He was ordained as a minister in 1583, and returned to Cambridge to study divinity. Harsnett rose through the ranks of the clergy to become Bishop of Chichester (1609), Bishop of Norwich (1619) and ultimately Archbishop of York (1629), but when he was involved in the case of John Darrell he was working as chaplain to Richard Bancroft, Bishop of London.

The impact of *A Discovery of the Fraudulent Practises of John Darrel*

The book is divided into five sections. The main thrust of the argument is summed up in the introduction, where Harsnett makes it clear that the practice of misleading people through magic is nothing new and can be traced back to ancient times. He also criticises the Catholic Church, and states that Catholic priests claim to carry out miracles as easily as a squirrel can crack a nut. He claims that because Catholics are so quick to perform tricks and miracles, such as those apparently carried out through the power of holy water, making the sign of the cross in order to perform a blessing and carrying out communion with bread and wine, they believe that rituals can solve any problem. The chief trick played by Catholics, however, is done when they claim to cast out devils through prayer and exorcism, which is also a form of ritual. Any casting out of devils can only be done by God, and anyone who attempts to take credit for God's work is a heretic and a fraud. The sections are then divided up as follows.

- The first section includes a survey of the people Darrell claimed to have exorcised, and an account of Harsnett's interrogation of Darrell. He claims that Darrell immediately called into question the reliability of witnesses, something that Harsnett says all guilty men will do. He then goes into detail about how Darrell was able to convince people that William Somers was possessed, and claims that Darrell is actually immoral and sinful because, in his hobby as an amateur musician, he has played blasphemous songs.

- The second section outlines how Darrell instructed Somers to feign possession, and how they conspired together to fake an exorcism.

- The third section recounts the confession made by William Somers, and Darrell's role in encouraging him to initially revoke it. It then details how Darrell and his associate George More argued that Somers had been forced to make a confession through threats or promises. Harsnett then claims that the fits experienced by Somers were not extraordinary, and had been misinterpreted.

- In the fourth section, Harsnett goes to great lengths to discredit Somers' fits. He says that the superhuman strength Somers was supposed to have displayed during his fits was nothing extraordinary, and there was no evidence that Somers became fluent in Greek, Latin and Hebrew during his fits, as Darrell had claimed. When Somers fell into a supposed fit in front of Harsnett he was asked questions in Greek, but laughed in response. When he was asked questions in Latin, he gave a few basic words.

- Harsnett dedicates the fifth section to the Boy of Burton case, and details how Darrell instructed Thomas Darling to act possessed, and how Darling confessed. He discredits a confession made by one woman suspected of being possessed and treated by Darrell years before, Katherine Wright. Wright ultimately confessed that she was beaten by her father-in-law for many years, and this made her weak and liable to hallucinations. Any apparitions she had seen were apparently fictitious, and she exaggerated her symptoms in order to avoid further beatings.

The pamphlet war

Harsnett started a pamphlet war that prompted a wider debate about witchcraft and possession.

- This led Darrell himself to respond to Harsnett with the provocatively titled *A detection of that sinful, shaming, lying, and ridiculous discours of Samuel Harsnett* (1600).

- John Deacon and John Walker, two ministers who had Puritan sympathies, questioned whether exorcism was a miracle and whether it was even possible in their pamphlet *Dialogicall discourses of spirits and divels* (1601). They argued that the Devil was unable to possess people, as only God had this power, and new bodies could not be created to do the Devil's work, as God would not allow this. They demanded proof from Darrell that he had the power to carry out exorcisms.

- Darrell responded in *The Replie of John Darrell to the answere of John Deacon and John Walker* (1602), where he repeated that he had witnessed all of the possessions that he claimed to have seen.

This pamphlet war was important, not only in revealing disagreements about the honesty of Darrell's patients, but in questioning the entire possibility of demonic possession and its cure by prayer and fasting. Darrell, however, still had much support. Joseph Hall, who became Bishop of Exeter and Norwich, wrote that Darrell did indeed perform exorcisms through his godly devotion, and that his critics were motivated by jealousy. The scepticism of Harsnett, Deacon and Walker was still a minority opinion.

Harsnett's own religious beliefs are contradictory and difficult to ascertain, and they may go some way to explain why he was so keen to attack beliefs in witchcraft. He was accused as a young minister of being sympathetic to the Catholic Church, and in 1596 he had supported Peter Baro, a professor at Cambridge who had shown **Arminian** tendencies. This may explain his immediate dislike for Darrell, who was a Puritan. Bishop Bancroft, with whom Harsnett worked closely, was also acknowledged to be a member of the Arminian faction. Despite this, in his criticism of Darrell, and in his *A Declaration of Egregious Popish Impostures* (1603), it is clear that he was deeply anti-Catholic, and he lays sole blame for witchcraft accusations at the Catholic Church.

The case of Darrell has been interpreted by historians to be one of factional fighting within the Church, as Darrell was a Puritan and Harsnett a Church of England conformist; however, the arguments of the Puritans Deacon and Walker suggest the truth is more complicated than this. The historian Keith Thomas argues that the entire controversy centres on whether prayer and fasting were accepted methods of exorcising spirits. In Puritan circles, these methods were widely used, but among the senior clergy they had long since been rejected.

ACTIVITY
KNOWLEDGE CHECK

Harsnett and Darrell
1 What do you think motivated Harsnett to attack Darrell?

2 Why do you think Harsnett's beliefs were still a minority opinion at the turn of the 17th century?

Thomas Ady's *A Candle in the Dark*, 1656

Thomas Ady's career
Little is known about the life of Thomas Ady, other than the fact that he published three books. Ady reveals that he lived in south-east England, and a document recording his marriage ceremony in 1634 suggests that he lived most of his life in Essex. His marriage record also states that he was a renowned doctor. He states in print that he had a familiarity with events in Essex and Suffolk, and

witnessed in person witchcraft trials in Bury St Edmunds (most likely those orchestrated by Matthew Hopkins). Nothing is known of his education, although his son studied at Cambridge and became a lawyer. His status as a doctor would suggest that Ady was highly educated.

A Candle in the Dark, a sceptical book about witchcraft, was published in 1656. This was followed in 1661 by *A Perfect Discovery of Witches*, which attacked the witch-hunts of the earlier 17th century. In *A Perfect Discovery*, Ady was critical of physicians who failed to understand diseases and were too quick to blame them on witchcraft. He was also critical of the attitude prevalent amongst the general population that witches were to blame for natural disasters and unexplained events. His final book was entitled *The Doctrine of Devils, Proved to be the grand Apostacy of these later Times* (1676). This book was initially published anonymously, and was heavily influenced by Joseph Mede's *The Apostacy of the Latter Times* (hence the similar title), published after Mede's death in 1644. Both Ady and Mede agreed that possession could be attributed to mental illness.

The significance of *A Candle in the Dark*

A Candle in the Dark uses the Bible as its only source, the same source used by witchfinders to justify their persecutions. In the preface Ady sets out his main argument that the actions of witchfinders and suspicions about witches cannot be found in written form anywhere in the Bible (Source 11). He goes on to explain that he was compelled to write the book because he knew of too many wrongful executions that had taken place as a result of witchcraft accusations, and that it was ridiculous to suggest that ordinary animals such as cats, mice or frogs can be taken to be witches' familiars.

Scot's *The Discoverie of Witchcraft* is mentioned as a direct influence, and Ady states that although Scot's work was taken seriously for a time, the English people had forgotten Scot's teachings. His work is essentially a revision of Scot's original message.

SOURCE

11 From Thomas Ady, *A Candle in the Dark* (1656).

Where is it written in all the old and new Testament, that a Witch is a murderer, or hath power to kill by Witchcraft, or to afflict with any disease or infirmity? Where is it written, that Witches have Imps sucking of their bodies?... Where is it written, that the Devil setteth privy marks upon Witches, whereby they should be known or searched out? or that any man or woman hath any mark upon their body any more than natural, or by some disease or hurt, which is preternatural? Where is it written, that the trial of a Witch should be by sinking or swimming in the water? or by... privy marks, or suspicion of people, to be signs of a Witch? Where is it written, that Witches can hurt corn or cattle, or transport corn by Witchcraft, or can fly in the air, and do many such strange wonders? Where is it written, that a Witch is such a man or woman that maketh a league with the Devil, written with his or her blood, and by virtue of that covenant to have the Devil at command?

The book is divided into three sections.

- In the first section, Ady describes what the definition of a witch is according to the Bible. The types of witches he identifies from the Bible include astrologers, jugglers, users of charms and those who attempt to communicate with the dead. He concedes that these types of magician could be seen as false prophets or **idolaters**, and states that if witches are people who encourage idolatry, then Catholic priests are guilty of witchcraft. He is particularly critical of the notion that witches had familiar spirits, as there is no evidence for this in the Bible.

- In the second section, Ady explains that the original scriptures have been misinterpreted, particularly by Catholics, in order to justify witch-hunts. He emphasises this with a number of examples of idolatry and corrupt priests from the Old Testament, who he directly compared to Catholic priests. He also notes that Catholics were the first to kill for religion and that this is unchristian. The 16th-century Danish theologian Hemingus is criticised, as well as the French philosopher Jean Bodin (1530–96), who claimed that torture was acceptable in witch trials because rumours about witches were almost always true. Andreas Hyperius (1511–64), the Flemish theologian, also comes under fire. Ady claims that these writers were Popish (Catholics), but in fact Hemingus and Hyperius were both Protestants.

KEY TERM

Idolater
A person who worships false idols.

- Most of Ady's contempt and anger is reserved for the third section, which contains a critique of a number of English works that promoted witch trials, and even criticises King James' *Daemonologie*. Ady claims that James' work was actually written by Bishop James Montague, a close ally of James who published his collected works. Ady is particularly critical because no scripture was referenced in *Daemonologie*.

Although the key arguments in the book are derived from close study of the Bible, Ady uses rational common sense to explain a number of concepts associated with witch-hunts. He is particularly critical of the swimming test (Source 12), which he claims can be manipulated easily. He is also critical of methods such as sleep deprivation, as used by Matthew Hopkins, who had been active in Essex and Suffolk in 1645–47, and is directly referenced by Ady.

SOURCE

12 From Thomas Ady, *A Candle in the Dark* (1656).

Then they cast them into the water, to see whether they will sink or swim, a mere Juggling delusion to blind people's eyes, for he that hath been used to the Art of Swimming may know, that few men or women being tied hand and feet together can sink quite away till they be drowned, or if he lay them flat on their back, and hold up their feet with a string, their fore-part will not sink, and therein they can use Juggling to blind the people's eyes for difference sake; for when they will save any man or woman, they will let loose the string which they hold in their hand, and let their feet sink first, and then all their body will sink, then they cry one to the people, Look you now, and see the difference betwixt an honest man or woman, and a Witch, take her out, she is an honest woman...

The reason of this difference is easy to conceive to men of knowledge; for, First; There is difference of constitution in peoples bodies; some are heavy of temper, and they sink most; some again are more light of temper, fuller of, vital spirits, and they sink not so much. Secondly, we must observe the Systole and Diastole of breathing; some happen to fall into the water when their bodies are full of breath, and they swim most; some happen to fall into the water when their breath is out of their bodies, before they can draw it up again, and they sink most. Some are kept long fasting in watching and torment, and then are cast into the water when their bowels and veins are empty of food and filled with Wind, and these swim more than those that are filled with nourishment; or perhaps they are kept fasting so long that they have scarce any life left, and then they happen to sink most, but if they do, it must not serve their turn, for the cruel Inquisitor will still torment them till he extort confession, if the party live long enough for his cruelty to take place. Some again are Women cast into the water, with their Coats tied close toward their feet, and Men with their apparel... Some again are Women, whose bodies are dilated with bearing of Children... more apt to swim than to sink.

Ady is highly critical of magicians and conjurors, and mentions a book published in 1634 called *Hocus Pocus Junior*. *Hocus Pocus Junior* was probably written by a leading magician of the time who used the stage name Hocus Pocus. (Incidentally, this is one of the earliest recorded uses of the phrase as a reference to magic.) Ady is critical of Hocus Pocus and the tricks performed by magicians, and goes some way to explaining how their tricks were carried out. Although these performers were claiming to perform miracles, they were able to convince people through sleight of hand or by planting assistants in crowds. He explains that cases of moving statues had been controlled by wires, and that weeping statues of saints were subtly fed by pipes. He also describes critically how some jugglers and swindlers would stuff dead rodents and attach them by springs to their clothes, claiming that they were familiars.

The significance of Ady's beliefs

Most crucially, Ady did believe that witches existed, but believed that the definition of a witch as found in the Bible did not resemble the 17th-century definition used in witch-hunts. To Ady, a witch was not someone who had supernatural powers, but someone who led others towards an ungodly path, either through idolatry or through practices associated with the Catholic Church. The real criminals were the idolaters and witch-hunters themselves. Reverend George Burroughs, the only minister to be executed in the Salem witch trials in 1692, quoted the book in his defence, but it failed to make an impact. In Britain, however, the steep decline in witch trials and increased scepticism in witchcraft after 1660 was certainly influenced by the work of Ady.

Thomas Ady

1 In what ways does *A Candle in the Dark* differ from other sceptical publications?

2 How does Ady explain the increase in false accusations and false confessions?

John Webster's *The Displaying of Supposed Witchcraft*, 1677

John Webster's career

Like Ady, Webster (1610–82) worked as a doctor, but made a name for himself as a preacher. Born in Yorkshire, in published works he suggests he had a familiarity with Cambridge University, although there is no record of him attending in the university registers. In 1634 he became the **curate** of Kildwick church. Before his ordination in 1632, he studied chemistry and medicine at Gresham College (Gresham is detailed further in Chapter 2), and became interested in the scientific method.

During the Civil War, Webster acted as a chaplain and surgeon in the Parliamentary army, and by 1648 he had left the Church of England and become a **nonconformist**. After the Civil War he preached at a number of Yorkshire churches, and engaged in public debates about the role of university education and astrology. He was living in Clitheroe in 1657, and in 1658 the Republican government seized his books, presumably because his religious views did not conform to those of the government, and he gave up preaching for medicine.

It was around this time that he began preparing *The Displaying of Supposed Witchcraft*, which was completed in 1673 but not published until 1677.

Webster's publication of *The Displaying of Supposed Witchcraft*

Webster's attitude was similar to that of Thomas Ady, and he agreed with Ady that beliefs that are not founded in the teachings of the Bible should be rejected. As with many sceptical publications, *The Displaying of Supposed Witchcraft* was written in response to other authors who claimed that witch-hunts were legitimate. In this case, Webster intended to rebuff Joseph Glanvill, who had claimed that the Demon Drummer of Tedworth case was genuine, and Meric Casaubon (1599–1671), the son of French intellectual Isaac Casaubon, who moved to England from France. Casaubon was a leading figure in the intellectual world after the Restoration of Charles II, and wrote in defence of the dominant view that witchcraft was genuine.

Webster's evidence

Webster's central belief was that witches did exist, but that they were not able to command supernatural powers. They did carry out evil acts, but they did this using their own power and did not have assistance from the Devil.

Webster was critical of the Demon Drummer of Tedworth case, and stated that the original complainant, John Mompesson, was responsible. He also comments on the Pendle Swindle of 1634, and claims that Edmund Robinson was instructed by his father to bring charges against the accused witches. Rather than being baseless speculation, Webster actually met Robinson when he was curate at Kildwick church in Yorkshire and was able to see first-hand a doubtful case. After noticing that his congregation was disturbed by the boy's presence, Webster went to see him at the house where he was staying, and found him there with two other men, presumably his uncle and father. The men refused to allow Webster access to the boy, but when he saw Robinson again in public he was able to speak with him and ask him if his story was true. The boy was hastily taken away by the two men.

Webster also cites the case of Roland Jenks from 1577. Jenks was a Catholic bookseller from Oxford who was in prison in 1577 for selling Catholic literature. At his trial, Jenks was said to have uttered a curse, and within a few days hundreds of people, including members of the jury and two judges, suddenly died. In reality, this was probably an outbreak of typhus, but two theories were put forward at the time. The first was that there was some sort of poisonous vapour rising from the prison and the prisoners themselves, and the other was that Jenks himself was responsible through sorcery. In Webster's account, he blames Jenks, but denies that witchcraft was responsible. Instead, he attributes blame to the use of entirely natural poisons. Webster argued that all accusations of harm done by witches could be ascribed to natural causes.

The impact of Webster's work

Although Webster never became a thinker of any significant stature, his work was relatively well received, and he engaged in public intellectual debate through pamphlets and books. The Oxford academic Seth Ward wrote a response to Webster's criticism of educational methods, as did John Wilkins, one of the founders of the Royal Society. The editor of Joseph Glanvill's works, Henry More, added a response to Webster's views on witchcraft when he published *Saducismus Triumphatus* in 1681. Webster also wrote on chemistry, minerals and metals, and was taken seriously by many members of the Royal Society. His methodical approach reflected the dawning of the new scientific age, and his thorough use of evidence, some of which was first-hand, meant that his credibility set him apart from many of the other sceptical authors.

The historian Hugh Trevor-Roper, in his influential *The Crisis of the Seventeenth Century: Religion, the Reformation and Social Change* (1967), discounts the importance of Webster's work. He argues that the origins of Webster's works can be found in the work of Weyer and Scot, published in 1563 and 1584 respectively, and that the intellectual debate had not progressed since then. Instead, according to Trevor-Roper, the witch craze declined because the power of the clergy over people's lives decreased in Protestant countries. It was no coincidence that witch-hunts continued for longer in Catholic countries, where the power of the clergy was stronger.

ACTIVITY
KNOWLEDGE CHECK

John Webster

1 What were Webster's main arguments?

2 How could it be argued that Webster's work is more reliable than other sceptical publications?

3 Which other sceptical writers does Webster agree with and why?

Publication of Balthasar Bekker's *The Enchanted World*, 1691

Balthasar Bekker's career

Bekker (1634–98) was a Dutch clergyman and made a name for himself as a **Cartesian** rationalist, writing about philosophy and theology as well as witchcraft. Born in Friesland, he was the son of a **Calvinist** minister and was deeply influenced by this religious tradition. He became a minister in 1657, and visited England in 1683, writing enthusiastically about his travels. In 1668

KEY TERMS

Cartesian
A follower of René Descartes (1596-1650), who employed logical analysis in his philosophy.

Calvinist
A follower of John Calvin (1509-64), a key figure in the Protestant Reformation. Calvin promoted the idea that God willed which souls were destined to go to heaven or hell, known as predestination.

he published *De Philosophia Cartesiana* (On Cartesian Philosophy), where he argued that natural events cannot be explained by reference to the Bible, an idea he would revive in *The Enchanted World*. A month after his death in 1698, he was accepted as a Fellow of the Royal Society.

SOURCE
13 Balthasar Bekker and another man, possibly the Dutch sceptical philosopher Christian Thomasius, sieve diseases from devils in order to rationalise witchcraft beliefs. From a Dutch engraving, c1695.

The significance of *The Enchanted World*

The Enchanted World has been described by historians Alan Kors and Edward Peters as the most influential critical work on witchcraft beliefs in the 17th century. Bekker's book was undoubtedly influenced by Reginald Scot, who he agreed with about the impossibility of witchcraft. Despite this agreement, his reasoning differed to Scot's. He again used the Bible as his primary source of evidence, but attempted to approach it in a reasoned and unbiased way, rather than relying on rumours and stories, as Scot often did. In this sense, Bekker's approach has much in common with that of Thomas Ady. As Source 14 shows, he was doubtful about the witchcraft cases he was aware of, and states that in every case there is some sort of deception or irregularity.

SOURCE 14 From Balthasar Bekker, *The Enchanted World* (1691).

Among all those [cases] I have cited, there is not a single example in which the chief circumstances are not incomplete, lacking something that would be necessarily if one desired to draw conclusions from them; there is not one whose certainty is not doubtful, and which doesn't lack solid evidence; there is not one in which one doesn't have good cause to suspect that there is deception…. all that is natural that is found in these is simply something unusual, of whose cause, for the most part, we are ignorant. There is, thus, no other Magic than that which is in the imagination of men; there are no Phantoms, no Divination, nor any obsession which is from the Devil.

Bekker used reason to argue that unless the Devil has a body, it would be impossible for him to possess and influence people on Earth. A rational interpretation of the Bible also suggests that the Devil is forever in hell, and cannot operate on Earth. Again, through his Cartesian methodology, he claimed that if the Devil is an instrument of God, and has no power of his own, then those who believe that the Devil has any power are **heretics**, because they are effectively practising a belief in two gods. An example of Bekker's reasoning is given in Source 15, where he points out that witches should not be blamed for causing events that could be attributed to nature. He believed, like Scot, that there was much that was unknown about nature, that the world of science would inevitably develop further, and that one day explanations would be found for apparent supernatural events.

SOURCE 15 From Balthasar Bekker, *The Enchanted World* (1691).

If I encounter something which has not yet been proven, but which nevertheless is of the same nature as something else, what reason do I have to look for another cause than that which I already have found at work in the other? Suppose that I see a new style of slippers that is beautiful, and such as I never have seen the likes of in the shop of any shoemaker, nor on anyone's feet: must I infer from this that it was neither a shoemaker nor his servant who made them, but rather a baker or a tinker? Nevertheless, it would not be so strange a thing that a baker or a tinker should have made a pair of slippers, since they have hands and feet just like other people, as it would be to say that a Spirit had done a corporeal thing [in bodily form], or, which is the same thing, that a body does spiritual things… I have not investigated the secrets of nature in such a way that I could know what she is yet capable of doing again, and I have not thumbed through books in such a way that there could not be in them certain things formerly known to be natural things, but that pass today for witchcraft.

The significance of Bekker's work: the views of historians

Historian Hugh Trevor-Roper argues that, like Webster, Bekker had no arguments to add to those that had been put forward by Weyer, Scot, or Webster. Instead, Bekker's work coincides with changes in witch beliefs because the intellectual climate had changed and new scientific approaches had been adopted (see Chapter 2). Keith Thomas (1971) claims that the end of the 17th century was a crucial time for the decline of witchcraft beliefs because advancements in science led intellectuals to believe they would soon be able to explain mysterious events through natural causes.

Robin Attfield (1985) has argued that Bekker is much more influential than many historians give him credit for. Within the first two months of *The Enchanted World* being published in Holland, 4,000 copies were sold. The fact that it was soon translated into German, Italian, French and English also underlines its significance. Bekker's publication also prompted a number of pamphlets to be produced in reply, criticising him for causing the decline in witchcraft beliefs. Attfield counts 131 contemporary Dutch works concerning Bekker, resulting in Bekker losing his job as a minister. He was put on trial for blasphemy and spreading atheism, but was acquitted. If his influence in Britain was limited, he seems to have genuinely worried German witch-hunters, who were still burning witches at the beginning of the 18th century. A number of German towns banned the book.

Conclusion: the end of the witch craze?

The repealing of witchcraft legislation in England in 1736 meant that sceptical publications were no longer needed to convince the authorities that change was necessary. In the public imagination, however, witchcraft was very much alive. The 1751 case of John and Ruth Osborne, who were pursued by a mob, was not an isolated incident, and occasional cases are recorded well into the 19th century. *Gentleman's Magazine* reported in 1785 that a suspected witch volunteered herself for the swimming test, and was found to be not guilty. In 1825, Isaac Stebbings of Wickham-Skeith, Suffolk, endured the swimming test several times until the local clergy intervened and stopped the investigation. In 1863, an elderly Frenchman living in Essex was suspected of witchcraft as he made a living as a fortune teller. He was subjected to the swimming test and died a month later from inflamed lungs. Bridget Cleary of Clonmel, Ireland, died in 1895 after her family and neighbours became suspicious that she was possessed by fairies. She was held over a fire and suffered significant burns. Her husband was found guilty of manslaughter.

In literature, witches were increasingly referred to in the realms of fiction rather than fact, but a number of writers continued to show support for witchcraft after the last trials. The founder of the Protestant Methodist Church, John Wesley (1703–91), wrote in 1768 that to disbelieve in witches was to disbelieve the teachings of the Bible, and was critical of the intellectual climate that had encouraged the repealing of witchcraft legislation. Despite Wesley's beliefs, the vast majority of learned individuals accepted the rationalism that came with the age of science and reason.

ACTIVITY
KNOWLEDGE CHECK

Balthasar Bekker

1 Why was Bekker's work controversial?

2 Do you agree with the view put forward by Trevor-Roper that Bekker added little to the study of witchcraft?

A Level Exam-Style Question Section C

How far do you agree that the publication of Thomas Ady's *A Candle in the Dark* (1656) was the most important development in changing attitudes towards witchcraft in the years c1580–c1780? (20 marks)

Tip
Dedicate a detailed discussion to the factor given in the question, in this case the publication of A Candle in the Dark. *Then evaluate this against other factors.*

ACTIVITY
SUMMARY

Sceptical attitudes, 1580–1750

1 Create a timeline showing the various dubious cases you have encountered in this chapter.

   a) Next to each case, provide an explanation about why that case was doubtful.

   b) Which case was the most influential? Why?

2 a) Create a table with the name of each sceptical author that you have come across in this chapter at the head of each column. Include the following categories in the table: influences, notable works, reasons for doubting contemporary witchcraft beliefs, reasons for doubting specific cases.

   b) Which authors are most influential? Why?

3 Do you agree that sceptical publications had an important impact on the decline in witchcraft beliefs? Explain your answer.

4 What other causes might account for the decline in witchcraft beliefs?

5 What was the biggest turning point in the decline of witchcraft beliefs? Explain your answer.

WIDER READING

Gaskill, M. *Witchcraft: A Very Short Introduction*, Oxford University Press (2010). Introduces witchcraft from a wider historical perspective.

Levack, B.P. *The Witch-hunt in Early Modern Europe*, Pearson (2006). A clearly written account of some of the major witch-hunts and doubtful cases.

Oldridge, D. *The Devil in Tudor and Stuart England*, The History Press (2000). Provides a sound analysis of religious beliefs and attitudes towards the Devil and witchcraft.

Pavlac, B. *Witch Hunts in the Western World*, Greenwood (2010). Provides a broad overview of many fraudulent cases.

Thomas, K. *Religion and the Decline of Magic*, Penguin, new edition (2003). First published in 1971 and still the major authority on changing attitudes to witchcraft.

Trevor-Roper, H.R. *The European Witch-Craze of the Sixteenth and Seventeenth Centuries*, Penguin (1991). Originally published in *The Crisis of the Seventeenth Century: Religion, the Reformation and Social Change*, Penguin (1967), but reprinted as a standalone text in 1991. A short but classic interpretation of the witch craze.

3.2 | The wider intellectual context: the coming of the age of science and reason

KEY QUESTIONS

- To what extent did understanding of the universe change in the years c1580–c1750?
- How did approaches to human understanding and knowledge change in the years c1580–c1750?

INTRODUCTION

What was the Scientific Revolution?

The Joseph Wright painting, *An Experiment on a Bird in the Air Pump* (1768), captures many of the key elements of the Scientific Revolution and the concerns of those who experienced it. Wright was painting towards the end of the Revolution, but displayed a keen interest in all things scientific and wanted to portray the difficult transition from an age where nature was said to be controlled by God, to one where humans could understand natural events from a rational perspective.

In the painting, a travelling scientist is seen demonstrating the effects of creating a vacuum by using a device known as an air pump. Inside the air pump is a bird, which will inevitably die through lack of oxygen if the scientist decides to continue the experiment, but could be saved if he lifts the lid on the device. The scientist is, in effect, playing God. Some of the audience cannot bear to watch, others are looking philosophically at the experiment, and the couple to the left are concerned with nothing but each other. The realisation that God does not control the world on a day-to-day basis is clear for all to see. This scene is a far cry from the superstitious witch trials of the previous century.

The 'Scientific Revolution' refers to the emergence of modern scientific beliefs and methods that took place between approximately 1550 and 1800, although new discoveries and debates peaked in the 17th century. New developments in biology, chemistry, physics, astronomy and mathematics helped to fundamentally alter established views of the natural world and the role of God in commanding nature. The revolution began when Nicolaus Copernicus (1473–1543) questioned the ancient astronomical belief that the Earth was at the centre of the universe. Other important contributors to the Scientific Revolution included Johannes Kepler (1571–1630), whose laws of planetary motion would inspire Newton's theory of gravity, and Galileo (1564–1642), whose many achievements include the discovery of four of the moons of Jupiter and an early appreciation for the role of tides in relation to the rotation of the Earth.

1597 - Gresham College founded

1609 - Johannes Kepler's *Astronomia Nova* published

| 1595 | 1600 | 1605 | 1610 | 1615 | 1620 | 1625 | 1630 | 1635 | 1640 |

1605 - Francis Bacon's *Of the Proficience and Advancement of Learning, Divine and Human* published

1632 - Galileo Galilei publishes *Dialogue Concerning Two Chief World Systems*

An Experiment on a Bird in the Air Pump by Joseph Wright of Derby (1768).

Two dominant ideas shaped **natural philosophy** during the Scientific Revolution:

- Aristotelian beliefs were based on the work of Aristotle (384–322 BC), who was perhaps the most influential figure in Ancient Greek natural philosophy. Aristotle's view of the universe was **homocentric**, and he believed that only simple circular motions could take place in space. Aristotle's wider approach was one of **empiricism**, or the processes of learning from observation and experience.

- Platonic beliefs were based on the work of Plato (427–347 BC). His approach was more theoretical, and he attempted to move away from observed knowledge towards knowledge based on thought alone. As the physical world can change there is no way of gaining certain knowledge from it. Ideas, however, do not change. Many natural philosophers were Neoplatonic, an approach that combines Aristotle's ordered and empirical approach with Plato's theoretical approach.

The methodology underlying the Scientific Revolution comprised two elements. Firstly, mathematics featured heavily in order to make precise calculations about how the world works. Secondly, experiment and observation were used to gain a better understanding of nature. When writers such as Scot, Ady and Webster adopted this rational approach, they concluded that witchcraft cases should not be taken at face value.

KEY TERMS

Natural philosophy
The study of the natural world. Natural philosophers were not scientists in the modern sense, as they were concerned with providing philosophical reasoning in order to explain the workings of nature. With the Scientific Revolution, they adopted the scientific method and the study changed from being strictly theoretical to one that adopted practical elements.

Homocentric
The belief that all rotations in the universe are centred on the Earth.

Empiricism
Empiricists believe that knowledge can only come about as a result of experience. They tend to seek out evidence and carry out experiments in order to formulate theories. Empirical ideas were essential to the development of the Scientific Revolution.

1655 – Thomas Hobbes publishes *De Corpore*

1660 – The Royal Society founded

1690 – John Locke publishes *Essay Concerning Human Understanding*

| 1645 | 1650 | 1655 | 1660 | 1665 | 1670 | 1675 | 1680 | 1685 | 1690 |

1658 – Thomas Hobbes' *De Homine* published

1687 – Isaac Newton's *Principia Mathematica* published

KEY TERM

Epicycle
A small circle on which a planet moves, from the Greek meaning 'on the circle'. This small circle moves along a larger circle (called a deferent) around a fixed point.

TO WHAT EXTENT DID UNDERSTANDING OF THE UNIVERSE CHANGE IN THE YEARS c1580–c1750?

The coexistence of new and older ideas

The influence of Claudius Ptolemy

Ptolemy (AD 90–168), who was born in Roman-occupied Egypt and wrote in Greek, believed, like Aristotle, that the Earth was at the centre of the universe. He produced tables to track and predict the position of the Sun, stars and planets, and his findings were generally accepted by scholars in medieval Europe. Towards the end of the Middle Ages, his system was beginning to be interpreted as a hypothetical one, as it provided mathematical models without observed evidence. Based on his models, Ptolemy had suggested that hypothetical bodies such as extra planets and stars might exist in the solar system, and although there was no evidence for this, his was the only system that seemed to work, and thus it was used well into the 16th century.

While Aristotle's view was that the Earth was at the centre of all things, and all heavenly bodies moved in perfect circles around the Earth, Ptolemy's mathematical approach suggested that planets move on an **epicycle**, although to make his calculations work, he had to assume that the epicycles did not move around the Earth but around another point not far from Earth (called the centre of deferent), halfway between the Earth and another point called the equant (see Figure 2.1). This meant that Ptolemy could account for the apparent changes in speed as the planets were in orbit but also maintain a system of perfect circles. As this system was refined and the number of circles used by astronomers increased, it became so complex that by the late Middle Ages it became almost unworkable. Before Copernicus, the Ancient Greek idea that the motion of all heavenly bodies must be perfectly uniform and circular was restricting progress. A new theory was needed.

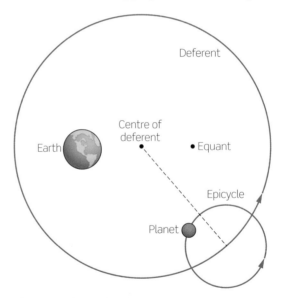

Figure 2.1 The Ptolemaic system.

EXTEND YOUR KNOWLEDGE

Astronomy before Ptolemy
The geocentric model of the universe, where the Earth is at the centre of all things, was already well established before Ptolemy.

In the 6th century BC, the Ancient Greek philosopher Anaximander postulated that the Earth was cylindrical in shape, and that surrounding the Earth were a number of invisible wheels. Inside the wheels, fire is burning constantly, and what we see as the Moon, stars and planets are actually holes in the invisible wheels, revealing the fire within.

According to Plato, the Earth was spherical in shape, but remained motionless at the centre of the universe, with all other celestial bodies moving in uniform circles around the Earth. These ideas heavily influenced Plato's student, Aristotle, who would develop them further.

Nicolaus Copernicus

Copernicus was born in Poland in 1473, but little is known about his early life other than that his father died when he was young and his uncle arranged for him to have a quality education. Copernicus studied at the University of Krakow and excelled at his studies. He became a **polymath**, but his most significant work was in the field of astronomy.

While the dates of the Scientific Revolution are debatable, it is generally agreed that the 1543 publication of Copernicus' *De revolutionibus orbium coelestium* (On the Revolutions of the Heavenly Spheres) marks its beginning. The book is based on over 30 years of research, and although Copernicus was hesitant to publish it at first, it was released shortly before his death. His continued commitment to Christianity is evident in the dedication he makes in the book to Pope Paul III.

The inadequacy of the long-standing Ptolemaic system was evident in its inability to explain all astronomical movements, but it also posed more practical problems, such as its inability to accurately set a date for Easter each year (it was decided in AD 325 that Easter should fall on the Sunday after the first full moon following the spring equinox). Crucially, Copernicus proposed that the universe is heliocentric, with the Sun at its centre, as opposed to the dominant view proposed by Ptolemy and others that the Earth was at the centre.

Copernicus agreed with both Aristotle and Ptolemy that heavenly bodies moved in perfect circles, but proposed that the universe was made up of eight spheres. The Sun is at the centre of the eight spheres, and does not move. The planets that were known to Copernicus revolved around the Sun, each in a separate sphere and did not interfere with each other (Mercury, Venus, Earth, Mars, Jupiter and Saturn). The Earth revolved on its own axis, and the Moon revolved in its own sphere around the Earth.

In order to avoid accusations of blasphemy, Copernicus had to present his work as Platonic theory rather than observed Aristotelian fact. In 1616, the book was banned by the Catholic Church when it was added to their *Index Librorum Prohibitorum* (List of Prohibited Books), and although scholars could access an edited version of the book, it was not removed from the *Index* until 1758. Despite the Church's attempts to censor the work of Copernicus, the book became hugely influential later and his findings were seen as accepted fact by many in intellectual circles, although not necessarily in his lifetime.

SOURCE

2 The Copernican view of the universe, with the Sun at the centre. From *De revolutionibus orbium coelestium* (1543).

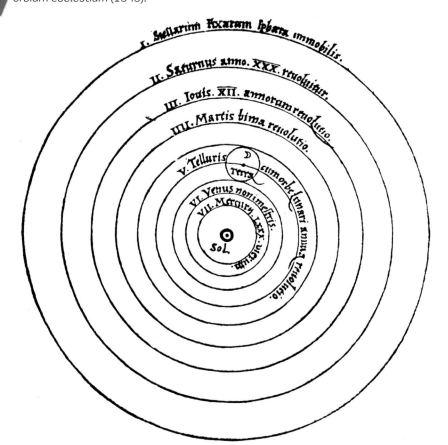

The limits of Copernicus' findings

There has been a tendency to view Copernicus as a conservative rather than revolutionary thinker.

- Like Ptolemy, he made theoretical conclusions rather than empirical observations.

- He continued to believe that the planets and stars moved on spheres (on a round trajectory), although he was not sure what these spheres were made of, or whether they could even be seen.

- He refused to change Ptolemy's underlying approach and believed that all planetary movements must be perfectly circular.

Most people who were aware of his book believed that Copernicus was simply presenting theory, and that his thoughts about the motion of the Earth were not to be taken seriously. The thought of the Earth moving was so counter-intuitive that it seemed impossible, and it contradicted biblical accounts that stated that the Earth stood still. This view was enforced by the fact that a preface was inserted by Andreas Osiander, a Protestant minister (Copernicus was too frail to oversee the publication himself), who stated that the book served simply to provide a model in order to aid astronomical calculations, and Copernicus' findings were unlikely to be accurate. A recent study has found that only ten thinkers accepted Copernicus' theory as physical truth before 1600.

ACTIVITY
KNOWLEDGE CHECK

Ptolemy and Copernicus

1 What was the Ancient Greek view of the universe, as promoted by Ptolemy?

2 In what ways were Copernicus' findings both similar and different to those of Ptolemy?

3 What were the limits of Copernicus' findings?

The impact of Johannes Kepler

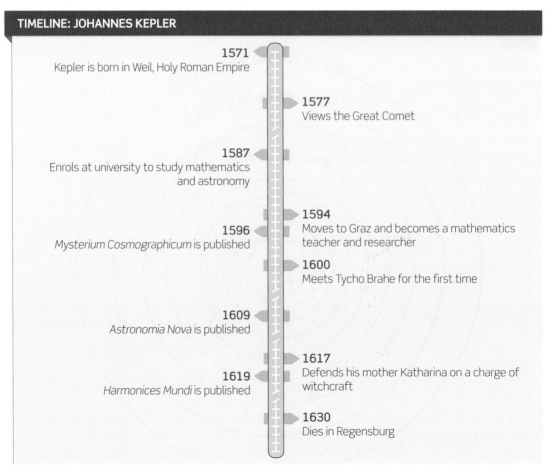

TIMELINE: JOHANNES KEPLER

1571
Kepler is born in Weil, Holy Roman Empire

1577
Views the Great Comet

1587
Enrols at university to study mathematics and astronomy

1594
Moves to Graz and becomes a mathematics teacher and researcher

1596
Mysterium Cosmographicum is published

1600
Meets Tycho Brahe for the first time

1609
Astronomia Nova is published

1617
Defends his mother Katharina on a charge of witchcraft

1619
Harmonices Mundi is published

1630
Dies in Regensburg

Copernicus was both groundbreaking and disappointingly conservative. His ideas were not taken seriously by a world still fixated on religious doctrine, just 57 years after the publication of the *Malleus Maleficarum*, and just a year after Henry VIII had passed the Witchcraft Act making magic and sorcery punishable by death in England. In slightly more enlightened times, Johannes Kepler (1571–1630) was able to make an impact by adopting a more Aristotelian, rather than a theoretical approach.

The influence of Tycho Brahe

In 1600 Kepler met the Danish astronomer Tycho Brahe (1546–1601) and began working for him. Brahe became the imperial astronomer for the Holy Roman Emperor in 1597, a post that would be taken up by Kepler on Brahe's death. As a nobleman, Brahe was free to dedicate significant time to his passion for astronomy, and although he was not involved in research at a university, he received a private education and read widely about astronomy and mathematics.

Brahe found a compromise position between those of Copernicus and Ptolemy. He believed that all planets circled the Sun, but that the Sun in turn circled the Earth, which was always stationary. This was clearly inaccurate, but was an important step in advancing understanding of orbits. Brahe generated perhaps more controversy in his observations rather than his mathematical calculations. In 1572, he observed a new **supernova** and published his findings. This new finding posed a problem for astronomers who followed the Aristotelian and Ptolemaic view of the universe, as it went against the established opinion that the universe was uniform and could not change. Brahe also observed a number of comets and published his findings in 1588. He concluded that they existed outside the atmosphere of Earth rather than inside it, as had been the established view. The path that was taken by these comets, according to Brahe, must mean that the idea that all heavenly bodies were controlled by perfect spheres was redundant.

KEY TERM

Supernova
A star that increases in brightness as it explodes.

Brahe believed that when medieval astronomers referred to spheres on which the planets travelled, they were referring to solid entities. He was able to refute this by stating that the planets moved independently through space, and did not always follow exactly the same paths, thus removing the requirement for spheres. This meant that an entirely new explanation was needed in order to understand the movement of celestial objects.

Kepler's career

Kepler was born in Weil, near Stuttgart, in the Holy Roman Empire, in 1571. In 1577 he witnessed the Great Comet, one of the three that Brahe had observed, and became passionate about astronomy. From a young age it was clear that he was an outstanding mathematician. When he attended university to study philosophy he became familiar with the work of Copernicus, agreeing with his heliocentric view of the world. He used his mathematical abilities at university to create horoscopes for other students, and although he considered becoming a priest he was offered a teaching position at a university in 1594 and began his research in earnest.

Kepler published *Mysterium Cosmographicum* (Cosmic Mystery) in 1596, where he asserted his strong religious faith by insisting that the universe was perfectly designed by God. Although the model he proposed was not without its faults, Kepler was able to adopt the heliocentric view of Copernicus but avoid his reliance on Ptolemaic spheres and epicycles. He proposed a complicated system whereby six layers of three-dimensional shapes (including cube, dodecahedron and octahedron) nestled together would correspond to the path of the six planets. Although Kepler later rejected this model himself, it provoked discussion and potential patrons began to take an interest.

Kepler's laws of planetary motion

Kepler moved to Prague in 1600 after he was noticed by Brahe, and assisted him with his research. In order to secure the patronage of Brahe, Kepler had to write a defence of his theories and after Brahe's death he continued his work with the help of his detailed observations. In 1609 he released *Astronomia Nova* (New Astronomy), which is notable for its inclusion of what became known as Kepler's first two laws of planetary motion.

KEY TERM

Elliptical
In the shape of an ellipse (an elongated or flattened circle). The discovery that planets moved in elliptical orbits was contradictory to the ancient view that all planetary movements took place in perfect circles.

- The first law is that the planets travel in **elliptical** orbits around the Sun.

- The second law is that planets do not travel at a consistent speed, as had been assumed since ancient times. The speed of planets varies as they circle the Sun; when an individual planet is closer to the Sun, it will move faster, and when it is further away, it will move more slowly.

Instead of providing mathematical theories to make his conclusions, Kepler provided a physical explanation based on his own observations and those of Tycho Brahe. In this way, he was using the approach of a natural philosopher as well as a mathematician. His approach is evident in Source 3 below. His belief that God is responsible for the form of the universe is clear, as well as his desire to continue the work of Brahe and discount Ptolemy's errors (in this case a missing eight minutes on Ptolemy's proposed orbit of Mars). This would not have been possible if he simply used mathematical formulae, but because he used observed statistics he was able to ascertain the true movement of Mars.

SOURCE

3 From Johannes Kepler, *Astronomia Nova* (1609).

To us, on whom Divine benevolence has bestowed the most diligent of observers, Tycho Brahe, from whose observations this eight-minute error of Ptolemy's in regard to Mars is deduced, it is fitting that we accept with grateful minds this gift from God, and both acknowledge and build upon it. So let us work upon it so as to at last track down the real form of celestial motions (these arguments giving support to our belief that the assumptions are incorrect). This is the path I shall, in my own way, strike out in what follows. For if I thought the eight minutes… were unimportant, I could make a sufficient correction… Now, because they could not be disregarded, these eight minutes alone will lead us along a path to the reform of the whole of Astronomy, and they are the matter for a great part of this work.

Kepler's mother was accused of witchcraft in 1617 and she was imprisoned in 1620. Although the accusations against her had nothing to do with the nature of his work, Kepler dedicated extensive time and energy to defending his mother, and in an effort to secure her release, his output slowed. She was released in 1621, and by this time Kepler had managed to complete and release *Harmonices Mundi* (Harmonies of the World), in which he established his third law. This law states that the distance from a planet to the Sun, cubed, is proportional to the time it takes for a planet to complete its orbit, squared. Through this he concluded that the further a planet is from the Sun, the longer it takes to complete its orbit. Because Kepler did not understand gravity properly he was not able to comprehend the gravitational pull of the Sun, and his theory was not taken any further until Isaac Newton's theory of gravity was developed.

Kepler and religion

Like many of the astronomers of the 16th and 17th centuries, Kepler was deeply religious. Although he abandoned plans to become a priest at a young age, his religious devotion informed much of what he did as an astronomer. He saw astronomy as a religious duty because it would help him understand the world that God created, and he believed that God had created the universe to a specific mathematical model. As God was all-knowing, the universe he created would have to be faultless. In all of his published works, and especially in *Harmonices Mundi*, Kepler concluded that the relationships between heavenly bodies that he had discovered were so perfect they could only have been made by God. Despite the fact that he was a great scientist, he was unaware of the impact that the Third Law would have, and seemed more preoccupied with his delight at discovering God's plan. Until Isaac Newton refined the third law and realised its importance, scholars saw it as little more than an interesting sideshow.

The impact of Kepler's theories

The most important impact of Kepler's findings was the shift from a belief in constant circular and linear motions always taking place in the universe, to a realisation that this was not the case. In the absence of invisible spheres somehow propelling the planets, questions were raised about what caused them to move. Kepler's use of mathematics to solve problems and explain how the physical world worked, rather than to simply describe theories, also had an impact on everyday life. Mathematics went through a revolution of its own, as civil engineering, canal building, warfare and navigation were improved as a result of applied mathematics. Kepler led the way for a new generation of natural philosophers and mathematicians, and the boundaries between the two professions blurred as more knowledge was shared and the importance of observation in order to prove a theory was acknowledged.

Johannes Kepler

1 Why were Tycho Brahe's findings significant?

2 Why were Kepler's findings groundbreaking?

3 In what ways could Kepler's beliefs be seen as conventional for the 17th century?

Galileo Galilei

TIMELINE: GALILEO'S LIFE AND WORKS

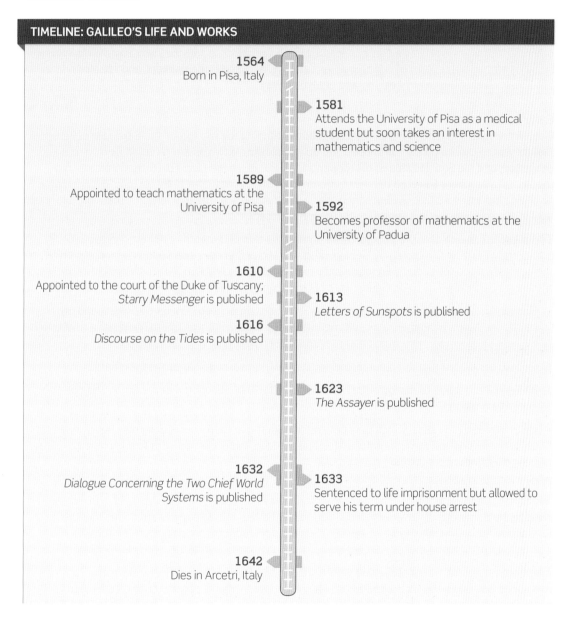

1564
Born in Pisa, Italy

1581
Attends the University of Pisa as a medical student but soon takes an interest in mathematics and science

1589
Appointed to teach mathematics at the University of Pisa

1592
Becomes professor of mathematics at the University of Padua

1610
Appointed to the court of the Duke of Tuscany; *Starry Messenger* is published

1613
Letters of Sunspots is published

1616
Discourse on the Tides is published

1623
The Assayer is published

1632
Dialogue Concerning the Two Chief World Systems is published

1633
Sentenced to life imprisonment but allowed to serve his term under house arrest

1642
Dies in Arcetri, Italy

Mathematics became a favoured interest of the upper classes throughout Europe in the early 17th century, and the universities were no longer the only places where valued research could be carried out. The enhanced status of mathematics is evident in the career of Galileo (1564–1642). When he started work as a university professor he was expected to defer to the higher-status natural philosophers, and as a result was paid a lower wage. He was able to negotiate a position at the court of Cosimo de' Medici, Duke of Tuscany, and received the title of philosopher, but more importantly, a level of respect that had previously been reserved only for natural philosophers. Times were changing.

Galileo's life and influences

Galileo was born in Pisa, Italy, in 1564 and studied medicine from 1581. He soon decided that he would rather study mathematics and left university without a degree. From 1589 he taught mathematics at the University of Pisa and in 1592 he was appointed professor of mathematics at the University of Padua. His time at Padua was productive, and he produced work on motion, ballistics, but most significantly astronomy. His most intense period of research came after 1610, when he was appointed to the court of the Duke of Tuscany.

Galileo wrote in a letter to Kepler in 1597 that he was deeply indebted to Copernicus, with whom he agreed on many fronts. He saw his own theories as the natural inheritance of Aristotle, and through him, Ptolemy. The influence of mathematicians such as Guidobaldo del Monte (1545–1607) can be found in his work, as well as medieval thinkers who developed theories about motion. There was not necessarily anything new in his method and approach, combining mathematical analysis with experiments and observation. Perhaps the most effective tool he had to make him stand out from other thinkers was his skill as a communicator. His *Dialogue Concerning the Two Chief World Systems* (1632) is written in the form of a dialogue, or a debate, between three thinkers, and enables him to put across his theories in a refreshing and analytical way.

Early controversy

Galileo concluded that tides were essential in understanding the motion of the Earth. He believed that they were caused by the Earth speeding up and slowing down as it rotated on its own axis and orbited around the Sun. He shared his thoughts in *Discourse on the Tides* (1616), and entered into the first of a number of heated debates with the Catholic Church. The Catholic Inquisition became involved, and assessed that Galileo's theory was contradictory to the teachings of the Bible. He was held in suspicion by the Inquisition for the next two decades.

Tycho Brahe's theory, that the planets move around the Sun and that the Sun revolves around a stationary Earth, was rejected by Galileo, despite the fact that the observations he made with the newly invented telescope were compatible with Brahe's findings. In *Siderius Nuncius* (Starry Messenger), published in 1610, Gaileo used his telescope to identify a number of new features.

- He found a number of features on the Moon that he claimed were similar to those found on Earth. The Moon contained seas and mountains like Earth, and was not made up of a mysterious element unknown to man, which had previously been believed.

- He also concluded that the natural motion of the Moon was circular around the Earth.

- He used a telescope to discover the moons of Jupiter, thus showing that the Earth was not unique in having a moon.

- He discovered new stars, which questioned the notion that there was a finite number of fixed stars, but which supported the Copernican idea that the stars cannot be set on a fixed sphere but must be spread throughout space.

In *The Assayer* (1623), Galileo argued that the study of the universe should be balanced between mathematics and experiment. The work was designed as an attack on mathematical astronomers. Despite the numerous discoveries that Galileo made, he did little to convince scholars that the ideas of Copernicus and Brahe should be questioned, and in fact did much to support their theories. Throughout his work he makes it clear that he is grateful to other thinkers, particularly Copernicus.

Like Copernicus, the works of Galileo were added to the *Index Librorum Prohibitorum* (List of Prohibited Books) by the Catholic Church. They took issue with his observations of tides and sunspots earlier in his career, but when *Dialogue Concerning the Two Chief World Systems* (1632) was published, which contradicted the Church-sponsored Aristotelian system, sale of his books was prohibited.

Galileo was found guilty of heresy, was made to sign a statement claiming that he had recanted his theories, and was placed under house arrest. The ban on printing Galileo's works was not lifted until 1718, although this did not include the *Dialogue*, and all of his works were removed from the *Index* in 1758. Despite the removal of all of Galileo's work from the list, it was stipulated that the *Dialogue* should still be censored.

Publication of *Dialogue Concerning the Two Chief World Systems* (1632)

Galileo saw himself as an heir to the work of both Aristotle and Copernicus. He was grateful for Aristotle's logical approach to astronomy, and he broadly agreed with the views of Copernicus regarding the make-up of the universe and firmly agreed with his view that the Sun was at the centre of the solar system. The *Two Chief World Systems* he refers to in his work were the Ptolemaic system (modified from Aristotle), and the Copernican system. The book is regarded as Galileo's most influential and his most controversial work.

SOURCE 4

The cover of Galileo's *Dialogue Concerning the Two Chief World Systems* (1632). Featured on the cover are Aristotle, Ptolemy and Copernicus in conversation. Galileo saw himself as the heir to the legacies of the great astronomers.

SOURCE 5

From Galileo Galilei, *Dialogue Concerning the Two Chief World Systems* (1632).

Now we, thanks to the telescope, have brought the heavens thirty or forty times closer to us than they were to Aristotle, so that we can discern many things in them that he could not see; among other things these sunspots, which were absolutely invisible to him. Therefore we can treat of the heavens and the sun more confidently than Aristotle could.

The structure of the *Dialogue*

The *Dialogue* is presented as a conversation between three thinkers.

- Salviati argues for the Copernican view of the universe, and gives what are essentially the views of Galileo. Amongst other arguments, he attacks the view of Aristotle that the universe is unchangeable, citing evidence of new stars and observations found through the telescope. He also argues that it is ridiculous to suggest that the Earth does not rotate and move like the other planets.

- Simplicio is an advocate of the Ptolemaic system, and presents the arguments against the Copernican model. He disagrees with Salviati over the motion of the Earth because, he argues, if the Earth was rotating, then a cannonball fired to the west would travel much further than one fired to the east, because the motion of the Earth westwards would help it to move further.

- Sagredo is a neutral. Whereas the other two men are philosophers, Sagredo is presented as an ordinary man.

A major difficulty of the Copernican theory was in explaining how a body as large and as heavy as the Earth could remain in perpetual motion. According to Aristotle, everything that moves in the universe must be pushed by something else, and Galileo had to simply reject this theory. Instead, he explained that if a ball was set in motion on an endless and frictionless incline, it would go on forever, and if it encountered an upward slope it would slow down. If there was a perfectly horizontal plane, once the ball was set in motion it would continue at the same speed forever. If the Earth moves round the Sun in a frictionless sphere, the same applies to the Earth, and it does not need any outside forces to constantly propel it. Of course, this theory would be completely undermined by Kepler's belief in elliptical, rather than circular, motion. Galileo, therefore, ignored many of Kepler's conclusions.

Galileo also attempted to build on Aristotle's theories of motion, which were seen by many contemporaries to be unsatisfactory. He refined Aristotle's theory that bodies fall with speeds proportional to their weight, to propose that acceleration and speed in free fall is constant for all bodies. He came close to a modern understanding of gravity when he proposed that a ball dropped from a tower would not fall to the west of the tower as the rotating Earth moved eastwards, but would instead fall to the bottom of the tower. He fell short of a true understanding of gravity because he proposed that this was because all things on Earth moved in a rotating motion, rather than the gravity of the Earth acting as a force on the ball.

The impact of Galileo

Despite being specifically told by the Inquisition not to write a defence of the Copernican theory Galileo did so anyway, with only minor adjustments. He rejected the right of the Church to act as an authority over scientific matters, and believed that the only way to find the truth was through reflection and experience. After his death in 1642, Pope Urban VIII protested against a plan by the Duke of Tuscany to give Galileo a ceremonial burial, owing to his heretical works.

Galileo's major works were published in Italian (which was unusual in a world where scholars always wrote in Latin), and were translated into a number of European languages. His influence then became widespread, and perhaps his biggest achievement was in developing a mathematical approach to the study of natural phenomena, which has ensured his lasting legacy among historians (see Extract 1). Although he and Kepler were contemporaries, they had quite different outlooks. Kepler was interested in mysticism and godly explanations for events, whereas Galileo was not convinced by superstition and was unwavering in his reliance on observation and empiricism.

EXTRACT

1 From Michael Sharratt, *Galileo: Decisive Innovator* (1996).

Galileo, the last man of science whom we customarily call by his first name, was the first scientific star: his work brought him European fame, and in his own day and since he stood out from even the ablest of his predecessors and contemporaries. If we had to name one founder of modern physical science, with its dependence upon mathematical reasoning in defiance of common sense, then most of us would pitch upon Galileo. He insisted that the same physics must apply to the Earth and the heavens; and he devised, and sometimes carried out, experimental tests of his reasoning. He did not invent the telescope but he perceived its importance, enabling us to see things (however blurred in the early models) never seen before, with momentous consequences for accepted beliefs about the world. Denounced to the Inquisition, he was, in his old age, condemned to house arrest after a show trial, which made him a kind of martyr to science and has assured his continuing fame.

He was in a hurry; he knew that he was right about the Earth going round the Sun and the new inertial physics that made sense of this idea, and he refused to say that this Copernican theory was a mere calculating device. A milder man might have got the new ideas admitted gradually (probably not in his lifetime); but Galileo's temperament put him on collision courses. He was, in his own estimation at least, a good Catholic; and he felt urgently that the Church must not commit itself to obsolete science. Belatedly, his Church has now vindicated him.

ACTIVITY
KNOWLEDGE CHECK

Galileo

1 a) Make a list of the scientific breakthroughs made by Galileo.

   b) For each, explain how it disagreed with previous accepted wisdom.

2 How could it be argued that Galileo was not entirely revolutionary?

3 Read Extract 1. Why was Galileo groundbreaking, according to the author?

Isaac Newton

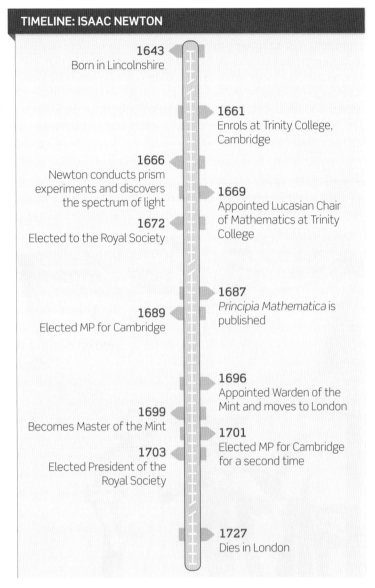

TIMELINE: ISAAC NEWTON

1643 Born in Lincolnshire

1661 Enrols at Trinity College, Cambridge

1666 Newton conducts prism experiments and discovers the spectrum of light

1669 Appointed Lucasian Chair of Mathematics at Trinity College

1672 Elected to the Royal Society

1687 *Principia Mathematica* is published

1689 Elected MP for Cambridge

1696 Appointed Warden of the Mint and moves to London

1699 Becomes Master of the Mint

1701 Elected MP for Cambridge for a second time

1703 Elected President of the Royal Society

1727 Dies in London

Isaac Newton (1643–1727) is widely recognised as one of the most influential scientists in history. His theories about calculus, classical mechanics, gravity and the laws of motion have remained relatively unaltered since his lifetime. His first letters to the Royal Society, written around 1672, concerned his research into the spectrum of light and he was soon invited to present his new invention, the reflective telescope. His work built on the advances in astronomy, mathematics and physics that had been made before him, including Kepler's laws of planetary motion. Indeed, he was so indebted to others that he famously stated 'If I have seen further, it is by standing upon the shoulders of giants'. By 1687, Newton was able to present his views on planetary and earthly motion, along with his most celebrated discovery of universal gravitation, in his most respected work, *Philosophiae Naturalis Principia Mathematica* (Mathematical Principles of Natural Philosophy).

Newton's forerunners: Descartes and Huygens

There is no doubt that Newton's *Principia Mathematica* is one of the most important works in the history of science. His theories and method can be traced back to some extent to the thinkers already outlined in this chapter, but also to his more immediate predecessors. Galileo had developed a system that fused together mathematics and natural philosophy, and this method was continued by René Descartes (1596–1650), the French mathematician, scientist and philosopher. Descartes took a great interest in astronomy, although it was not his primary field of study. He came close to publishing *The World* in 1653, meant as a further mathematical explanation for events in the universe, but withdrew his work in fear of being condemned by the Inquisition.

Christiaan Huygens (1629–95) has been viewed by historians as a forerunner to Newton. He wrote about a number of topics, including optics, pendulums and the rings of Saturn, but it was his work on motion and gravity that most influenced Newton's ideas. In the 1650s and 60s his research on motion led him to propose a formula very similar to the one known later as Newton's second law of motion. It was published in 1673, 14 years before Newton's *Principia Mathematica*.

Newton's career

Born in Lincolnshire in 1643, Newton enrolled at Trinity College, Cambridge in 1661 and became Lucasian Professor of Mathematics there in 1669. He remained at the University until 1696. Although he produced numerous published works on a variety of topics, his *Principia Mathematica*, which derived from an intense period of study in the 1660s (after he had famously conceived his theory of gravity when he saw an apple fall from a tree in 1665 or 1666), is his most important work. He was elected MP for Cambridge in the **Convention Parliament** of 1689 as a result of his resistance to the attempt by James II to turn the universities into Catholic institutions, and was elected again in 1701. He moved to London in 1696 to become Warden of the **Royal Mint**, and became Master of the Mint in 1699. He was elected as fellow of the Royal Society in 1672, and became President in 1703. He was re-elected each year until his death in 1727.

The *Principia Mathematica* is most famous for establishing that the force propelling planets in orbit around the Sun is the same force acting to keep people and objects on the ground on Earth: gravity. A number of other theories and observations were made.

- Newton demonstrated that Kepler's laws of planetary motion could be proven mathematically.

- He questioned the long-accepted view first proposed by Aristotle that physics on Earth worked differently to the rest of the universe.

- Newton was able to adequately explain **centrifugal force**.

- He developed a theory of **acoustics**, whereby sound varied depending on the density of the medium through which it passed.

Most significantly for improving man's understanding of the universe, Newton proposed three laws of motion and his law of universal gravitation, which can be summed up as follows.

- The first law of motion states that every object will remain in a uniform straight line or at rest unless an external force compels it to change direction.

- The second law states that the external force on an object is equal to the mass of the object times its rate of acceleration.

- The third law states that for every force (action) in nature there is an equal and opposite force (reaction).

- Newton's theory of gravitation had a significant impact on the understanding of the universe and in particular of orbits. Whereas Kepler had argued that in order for planets to move in orbit, something must be pushing them from behind, Newton was able to show that the planets are pulled towards the gravity of the Sun (Figure 2.2). The natural path of the planets (a straight line if undisturbed by any force) forms a circular orbit because just enough force is placed on the planet by gravity. The same principle applies to the relationship between the Earth and the Moon.

KEY TERMS

Convention Parliament
A parliament assembled without the formal authority of a monarch. The Catholic James II had vacated the throne in late 1688, and the Convention Parliament offered the throne to the Protestant Prince William of Orange and his wife Mary in what became known as the 'Glorious Revolution'.

Royal Mint
The organisation given the sole right to manufacture coins in England.

Centrifugal force
A force that appears to act on an object moving in a circular pattern, causing it to move away from the centre of its path.

Acoustics
The branch of physics associated with the study of sound.

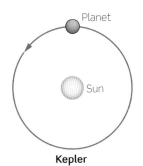

Kepler

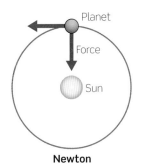

Newton

Figure 2.2 The orbit of planets according to Kepler and Newton.

The impact of Newton's theories

Despite his achievements, Newton was well aware of the fact that he would not have been so successful if it was not for the earlier thinkers who began the Scientific Revolution. His work represents the final stage of a long process of theory and discovery that had been evolving for over 100 years. *Principia Mathematica* represents an important break from the mindset of the Middle Ages and, although his works were not accessible to many at first (partly because they were published in Latin), later interpreters such as Voltaire provided simpler versions of his work for the masses.

Historians have made the judgement that Newton completed the 'mathematisation' of natural philosophy because unlike earlier thinkers he succeeded in making all of his calculations work, leaving no mysteries or grey areas. Newton's importance in the history of science is summed up by John Henry in Extract 2.

EXTRACT

2 From John Henry, *The Scientific Revolution and the Origins of Modern Science* (2008).

Newton himself did not have to justify the mathematical approach; he could safely assume that there was an audience for his book, who, even if they could not follow its mathematics, took for granted the validity of mathematics for understanding the workings of the world. Before the intellectual status of mathematicians had been raised by Copernicus and other renaissance *mathematici* there was natural philosophy and there was mathematics and they were essentially separate and distinct. Newton's [book] title therefore would have been scarcely conceivable. By the final decades of the seventeenth century, however, the notion that there could be mathematical principles of natural philosophy could be taken for granted. Although his book met with some fierce criticism, not a murmur was raised against it in this regard.

Newton and magic

Despite his reputation as a deeply rational and mathematical thinker, Newton, like Kepler, still believed in arcane knowledge and the power of magic. In early drafts of *Principia Mathematica*, he speculates that gravity may be the result of magic of some kind. He claims that the followers of the Ancient Greek philosopher Pythagoras had a rudimentary understanding of gravity and were aware of the fact that the planets circle the Sun. He cites the regular symbolism used by Pythagorean followers of the sun-god Apollo playing a seven-stringed lyre as evidence. Newton seemed obsessed with the numerological significance of the number seven, and in his presentations to the Royal Society on the colours of the spectrum of light he makes comparisons with the seven musical notes of the octave. Newton's belief in so-called cosmic harmonies followed Kepler's belief in a harmonious universe, where God had created six planets to fit in with a perfect geometric plan.

Newton, like a number of his contemporaries in the Royal Society, was also an **alchemist**. He believed that different particles could be attracted to each other across empty space, and his confidence in the power of light and gravity stems from a genuine belief that supernatural or occult forces were responsible. Robert Boyle (1627–91), one of the most respected members of the Royal Society, also practised alchemy, and his approach to natural philosophy was based on the principles of alchemists.

Finally, Newton's study of the Bible was as dedicated as his scientific work. He was concerned with prophecies that he thought could be found in the books of Daniel and of Revelation. He wrestled with their meanings from a young age, and was still mystified by them when he died. Later in life, he wrote down many of the supposed hidden messages he had found (the majority unpublished), including speculation about when the world would end.

KEY TERM

Alchemist
Someone who attempts to transform common substances such as base metals and liquids into gold or potions used to cure diseases.

ACTIVITY
KNOWLEDGE CHECK

Isaac Newton

1 How did Newton improve man's understanding of the universe?

2 Do you think Newton's findings would have been possible without thinkers such as Tycho Brahe, Galileo and Johannes Kepler?

3 How could it be argued that Newton was not a truly modern scientist?

THINKING HISTORICALLY Change (8a, b & c) (I)

Imposing realities

The shape of history is imposed by people looking back. People who lived through the 'history' did not always perceive the patterns that later historians identify. For example, some people living through the Industrial Revolution may have understood that great change was taking place, but they would not have been able to understand the massive economic, social and political consequences of industrialisation.

1 Consider the Scientific Revolution.

   a) Who would have made the decision as to when the Scientific Revolution began?

   b) Could anybody have challenged this decision?

   c) Explain why someone living in the 16th century would have been unable to make a judgement about the beginning of a new era.

2 Who living at the present time might regard the beginning of the Scientific Revolution as an important event?

3 What do your answers to the above questions tell us about the structure of history as we understand it?

HOW DID APPROACHES TO HUMAN UNDERSTANDING AND KNOWLEDGE CHANGE IN THE YEARS c1580–c1750?

Francis Bacon and the empirical scientific approach

TIMELINE: FRANCIS BACON

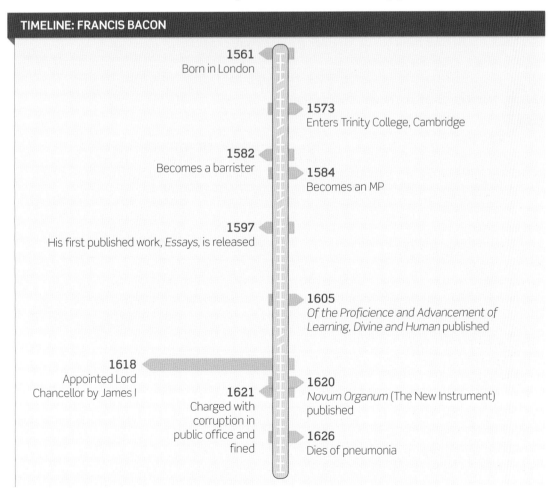

1561
Born in London

1573
Enters Trinity College, Cambridge

1582
Becomes a barrister

1584
Becomes an MP

1597
His first published work, *Essays*, is released

1605
Of the Proficience and Advancement of Learning, Divine and Human published

1618
Appointed Lord Chancellor by James I

1620
Novum Organum (The New Instrument) published

1621
Charged with corruption in public office and fined

1626
Dies of pneumonia

One of the most important contributors to scientific discovery never carried out a scientific experiment.

While the other great mind of English science, Isaac Newton, came to prominence towards the end of the 17th century, Bacon was active much earlier. Born into a well-connected family in London in 1561, Bacon enrolled at Trinity College, Cambridge at the age of 12, where he lived for three years with his older brother. Already recognised as an outstanding intellectual in his teens, he trained in law and became a barrister in 1582, and then an MP in 1584. This marked the beginning of a notable career in public service for a time, where he rose to become a member of the Privy Council. He wrote widely on a number of topics, including law, philosophy and religion.

KEY TERMS

Inductive reasoning
Reasoning based on evidence. The inductive approach allows for an original hypothesis to be proved false.

Deductive reasoning
When a conclusion is made based on something already known or assumed. If deductive reasoning is being followed, a rule that applies to one instance would also apply to other instances, such as the assumption that because gravity is a force on all things on Earth, an object falling to the ground must be because of gravity. Aristotle is known as the founding father of deductive reasoning.

The experimental method

As Sources 6 and 7 make clear, Bacon focused heavily on collecting evidence in order to formulate theories, through an emphasis on **inductive** rather than **deductive reasoning**.

Bacon wanted to pursue the 'experimental and the rational', concepts that appear normal to the scientists of today but were not part of the vocabulary of pre-17th-century thinkers. At the time, scientific thinking was heavily influenced by the beliefs of the Church and this restricted scientific advancement for centuries. There are a number of key elements to Bacon's method.

- Bacon believed that scientific discovery is best aided by accumulating as much data about the subject as possible.

- His method involved rejecting any preconceived theories or conclusions about the subject matter.

- He thought that the methodical and meticulous observation of facts was the best way to understand natural phenomena.

After his death in 1626, other scientists attempted to emulate his 'Baconian Method' and the empirical nature of his work was developed by philosophers such as John Locke. His ideas about science were not widely implemented before 1640 but, with the change in social attitudes that came about as a result of the Civil War, his work was revisited and emulated by others. Perhaps the best evidence of Bacon's influence is in the founding of the Royal Society (see page 55) nearly 40 years after his death. Regular mentions of his guiding genius were cited at early meetings.

SOURCE

6 From Francis Bacon, *Novum Organum* (1620).

Those who have taken upon them to lay down the law of nature as a thing already searched out and understood, whether they have spoken in simple assurance or professional affectation, have therein done philosophy and the sciences great injury. For as they have been successful in inducing belief, so they have been effective in quenching and stopping inquiry; and have done more harm by spoiling and putting an end to other men's efforts than good by their own. Those on the other hand who have taken a contrary course, and asserted that absolutely nothing can be known… have certainly advanced reasons for it that are not to be despised; but yet they have neither started from true principles nor rested in the just conclusion, zeal and affectation having carried them much too far. The more ancient of the Greeks (whose writings are lost) took up with better judgment a position between these two extremes – between the presumption of pronouncing on everything, and the despair of comprehending anything; and though frequently and bitterly complaining of the difficulty of inquiry and the obscurity of things, and like impatient horses champing at the bit, they did not the less follow up their object and engage with nature, thinking… whether or not anything can be known – was to be settled not by arguing, but by trying. And yet they too, trusting entirely to the force of their understanding, applied no rule, but made everything turn upon hard thinking and perpetual working and exercise of the mind.

Now my method, though hard to practice, is easy to explain; and it is this. I propose to establish progressive stages of certainty. The evidence of the sense, helped and guarded by a certain process of correction, I retain. But the mental operation which follows the act of sense I for the most part reject; and instead of it I open and lay out a new and certain path for the mind to proceed in, starting directly from the simple sensuous perception.

SOURCE

7

From Francis Bacon, *Novum Organum* (1620).

The men of experiment are like the ant; they only collect and use: the reasoners resemble spiders, who make cobwebs out of their own substance. But the bee takes a middle course, it gathers its material from the flowers of the garden and of the field, but transforms and digests it by a power of its own. Not unlike the true business of philosophy; for it neither relies solely or chiefly on the powers of the mind, nor does it take the matter which it gathers from natural history and mechanical experiments and lay it up in the memory whole, as it finds it; but lays it up in the understanding altered and digested. Therefore from a closer and purer league between these two faculties, the experimental and the rational (such as has never yet been made) much may be hoped.

SOURCE

8

The title page of Bacon's *Instauratio Magna* (1620). It depicts a ship sailing past Gibraltar, between the mythical Pillars of Hercules, representing the limits of exploration and learning in the age of Aristotle. The ship is sailing out of the Mediterranean and onwards to the great expanse of the Atlantic Ocean.

While Bacon applied his empirical thinking to the study of nature, others adopted his ideas when they attempted to gain a greater understanding of religion. Lord Falkland (1610–43) opened his house and estate at Great Tew in Oxfordshire to learned thinkers, where they used the rational method to question the problems that faced the Church of England, such as the agreed date for the end of the world. Falkland's group reached the conclusion that the Church would benefit from religious toleration, as a rational interpretation of the Bible shows that it contains many contradictions that will inevitably be interpreted in different ways by different people. Because of this, no single denomination has the right to dictate the way people worship. This idea became popular during the Civil War (1642–46) and in the years that followed. The rational method also spread to be used in the study of society, philosophy and eventually history.

The importance of inductive reasoning

Bacon believed that preconceived theories could mislead scientists and philosophers. His reasoning was carried out through the production of so-called 'Tables of Instances', where all the information about a subject could be recorded. Once all the facts about the subject were recorded in the table, a theory would then emerge.

One example of this reasoning that Bacon supplied was in relation to the generation of heat. Once all of the facts known about the generation of heat had been recorded in the Table of Instances, Bacon concluded that heat is a form of motion. This theory fits in relatively well with modern theories of kinetics, where heat is produced as particles increase in motion.

Bacon and magic

Despite being hugely influential in scientific circles, Bacon's method actually served to preserve a belief in magic and the occult. When he rejected deductive for inductive reasoning, he was actually reverting back to the sort of logic used by those who studied natural magic, whose conclusions came largely from observations in nature. By setting down all observed facts about an object of study in 'Tables of Instances', Bacon was dismissing the distinction between magical and rational qualities that many scientists were starting to make. His method allowed for unexplained or supernatural physical phenomena to exist as long as they were observed as part of the scientific process.

The influence of Bacon's works

Bacon produced two works that promoted his scientific method.

- His first major work of philosophy was *Of the Proficience and Advancement of Learning, Divine and Human* (1605), usually referred to as *The Advancement of Learning*. Here he argued that empirical knowledge, learnt from experience and observation, is the most superior form of knowledge. He states that if men begin with certainties, they end with doubts, but if they begin with doubts but observe known facts, they will end with certainties.

- Bacon intended to produce a six-volume *Instauratio Magna* (Great Restoration), although much was never completed. The second part, known as the *Novum Organum* (The New

KEY TERM

Utopian
An idealised, perfect society.

Instrument) became the most influential and was released in 1620. Here, Bacon succinctly argues for his experimental method, and although it contains no new scientific discoveries, it became an important guidebook for the men who founded the Royal Society later in the century.

- In *The New Atlantis* (1626), Bacon described a **utopian** state, where scientific knowledge is exploited and valued.

EXTEND YOUR KNOWLEDGE

The experiment that killed Francis Bacon
In April 1626, Bacon was travelling from central London to Highgate in cold weather. According to John Aubrey, writing in the late 17th century, Bacon was inspired to carry out an experiment to see if snow could preserve meat.

Stopping the coach that he was travelling in, Bacon bought a fowl and stuffed it with snow. Before he could witness the results of his experiment, he caught pneumonia and died a few days later. Aubrey, in his *Brief Lives*, presents this as a story of Bacon's absolute commitment to the discovery of knowledge, and calls him a martyr to his scientific method.

ACTIVITY
KNOWLEDGE CHECK

Francis Bacon and the experimental method
1 Read Sources 6 and 7. Why does Bacon feel his method is superior, according to these extracts?

2 Why was his focus on inductive reasoning so influential?

3 What are the drawbacks to Bacon's approach?

The foundation of Gresham College and the Royal Society

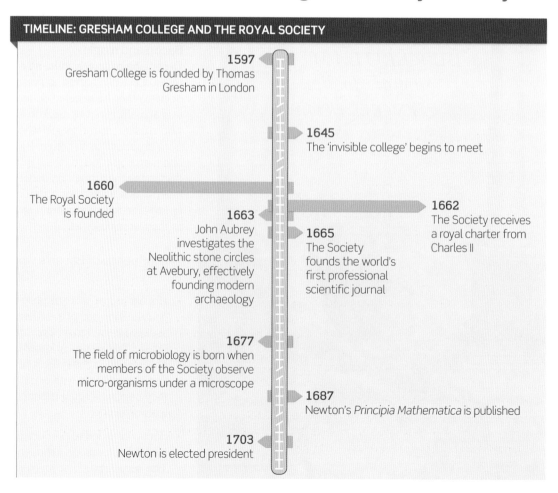

TIMELINE: GRESHAM COLLEGE AND THE ROYAL SOCIETY

1597
Gresham College is founded by Thomas Gresham in London

1645
The 'invisible college' begins to meet

1660
The Royal Society is founded

1662
The Society receives a royal charter from Charles II

1663
John Aubrey investigates the Neolithic stone circles at Avebury, effectively founding modern archaeology

1665
The Society founds the world's first professional scientific journal

1677
The field of microbiology is born when members of the Society observe micro-organisms under a microscope

1687
Newton's *Principia Mathematica* is published

1703
Newton is elected president

Gresham College

The need for a national scientific association was understood as early as 1645, when a group of natural philosophers formed what became known as the 'invisible college', a loosely organised collective who shared an interest in experimental investigation, and had connections to Gresham College, London, which had been founded in 1597. This group would often meet after the astronomy lecture at Gresham, usually in the rooms of the Gresham Professor of Astronomy, and many of the group would go on to form the Royal Society. The early followers of the Royal Society were referred to as 'Greshamites' in contemporary literature.

Gresham was, however, crucially important in the development of knowledge from its foundation. Sir Thomas Gresham, who made a substantial fortune as a financier in London, died in 1579. The Royal Exchange, the first commercial building in Britain, was opened by Gresham in 1571 and provided space for brokers to do deals. In his will he bequeathed all of his estate to the City of London authorities. In return they were expected to support from the profits of the Royal Exchange seven professors, who were to be lodged at his mansion house and who would deliver public lectures on their respective faculties of law, rhetoric, divinity, music, physics, geometry and astronomy.

The opening of Gresham College was the result of a long effort to establish a permanent organisation that would be responsible for research in the mathematical sciences. Academic positions in the study of medicine had been established at Oxford and Cambridge in the early 16th century, and a lectureship in surgery was created by the Royal College of Physicians in 1583. Astronomy and geometry, the two fields that were essential for understanding the workings of the Earth and the rest of the universe, were not fully recognised until professorships were created by Gresham. It was not until 1619 that professorships in astronomy and geometry were founded at Oxford, and those who filled these vacancies in the first decades were chosen from Gresham.

A number of achievements can be attributed to those involved in Gresham College before the initial meetings of the 'invisible college' in 1645.

- The first professor of geometry, Henry Briggs, popularised the use of **logarithms**.

- A close associate of Briggs, who was able to flourish through his connections with Gresham, was William Bedwell. Bedwell translated a number of important mathematical works into English and invented a new type of ruler for carrying out geometric calculations.

- Edmund Gunter became professor of astronomy in 1619. He worked closely with a group of naval officials to improve navigation.

> **KEY TERM**
>
> **Logarithm**
> In mathematics, the power (number of times) to which a base number must be multiplied by itself in order to produce a given number.

The Royal Society

It was not until the Restoration of the monarchy in 1660 that the political climate was suited to the formation of a more formal and recognised organisation, and Charles II's interest in science inevitably contributed to the swift royal charter given to the Society. The Society was formally proposed in November 1660, at a lecture by the architect Christopher Wren, and was established in July 1662. It met once a week and its membership included men from all areas of intellectual study. John Locke, philosopher; Samuel Pepys, diarist and civil servant; John Dryden, poet; and the Earl of Sandwich joined an array of botanists, astronomers, mathematicians, chemists and biologists. The aims of the Society are outlined in Source 10 (on page 57).

The Society was divided into a number of committees, each responsible for a different area of study. The first few years were marked by a genuine variety of research in areas other than science, including an investigation into the best way to improve the English language. Most early experiments followed Bacon's method in all areas of intellectual endeavour, and it was only after 1684 that the Society dedicated itself solely to scientific pursuits. Isaac Newton, who was working at Cambridge University at the time, was consulted about his theory of gravity and so began a long relationship with the Society, of which he was president for 24 years. In fact, the pull of Oxford and Cambridge was not as great as that of the Royal Society in the post-Restoration period, and the universities appeared to be falling behind as they were not always able to attract the best scholars. Religious nonconformists were excluded from both universities, and many would attend for the status that a degree gave them rather than for any serious desire to learn. Those who were genuinely engaged in pushing the boundaries of science did so through the Society.

Frontispiece to Thomas Sprat's *The History of the Royal Society* (1667). The first president, William Brouncker and Francis Bacon are featured, with a bust of the Society's first patron, Charles II. Below Bacon, the words *artium instaurator* (restorer of the arts) are inscribed, and objects from the Society's early history are featured, including an air pump and a telescope.

SOURCE 10 From the Second Charter of the Royal Society (1663).

We [King Charles II] have long and fully resolved with Ourself to extend not only the boundaries of the Empire, but also the very arts and sciences. Therefore we look with favour upon all forms of learning, but with particular grace we encourage philosophical studies, especially those which by actual experiments attempt either to shape out a new philosophy or to perfect the old. In order, therefore, that such studies, which have not hitherto been sufficiently brilliant in any part of the world, may shine conspicuously amongst our people, and that at length the whole world of letters may always recognise us not only as Defender of the Faith, but also as the universal lover and patron of every king of truth.

The Society has been seen by some historians as not particularly significant, as it was simply a channel for scientists to air their discoveries, and did not necessarily give them any assistance. However, its Baconian aim to gather all knowledge about nature made it extremely well respected. The Society also agreed that the knowledge it would gather would only be used for the public good, rather than to fulfil the interests of a small clique of intellectuals. As well as English scientists, the Society encouraged foreign scholars to share their discoveries and, from 1665, these discoveries were presented in the first scientific journal, *Philosophical Transactions*. This sharing of information was perhaps its greatest strength. For example, in 1661, Marcello Malpighi wrote to the Society after he observed capillary action in the lungs of frogs. This turned out to be the missing link in William Harvey's theory of blood circulation. The Society also created a model that would be followed by groups on the continent. In 1666, the French Royal Academy of Sciences was established and the Prussian Academy of Sciences was founded in Berlin in 1700.

The Royal Society could not survive without funding, and this came in the form of endowments from wealthy supporters, as well as gifts from wealthy men from all over Europe who viewed themselves as amateur scientists. The aim to carry out work that was beneficial to the public good was achieved through regular public demonstrations and a number of members carried out public anatomy lessons, with dissections taking place on the bodies of criminals. Crucially, by the early 18th century, science was part of the public consciousness, was no longer viewed with suspicion and had been greatly supported by Charles II. The Society gave a boost to the increasing belief in Europe that humans could progress without divine assistance and contributed to the overall aims of the Enlightenment, or Age of Reason, which had begun in the 1650s.

The Royal Society and magic

A number of historians, including Henry Lyons, have claimed that the Royal Society significantly undermined belief in witchcraft and magic through its focus on critical investigation. Indeed, the first history of the Society, written by Thomas Sprat in 1667, claims that astrologers only serve to deceive people and that alchemists are essentially fraudulent. The manuscript of Webster's *The Displaying of Supposed Witchcraft* (1677) was dedicated to the Society.

Despite the Society's focus on the scientific and experimental, many of its early members were interested in magical areas of study. Robert Boyle, Isaac Newton, John Aubrey and Thomas Henshaw all took an interest in astrology or alchemy. A number of laboratory-based investigations relating to alchemy can be found in early editions of *Philosophical Transactions*, although these were rare. As we have seen in Chapter 1, from 1666, Joseph Glanvill made much of his reputation as a member of the Royal Society when he argued for the existence of witches. True to the Baconian method, he endeavoured to establish matters of fact about witches. Although other members may have shared his interests, the Society itself had no time for Glanvill's suggestion that witchcraft be studied formally. In 1666, an Irish healer named Valentine Greatrakes visited England, and caused a stir when he apparently cured people of disease by laying his hands on them. Robert Boyle, who was a member of the Society, took great interest in the case, and recorded Greatrakes' achievements in a log. Boyle brought in other members of the Society, but as in the case of Glanvill, the Society as an organisation took no interest, and the minutes of its meetings during 1666 show only discussions of gravity, friction, medicine and the planets.

EXTRACT

3 From Michael Hunter, 'The Royal Society and the Decline of Magic' in *Notes and Records of the Royal Society of London* (2011).

The early Royal Society had a rather paradoxical role in relation to magical beliefs. Through its negative institutional stance concerning magic phenomena, the Society had an important – if probably unwitting – definitional significance in this area. But what is curious is the permutation through which the Society's role then went, in the context in which orthodox thinkers began hesitantly to follow in the footsteps of the free-thinkers who had pioneered sceptical attitudes in the late seventeenth and early eighteenth centuries.

ACTIVITY
KNOWLEDGE CHECK

Gresham College and the Royal Society

1 Why was the foundation of Gresham College significant?

2 How did the structure of the Royal Society enable it to facilitate scientific discovery?

3 Why do you think members of the Society continued to give credence to the notions of witchcraft and magic?

Thomas Hobbes' deductive reasoning and materialism

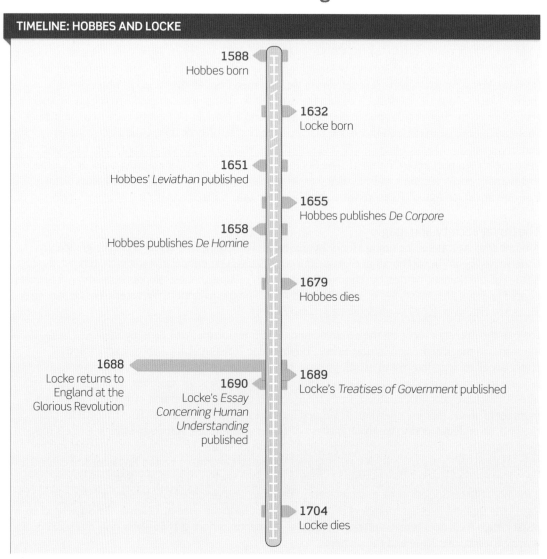

TIMELINE: HOBBES AND LOCKE

1588 Hobbes born

1632 Locke born

1651 Hobbes' *Leviathan* published

1655 Hobbes publishes *De Corpore*

1658 Hobbes publishes *De Homine*

1679 Hobbes dies

1688 Locke returns to England at the Glorious Revolution

1690 Locke's *Essay Concerning Human Understanding* published

1689 Locke's *Treatises of Government* published

1704 Locke dies

Unlike the inductive, evidence-based approach of Francis Bacon, the philosopher Thomas Hobbes championed a more deductive approach to human understanding.

The career of Thomas Hobbes

The son of a vicar, Hobbes was born in 1588 and attended Oxford University. He worked as a tutor to the sons of the landed elite and travelled extensively throughout Europe, where he developed an interest in philosophy. He worked as a tutor to the aristocratic Cavendish family and for a time was secretary to Francis Bacon. When the Civil War broke out in 1642 he was in Paris, after fleeing there fearing that he would be targeted for his Royalist sympathies. While in Paris he worked for a time as tutor to the young Charles II, and it was here that he began to formulate his most important political ideas, published in 1651 in his book *Leviathan*. In this work Hobbes advocated a strong government led by a single leader – in clear reaction to the recent execution of Charles I and beginning of republican rule. Two of his other great works of philosophy were published later in the 1650s, *De Corpore* (On the Body) in 1655 and *De Homine* (On Man) in 1658.

Deductive reasoning

In all of his works, Hobbes' focus on deductive rather than inductive reasoning is clear. When he travelled around Europe in the 1630s and 40s, he met a number of continental philosophers, including Descartes. Although he disagreed with many of Descartes' views, they shared the same opinion that knowledge should be based on certain indisputable principles. For Hobbes, the inductive method of Bacon was inadequate for a number of reasons.

- It is too experimental.

- It never provides secure knowledge that is irrefutable.

- Whenever the inductive method is used, an element of doubt can always exist when some observed facts cannot be explained.

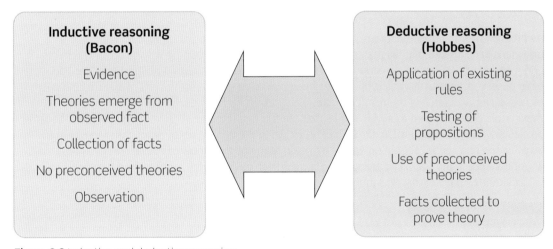

Figure 2.3 Inductive and deductive reasoning.

According to his biographer, John Aubrey, Hobbes concluded that deductive reasoning was the right approach at the age of around 40, when he read a section of the ancient Greek mathematician Euclid's *Elements*, one of the most influential books on mathematics ever written. When he first read Euclid's explanation of Pythagoras' theorem, he was supposed to have exclaimed that it was impossible. When he went on to read Euclid's explanation, he could see that he based his justification on deductive reasoning and was satisfied with it. An example Hobbes gives of deductive logic is as follows.

- Every man is a living creature.

- Every living creature is a body.

- Therefore, every man is a body.

As Hobbes was concerned with defending the notion of a powerful monarchy, he used deductive reasoning to prove his point.

- All men are born bad.

- Nero was a bad (Roman) emperor.

- Therefore, Nero was a bad emperor because he was born bad, not because of the system that he was placed in charge of.

Hobbes argued that it is not the system (e.g. monarchy or democracy) that creates corrupt, tyrannical or self-seeking politicians, but the politicians themselves, because of his original premise that all men are born flawed. He used deductive reasoning to promote his own ideological view, and the logical view that powerful monarchy could result in negative consequences is ignored. Likewise, he attempted to dismiss the role of group discussion and assemblies in politics by arguing that defeated men will always attempt to make the victor's job difficult. If group discussion takes place over policies, there will always be a victor and there will always be a loser and therefore the victor's job will be made difficult. This demonstrates the problem with beginning a deductive argument with a questionable premise.

If both the original premise and the concluding premise seem to be true, then they can be seen to be deductively valid, and Hobbes would accept them. Another premise, such as the idea that God rules the universe alone, and that God appoints monarchs, so monarchs should be allowed to rule alone, is not deductively valid because one can find examples from history to show that absolute monarchs can abuse their powers.

Hobbes, materialism and magic

An important concept in all of Hobbes' work is that of materialism – the idea that everything is created by **matter**, and that all observed events, including those to do with the mind and spirituality, are the result of matter acting on matter. As Hobbes was a complete materialist, this allowed no room for a belief in the supernatural or magic, because they were not founded on matter. Because of this strongly held belief, concepts such as the soul and the existence of angels could be questioned.

As Hobbes was so influential during his long life (he died at 91) and after his death, a number of historians have argued that his materialism goes some way to explaining why belief in witchcraft and magic declined, especially after 1660. According to Hobbes, unusual phenomena that had been observed, such as miracles, had never been proven to go against the law of nature, and cases of possession were in fact the result of madness or epilepsy. Hobbes did not deny, however, that there could be spirits with material bodies that are too fine to be seen by humans. His ideas became particularly fashionable in the early 18th century, when the final cases of witchcraft were being investigated and sceptical opinion was at its peak. Many of the writers discussed in Chapter 1, such as John Webster and Balthasar Bekker, and judges such as John Holt, approached cases of witchcraft with a rational mindset that was influenced by the work of Hobbes.

> **KEY TERM**
>
> **Matter**
> A physical substance that occupies space and has a mass.

ACTIVITY
KNOWLEDGE CHECK

Thomas Hobbes

1 What are the advantages of deductive reasoning?

2 What are the drawbacks of deductive reasoning?

3 Explain why the approach of Hobbes coincides with the decline of magic and witchcraft.

John Locke and his *Essay Concerning Human Understanding* (1690)

John Locke is best known for helping to shape a new era of liberal philosophy, which set the political agenda for the next three centuries. His political ideas helped to inspire the French and American Revolutions, and he is generally viewed as an opponent of absolute monarchy in favour of individual rights and liberties, in contrast to Hobbes' justification for a strong state. He also became internationally famous for his *Essay Concerning Human Understanding* (1690), which discussed human knowledge and understanding.

Locke's career

Locke was born in 1632 and his puritan father fought for parliament during the Civil War. He studied medicine at Oxford, although he also spent much time learning about ancient philosophy, which he quickly grew tired of as he felt it was inadequate in explaining the problems of the age. He entered the service of the Earl of Shaftesbury, a prominent founder of the Whig movement and England's Lord Chancellor, and, as a result of his patronage, was able to write and publish a number of important works of political philosophy. When Shaftesbury's political career appeared to be floundering in 1675, Locke fled to Holland and after settling again in England in 1679 he left again and only returned permanently at the Glorious Revolution in 1688, accompanying the new queen, Mary.

Although Locke had been writing for a number of years, it was only after the Glorious Revolution that the majority of his works were published. His ideas became influential extremely quickly and, by the time of his death in 1704, his theories were well known and his political ideas had been applied in the Glorious Revolution of 1688–89. Locke is seen as the father of modern empiricism, as he sought to make his conclusions only through experience or through observing the experiences of others. As well as the *Essay Concerning Human Understanding*, his ethical and philosophical ideas were published in *Treatises of Government* (1689).

The significance of the *Essay*

In the *Essay*, Locke presents a detailed interpretation of the workings of the mind. He questions how we think, how we perceive the world around us and the nature of religious practices. He ultimately concludes that experience is the most important source of human knowledge (Source 11).

SOURCE

11 From John Locke, *Essay Concerning Human Understanding* (1690).

Let us then suppose the mind to be, as we say, white paper, void of all characters, without any ideas: How comes it to be furnished? Whence comes it by that vast store which the busy and boundless fancy of man has painted on it with an almost endless variety? Whence has it all the MATERIALS of reason and knowledge? To this I answer, in one word, from EXPERIENCE. In that all our knowledge is founded; and from that it ultimately derives itself. Our observation employed either, about external sensible objects, or about the internal operations of our minds perceived and reflected or by ourselves, is that which supplies our understandings with all the MATERIALS of thinking. These two are the fountains of knowledge, from whence all the ideas we have, or can naturally have, do spring.

The *Essay* is divided into a number of books, which each deal with a different topic.

- Book I is dedicated to the idea that humans are not born with any knowledge. As is evidenced in Source 11, Locke sees the mind as completely blank at birth, and says that it is filled through experience alone. There can be no innate ideas at birth.

- Book II contains the argument that knowledge can only come from experience.

- Book III focuses on language, and in particular why humans may use one word to categorise many different things (such as the word 'tree' to denote a large number of different types of tree).

- In Book IV, Locke questions whether knowledge can ever be entirely accurate or truthful, because every person's knowledge is unique to them and their own point of view.

Like Hobbes, Locke also put forward an argument that all things consist only of matter, and that the 'primary' qualities of an object (size, shape, etc.) are the same regardless of how someone perceives them. Secondary qualities, such as colour, smell and taste are perceived depending on conditions. He saw no point in focusing on secondary qualities, because primary qualities are unchangeable and accepted by all.

The *Essay*'s significance for magic and witchcraft

Because Locke was a materialist, and because he was a strong believer in empiricism, he made no allowances for the supernatural. He did not, however, say that spirits did not exist. Instead, he thought it was impossible to arrive at any certain knowledge of them because he had not experienced them for himself. As spirits do not have primary qualities, their nature and even their existence is based on personal perceptions, and thus can never be proved.

Surprisingly, Locke did have some belief in astrology, and claimed that it could be useful, for example in determining which medicinal herbs to use at different times of the year. He was able to form this view because he felt that experience showed him that different medicinal herbs had worked at different times. Ultimately, Locke's denial of innate ideas was interpreted by some contemporaries as heretical, because it suggested that man, and not God, was responsible for learning.

ACTIVITY
KNOWLEDGE CHECK

John Locke

1 In what ways are the ideas of Locke similar to those of Hobbes and in what ways are they different?

2 What is the significance of Locke for understanding the decline of magic and witchcraft?

Conclusion: Did belief in magic and witchcraft decline with the advancement of science and reason?

It can be no coincidence that accusations of witchcraft declined as the Scientific Revolution took hold. There were a number of important breakthroughs in the understanding of the universe, such as Copernicus' heliocentric solar system, Kepler's laws of planetary motion and Newton's theory of gravity. This subject matter had previously been associated with the actions of the supernatural. There was also a growing acceptance of the experimental method of Bacon, and the rational beliefs associated with the growth of science were reflected in sceptical publications. Johan Weyer and Reginald Scot, for example, concluded that many witches were suffering from mental illness after rational

investigation. Balthasar Bekker's criticism of witchcraft cases at the end of the 17th century was also clearly influenced by scientific ideas. The fact that Hobbes and Locke were materialists meant that they did not allow for the presence of the supernatural, and the use of deductive logic by Hobbes had a damaging effect on established beliefs, as arguments for the supernatural were not deductively valid.

The decline in belief was not steady, however, and was clearly much faster after 1660. Many of the great thinkers of the age, such as Bacon, Copernicus and Kepler, were active much earlier than this, when belief in witchcraft was still widespread. Even later thinkers, such as Joseph Glanvill and Isaac Newton, who were both members of the Royal Society, had strong supernatural beliefs. Kepler and Newton believed that they had discovered God's plan for the universe through their research, and sceptical writers such as Thomas Ady felt that suspected witches were straying from God's path, rather than being complete frauds. As well as this, the inductive method that Bacon had introduced actually meant that it was easier to put forward supernatural explanations for events.

Finally, other factors contributed to the decline in beliefs that had nothing at all to do with understanding and knowledge. For example, the issue of poverty, although not eradicated, had improved somewhat by the 18th century as a result of increased poor relief. This led to less suspicion between poverty-stricken neighbours and fewer vengeful accusations of witchcraft. The growth of an English empire in the late 17th century, accompanied with more trade and the growth of insurance, led to greater prosperity generally. The growth of insurance in particular meant that merchants were making an attempt to safeguard against chance events, and did not need to blame witches for their misfortunes if their losses were covered by insurance.

THINKING HISTORICALLY Change (7a)

Convergence and divergence

Developments in astronomy and the study of the universe c1540–1750

1543	1588	1609	1632	1687
Copernicus publishes *De revolutionibus orbium coelestium* (On the Revolutions of the Heavenly Spheres)	Tycho Brahe challenges the view that comets exist within the atmosphere	Kepler's *Astronomia Nova* (New Astronomy) is published	Galileo's *Dialogue Concerning the Two Chief World Systems* is published	Newton's *Philosophiae Naturalis Principia Mathematica* (Mathematical Principles of Natural Philosophy) is published

Developments in human understanding and knowledge c1580–1750

1597	1605	1655	1660	1690
Gresham College founded	Francis Bacon's *The Advancement of Learning* published	Thomas Hobbes publishes *De Corpore* (On the Body)	The Royal Society founded	John Locke publishes *Essay Concerning Human Understanding*

1 Draw a timeline across the middle of a landscape piece of A3 paper. Cut out ten small rectangular cards and write on them the changes shown in the two tables above. Then place the cards on the timeline, with events in astronomy above the line and changes in understanding and knowledge below. Make sure there is a lot of space between the changes and the line.

2 Draw a line and write a link between each change within each strand, so that you have four links that join up the changes in the astronomy part of the timeline and four that join the understanding and knowledge changes. You will then have two strands of change.

3 Now make as many links as possible across the timeline between astronomical change and understanding and knowledge. Think about how they are affected by one another and think about how things can link across long periods of time. You should end up with something like the diagram below.

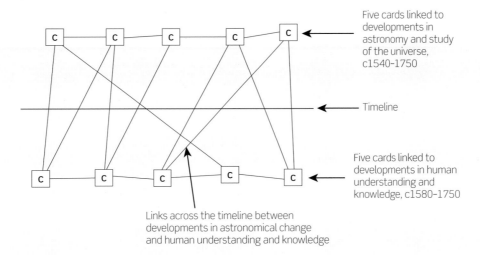

Five cards linked to developments in astronomy and study of the universe, c1540–1750

Timeline

Five cards linked to developments in human understanding and knowledge, c1580–1750

Links across the timeline between developments in astronomical change and human understanding and knowledge

4 Answer the following questions.

a) How far do different strands of history interact with one another? Illustrate your answer with two well-explained examples.

b) At what point do the two strands of development converge (i.e. when do the changes have the biggest impact on one another)?

c) How useful are the strands in understanding the decline of beliefs in the supernatural, witchcraft and magic?

ACTIVITY
SUMMARY

Society in the 17th century

1 Create a graph showing the major changes in human understanding and the universe between c1580 and c1750. The x-axis should denote time, and the y-axis should represent periods of significant change. From this you should be able to establish when the most significant changes took place.

2 Choose three changes that you feel are the most noteworthy, and explain why they are important.

3 Does your graph support the view that the Scientific Revolution and an increased understanding of human knowledge contributed to the decline of magic and witchcraft? Explain your answer.

A Level Exam-Style Question Section C

To what extent did the coming of the age of science and reason result in the end of a belief in magic and witchcraft in the years c1580–c1750? (20 marks)

Tip
The decline of witchcraft was not steady, and it should be noted that the speed of decline was faster in the second half of the period.

WIDER READING

Henry, J. *The Scientific Revolution and the Origins of Modern Science*, Palgrave Macmillan (2008)

Israel, J. *Radical Enlightenment: Philosophy and the making of Modernity 1650–1750*, Oxford University Press (2001)

Principe, L. *The Scientific Revolution: a Very Short Introduction*, Oxford University Press (2011)

Thomas, K. *Religion and the Decline of Magic*, Penguin, new edition (2003)

3.3

The North Berwick witches in Scotland, 1590–91 and the aftermath to 1597

KEY QUESTIONS

- Why did the persecutions begin?
- What was the impact of confessions, trials and executions in the years 1590–91?
- Why were persecutions widespread in the years to 1597?

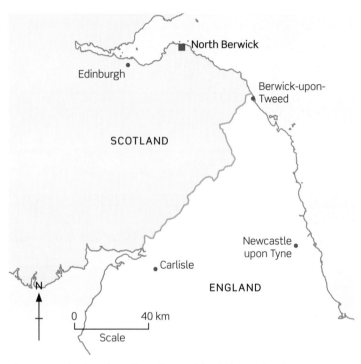

Figure 3.1 The location of North Berwick within Scotland.

INTRODUCTION

The importance of North Berwick

The North Berwick witch-hunt contains many of the typical elements of 16th- and 17th-century persecutions.

- A large number of women were accused (along with a minority of men).
- They were charged with fraternising with the Devil.
- A case of *maleficium* was central to the case.

What makes the North Berwick hunt unique, however, is the involvement of royalty. James VI of Scotland (later to become James I of England on the death of Elizabeth in 1603) took a personal interest in events, and one of the central charges against the accused was conjuring a storm to prevent James and his new wife, Anne of Denmark, from travelling to Scotland after their marriage.

Witch-hunting in Scotland

Witch-hunting in Scotland was always more widespread and more intense than in England (see Figure 3.2), with a relatively large number of executions and extensive use of torture. A number of reasons have been put forward by historians to explain this.

1563 - Scottish Witchcraft Act passed

1555	1560	1565	1570	1575

- Scotland had a less complex system of government than England. With fewer royal agents at the monarch's disposal, local officials were usually allowed to pursue witch-hunts without interference, resulting in trials dominated and directed by the paranoid neighbours of suspected witches.

- According to the law, torture could only be used with the consent of the Privy Council or parliament of Scotland, but as the Scottish monarchy was relatively weak, local judges often allowed torture without suffering repercussions. Unlike in England, the swimming test was hardly used.

- Although Scotland had a jury system a simple majority was needed to find a defendant guilty, rather than a unanimous decision.

- The nature of religion in Scotland also played a part in increasing the intensity of witch-hunting. Like England, Scotland witnessed a Protestant reformation, but on stricter, Calvinist lines. An air of anti-Catholic feeling heightened an already well-established suspicion of rituals and traditions, the use of which was increasingly blamed on witches.

- Compared with England, Scotland was relatively poor. In this context, the appeal of the notion that the Devil was able to offer people eternal riches and a fruitful life while they were on Earth can be understood. The Christian Church made promises of eternal rewards in the afterlife, only after a life of virtue and godliness on Earth first.

- The children of accused witches would suffer the same reputation as their parents, and were referred to as 'witch's get'. In a deeply patriarchal society, women who were antisocial or caused their neighbours distress were often so labelled.

- As well as belief in witchcraft, there was a deeply held belief in fairies and folk magic used for helpful purposes. This could, however, result in accusations of wrongdoing.

Region	Years	Confirmed trials	Executions	% executed
Geneva, Switzerland	1537–1662	318	68	21
Luxembourg	1509–1687	547	358	69
Finland	1520–1699	710	115	16
Norway	1551–1760	730	280	38
Essex, England	1560–1672	291	74	24
Scotland	1563–1727	402	216	54

Figure 3.2 Execution rates for witchcraft by region.

1591 – Execution of Agnes Sampson and others

1597 – The witch-hunt of 1597

1597 – James VI publishes *Daemonologie*, justifying witch persecutions

1589 – James VI and Anne of Denmark marry by proxy

1591 – Earl of Bothwell implicated

| 1580 | 1585 | 1590 | 1595 | 1600 |

1590 – James VI's return to Scotland from Denmark impeded by severe storms

1595 – Bothwell is found guilty of treason and goes into exile

1590 – Gilly Duncan arrested and confesses to witchcraft

WHY DID THE PERSECUTIONS BEGIN?

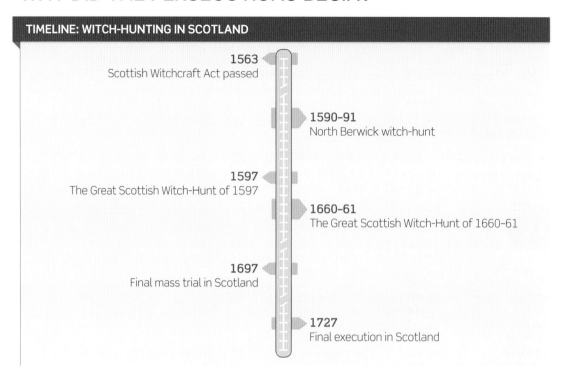

TIMELINE: WITCH-HUNTING IN SCOTLAND

1563
Scottish Witchcraft Act passed

1590–91
North Berwick witch-hunt

1597
The Great Scottish Witch-Hunt of 1597

1660–61
The Great Scottish Witch-Hunt of 1660-61

1697
Final mass trial in Scotland

1727
Final execution in Scotland

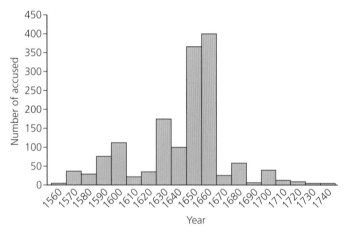

Figure 3.3 Number of accused witches in Scotland, by decade, based on data from the Survey of Scottish Witchcraft.

Witch-hunting in the late 16th century

Witch-hunting started relatively late in Scotland, with the first major hunts occurring toward the end of the 16th century. The majority of hunts took place in the south, where people had more contact with England, and away from the Highlands. The Scottish Witchcraft Act was passed in 1563 under Mary Stuart, Queen of Scots – mother of James I – and it was heavily influenced by Calvinist clergymen keen to enforce godly morals.

Commissions of judges could be set up under the Witchcraft Act in order to investigate cases, and they were sent around the country when required. This meant that witchcraft became one of the few crimes that could be dealt with on a national, rather than local level. At first, the number of accused persons was low, as can be seen in Figure 3.3. The years 1590 and 1591 were some of the most intense for witch-hunting that Scotland had seen, until accusations peaked in the mid-17th century and then declined rapidly. Accusations tended to peak at times of crisis or economic difficulty, such as years of poor harvest, political upheaval or war.

Gilly Duncan's confession

The persecutions at North Berwick began with the confession of a young woman named Gilly (or Gellie) Duncan, who was reputed to have unnatural healing abilities. Although she had never attempted healing before, she began visiting those who were sick and disabled in her neighbourhood in an effort to help them. When her efforts were apparently rewarded and her patients made miraculous recoveries, some of her neighbours began whispering that dark, supernatural forces may be to blame. Duncan was not a typical witch, as she was neither old nor particularly isolated from her community.

Duncan worked as a maidservant for David Seaton, the local deputy-bailiff, who decided to question her about where she acquired her remarkable skills, as well as why she had been stealing from his house and disappearing for days at a time. Duncan remained stubbornly silent throughout Seaton's questioning, and then the torture began. Seaton was assisted by others in this torture, and Duncan was subject to the most painful methods available.

- She was tortured with 'pilliwinks', or thumb-screws. These would be tightened gradually as a question was repeated.

- She was also tortured with cords around her head. This was a common method of torture in Scotland, whereby the cords would be jerked about in order to rattle the brain.

- Duncan continued to deny her involvement in witchcraft, so Seaton set about searching for a Witch's mark. As Source 1 attests, this was found in the front of her throat, and its discovery was enough for her to confess. This source is taken from a pamphlet, *Newes from Scotland*, printed shortly after the events, and serves as one of the most detailed primary accounts of the witch-hunt.

Duncan stated that her cures had been the work of the Devil, and she was sent to prison, where she started to name other witches.

SOURCE

1

From *Newes from Scotland* (1591). An anonymous pamphlet, but probably written by James Carmichael, minister of Haddington, and circulated in both Scotland and England. It was later reproduced in some editions of King James' *Daemonologie*.

They... found the enemies [Devil's] mark to be on her fore crag, or fore part of her throat; which being found, she confessed that all her doings was done by the wicked allurements and enticements of the Devil, and that she did them by witchcraft. After this her confession, she was committed to prison, where she continued a season, where immediately she accused these persons following to bee notorious witches, and caused them forthwith to be apprehended, one after another... Agnes Sampson the eldest witch of them all, dwelling in Haddington; Agnes Tompson of Edinburgh; Doctor Fian alias John Cunningham master of the school at Saltpans in Lowthian, of whose life and strange acts you shall hear more largely in the end of this discourse. These were by the said Geillis Duncan accused, as also George Motts wife, dwelling in Lothian; Robert Grierson, skipper; and Jannet Blandilands; with the potter's wife of Seaton: the smith at the Brigge Hallis, with innumerable others in those parts, and dwelling in those bounds aforesaid; of whom some are already executed, the rest remain in prison to receive the doom of judgement at the King's Majesties will and pleasure.

Duncan's employer, David Seaton, seems to have had little compassion or understanding of why Duncan would want to help others, or why someone of her humble background would have knowledge of medical techniques such as the use of leeches. His motivation for pressing ahead with torture may have been due to her stealing from him or being absent from work, and some historians have even suggested the two had previously entered into an affair that ended shortly before the accusations were made. Some of the accomplices she named were the wives of respectable Edinburgh gentlemen, whose previous reputations had been impeccable.

ACTIVITY

KNOWLEDGE CHECK

The nature of witch-hunting in Scotland and Gilly Duncan's confession

1 Why were executions and the use of torture more widespread in Scotland than England?

2 Read Source 1. From what you know so far about the people accused by Gilly Duncan, what was her motive in naming them?

The impact of James VI's voyage from Denmark

James' voyage to Denmark

James had married the 14-year-old Anne of Denmark by proxy, and she attempted to set sail for Scotland three times, starting her first voyage on 1 September 1589, but each time her fleet was driven back by storms. The Danish admiral, Peter Munk, could not recall ever witnessing storms as dangerous, and he attributed them to witchcraft. Munk may have had other reasons for suggesting witchcraft was to blame, as he seemed concerned that he may have been accused of negligence himself.

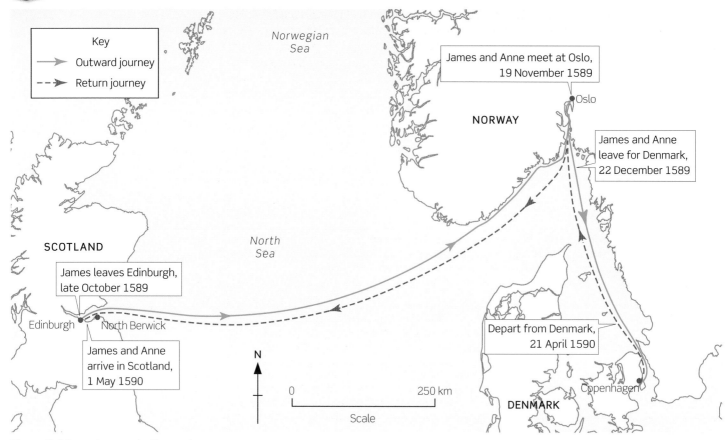

Figure 3.4 James' voyage to Denmark.

James ordered his cousin, Francis Stewart, Earl of Bothwell, who was Admiral of Scotland, to fetch his bride. Bothwell submitted his estimated costs for the trip to the Chancellor, who rejected them as too expensive, and so the Treasury and Bothwell suggested that James travel to Denmark in person. He departed in October in a vessel packed with large quantities of food and wine, arrived in Norway after a stormy journey, and proceeded to Denmark, where he stayed until spring.

While in Denmark James met a number of scientists and philosophers, and his royal engagements included a visit to astronomer Tycho Brahe's home at Uraniborg. He also met with a leading Danish theologian, Niels Hemmingsen, with whom he discussed Calvinism at length. Finally, he met a number of courtiers who held strong beliefs in group witch trials.

James and Anne sailed back to Scotland as part of a fleet, and the journey was perilous. One ship was lost, and witches were again blamed by some. A few months later, members of the Danish court made a visit to Scotland and James' conviction against witches was again strengthened in conversation with leading courtiers.

Did James' voyage encourage his belief in witches?

There is no evidence that James was interested in witchcraft before 1590, and there were few books on witchcraft and magic printed or imported into Scotland. There is a chance that James was present at a performance of a play called *Flyting* around 1580, which contained some references to fairies and witches, and he quoted from it in an essay he wrote in 1584.

The Witchcraft Act of 1563 did forbid anyone to use witchcraft or sorcery, or to consult with anyone claiming to be a witch, but even the wording of the Act treated the existence of witchcraft with a degree of scepticism. Witches are referred to as abusers of the people rather than genuine Devil-worshippers, reflecting the fact that most Scots saw witchcraft as a fraudulent practice. Before James' voyage, the Act was rarely enforced to the letter – in 1573 an order was given by the General Assembly of the **Kirk** that witches simply repent for their sins, and shows no interest in executing them. This is not to say that James would have been entirely ignorant of continental notions of witchcraft, and references are made to a diabolic pact with the Devil from a case tried in 1552, that James would have been aware of.

KEY TERM

Kirk
The Scottish Church.

Historians Christina Larner and P.G. Maxwell-Stuart have suggested that it was James' meeting with theologian Niels Hemmingsen that may have fired his belief in witchcraft. Hemmingsen was well respected and had written a book on magic and related subjects in 1575, entitled *Admonitio de Superstitionibus Magicis Vitandis* (Avoiding Magic and Superstition). In his book, Hemmingsen accepted that witches were able to carry out acts of *maleficium*, but he denied that a pact with the Devil could take place.

The idea that James' visit to Denmark had a significant impact on his thinking has been questioned, however. The historian Thomas Riis has argued that as witchcraft accusations in Denmark were generally based on localised cases of *maleficium* and not pacts with the Devil, the voyage would have had little impact on James.

The extent to which Danish witch-hunting influenced events in Scotland

Witchcraft in Denmark

Denmark of the late 16th century had inherited a long history of medieval suspicion and legal action against witches, although witch-hunting in earnest arrived relatively late. Suspected witches had a remarkable amount of state protection after laws were passed in 1547 to ensure fair trials. Torture was not allowed, and testimony from disreputable individuals was also excluded from trials. Further reform was carried out in 1576, which guaranteed that appeals against local court decisions could be heard in the high court in Copenhagen. Danish trials rarely made reference to a satanic pact.

Despite the safeguards against torture and miscarriages of justice, there were a number of high-profile witch-hunts that undoubtedly influenced events in Scotland. Early in the Protestant Reformation, high-profile clergy had taken to labelling those who opposed them as witches. The **Lutheran** Bishop, Peter Palladius (1503–60) encouraged good Christians to speak up if they suspected someone of witchcraft, and he reported that 52 witches were burned in just one hunt, after each confessed the names of others when they were found guilty.

Scotland's Protestant Reformation shared many characteristics with that which took place in Denmark, and events in Denmark reinforced Scottish prejudices. Long before the North Berwick trials, Bessie Dunlop was accused of witchcraft in Ayr in 1576. She was charged with conversing with the Devil, who invited her to become a Catholic. Bessie confessed under torture that the ghost of a dead soldier had assisted her in healing animals and finding stolen goods. Similar trials in Denmark were based on accusations of hidden Catholicism.

In the North Berwick case, the connection between Danish and Scottish witchcraft was first made in early July 1590, when a crazed woman arrived in Leith and prophesised than James would carry out noble acts. Later that month the news reached Scotland that a number of witches in Denmark had been arrested for conjuring up the storms that had prevented Anne from travelling.

The role of Anna Koldings

A letter dated 23 July 1590 from a spy of the English statesman Lord Burghley stated that the Danish admiral Peter Munk had demanded that five or six suspected witches be taken to Copenhagen. They were alleged to have used witchcraft to disturb the voyages of Anne and James.

One of the women suspected was Anna Koldings, who was interrogated and possibly tortured, despite this being illegal in Denmark. In fear of further torture she gave up the names of five other women who were involved, one of whom was the wife of the **borgmaster** of Copenhagen. Ultimately, all of the women confessed to raising a storm to sink Anne's ship and to sending demons to climb onto the ship and pull it under the waves. Koldings said that the women participated in meetings at the house of a woman named Karen the Weaver. Koldings was burned at the stake and at least 12 other women were executed in the course of the witch-hunt.

Interestingly, the authorities in Denmark initially looked for other reasons to explain the fate of the fleet before they turned to witchcraft. The minister of finance, Christopher Valkendorff, was initially accused of providing an inadequate and poorly constructed fleet. He responded that the witches, particularly Karen the Weaver, were responsible.

KEY TERMS

Lutheran
A follower of the Protestant reformer Martin Luther. Lutheranism is the oldest Protestant denomination, and is based on the doctrine of justification by faith alone and the authority of Scripture.

Borgmaster
The principal magistrate of a Danish town, similar in stature to a mayor.

ACTIVITY
KNOWLEDGE CHECK

The Danish connection

1 Create a table with the following information.

 a) On one column, include evidence that James' views on witchcraft changed as a result of his voyage to Denmark.

 b) On the other column, include evidence that a widespread witch-hunt in Scotland was already possible in 1590–91.

2 What parallels exist between Danish and Scottish witch-hunting?

WHAT WAS THE IMPACT OF CONFESSIONS, TRIALS AND EXECUTIONS IN THE YEARS 1590–91?

The case of Agnes Sampson and John Fian

Agnes Sampson accused

After Gilly Duncan, the next suspected witch to be implicated in North Berwick was an old woman called Agnes Sampson. She had a long-standing reputation as a midwife, healer and cunning-woman and seems to fit the description of a typical suspect, although unusually she was relatively well educated. It has been speculated that Gilly Duncan's sudden skill in healing may have been acquired as a result of her friendship with Sampson. King James himself interrogated and examined her at Holyrood Palace in Edinburgh, after officials had already discovered the Devil's mark on her body. She was interrogated with a number of devices.

- While she was not being questioned, a witch's bridle, a device that kept the mouth open with a number of prongs, was used on her in order to prevent her from reciting charms.

- She also had cords tied round her limbs and twisted tightly, causing extreme pain.

- Finally, she was kept awake for several days and nights.

The answers offered by Sampson under interrogation were calm and logical, despite the pressures she was under. One charge against Sampson accused her of communicating with another witch through letters, and ordering the other witch to instruct further members of their **coven** to raise a storm to prevent Anne of Denmark's arrival in Scotland.

Sampson was the first accused witch to be questioned in depth, and the list of accusations made against her is longer than the others and includes some that were seemingly harmless. Her charges included:

- healing the sick

- discovering information of a personal nature on behalf of others

- sailing across the sea in a sieve

- calling on the Devil in the shape of a dog named Elva in order to assist her with healing, although she denied the spirits that she met were the Devil.

James first became interested in Sampson's case in late 1590, several months after he had returned from Denmark with Anne. It is likely that his attention was drawn to the case because Sampson was asked if she had been responsible for the storms that delayed the royal rendezvous. After losing her dignity as a result of being shaved and probed for marks, together with the pain of her torture and sleep deprivation, it seems she confessed to anything that was asked of her.

The impact of Sampson's confession

Despite the obvious pressure put on Sampson to confess, she still seems to have been proud of her abilities as a cunning-woman. During her interrogation by James, he suggested that the things she had confessed to were so miraculous and strange that she was in fact a liar. She took him aside, and

KEY TERM

Coven
An assembly or group of witches, often believed to consist of 13 people.

repeated the exact words that had passed between James and Anne on their first night of marriage in Oslo. From this moment James was convinced by Sampson's confession. Many of the acts that were supposed to have been carried out by the witches were related by Sampson in her confession, including the theft of a corpse in order to use its knucklebones for magical purposes, and the throwing of a cat into the sea to cause a storm. This precise knowledge of witchcraft seems to come from her genuine experience as a healer, but not necessarily as someone who was in league with the Devil.

The magistrates seem to have agreed that Sampson was a leader of the coven of witches, but the accusations soon moved away from the limited region around North Berwick towards Edinburgh. As a healer and midwife, Sampson had travelled further than most, and had mixed in relatively high social circles.

- One of those she accused was Barbara Napier, who was a friend of the Earl of Bothwell (discussed later in the chapter). She even wrote to Bothwell while he was on trial, but the contents of her letter found their way to the king, who became even more incensed against Bothwell.

- Another of the accused was a royal courtier named Richard Graham, who was taken into custody in 1590 as a magician. He also knew Bothwell, and according to the earl's testimony at his own trial in 1593, once tried to sell him a ring containing a familiar spirit.

- Effie McCalyan was also accused. She was the daughter of Lord Cliftonhall and was well respected. She was accused of wanting to take revenge on her father-in-law, and her trial contained details of at least four coven meetings. She was also accused of using magic to transfer her childbirth pains for two births to a dog and a cat, and using her servants to deliver materials to other witches. Her servants betrayed her in court by testifying against her.

John Fian

John Fian was a schoolmaster from Saltpans, a few miles from North Berwick. He was arrested on 20 December 1590 and charged with 20 counts of witchcraft and high treason. As with Gilly Duncan and Agnes Sampson, he was tortured in order to identify the other witches in his coven. When he was initially imprisoned, he claimed that he had entirely renounced the Devil, but the evening after he had done this, the Devil came to him and told him he would never be able to escape his clutches and that he would take him under his control when he died. Fian was then able to escape for a short time, but was recaptured and tortured under command of the king.

His torture included many of the methods already well used in Scotland.

- His head was twisted with rope.
- Needles were driven under his fingernails.
- He was placed in a device known as the '**boots**' (see Source 4 on page 73).

Fian's refusal to confess made his interrogators even more enthusiastic about his torture, as it was believed that if a witch refused to confess it meant that the Devil was particularly entrenched in their soul. He was accused of involvement in the same events that Agnes Sampson had described (Source 2), including the casting into the sea of a cat.

> **KEY TERM**
>
> **Boots**
> Screws for the legs that would be gradually tightened. In the case of John Fian, this method resulted in his bones bursting.

SOURCE

2 From the charges against John Fian (1590), reproduced in King James VI, *Daemonologie* (1597).

ITEM, for the raising of winds at the King's passing to Denmark, and for the sending of a letter to Marian Linkup in Leith, to the effect, bidding her to meet him and the rest on the sea within five days; where Satan delivering a cat out of his hand to Robert Grierson, and gave the word to 'Cast the same in the sea, *hola!*' And thereafter, being mounted in a ship and drunk like unto others, where Satan said, 'You shall sink the ship;' like as they thought that did.

ITEM, for the assembling himself with Satan, at the King's returning from Denmark, where Satan promised to raise a mist, and cast the King's Majesty in England: and for performing thereof, he took a thing like to a soot-ball, which appeared to the said John like a wisp, and cast the same in the sea; which caused a vapour and a reek to rise.

As well as being accused of taking part in the treason against James, Fian was accused of a long list of other crimes of sorcery and witchcraft:

- acting as secretary at the coven meetings, where he recorded the oaths of allegiance to the Devil and played a central role in discussions

- giving the **kiss of shame** to the Devil

- falling into trances where his spirit was transported to mountains

- bewitching a man to suffer a spell of lunacy once a day because he was in love with the same woman as Fian

- attempting to bewitch the same woman to fall in love with him, but instead bewitching a cow that followed him everywhere he went, to the amusement of his neighbours

- together with the other witches, robbing graves for body parts to use in charms

- chasing cats after the Devil had told him to collect them to use in charms

- dismembering unbaptised babies

- predicting the future to discover how and when people would die, using his knowledge of their birthdays

- burning down a house in revenge for not keeping a promise

- flying through the air

- attaching magical candles to his horse (see Source 3), which enabled him to turn night into day as he travelled.

KEY TERM

Kiss of shame

An initiation rite among witches that appears in cases from as early as the 14th century. An initiate was expected to kiss the Devil's buttocks, although some witches alleged that the Devil had a second face located on his posterior. The kiss would take place at the beginning of a coven meeting after the Devil had read out the names of his followers.

SOURCE

3 John Fian makes cattle sick and sets fire to churches. Taken from an illustration in the contemporary pamphlet, *Newes from Scotland* (1591).

Why was John Fian accused?

John Fian features prominently in the surviving account, *Newes from Scotland* (see Source 4), but in reality he seems to be an unlikely witch. Unlike Agnes Sampson, there is no evidence to suggest he knew magic or was interested in healing. In reality it seems as though he was an easy target for accusations; as a schoolmaster he came into contact with many locals, and he also seems to have conducted affairs with a number of married women. As he was one of the few well-educated people in his community, and owned and taught from Latin and Greek texts, he would have been suspected by illiterate locals of possessing some sort of hidden knowledge.

SOURCE

 Adapted from *Newes from Scotland* (1591). This was probably written by James Carmichael, minister of Haddington, six miles from North Berwick. It was reproduced in some editions of King James' *Daemonologie*.

He [Fian] stole the key of the prison door... which in the night he opened and fled away... the King's majesty... presently commanded diligent inquiry to be made for his apprehension, and... sent public proclamations into all parts of his land to the same effect. By means of whose hot and hard pursuit, he was again taken and brought to prison, and then being called before the kings highness, reexamined as well touching his departure, as also... all that had before happened.

Whereupon the king's majesty perceiving his stubborn wilfulness, conceived... that in the time of his absence he had entered into new conference and league with the devil his master, and that he had been again newly marked, for the which he was narrowly searched, but it could not in any wise be found, yet for more trial of him to make him confess, he was commanded to have a most strange torment which was done in this manner following.

His nails... were risen and pulled off with an instrument called in Scottish a *Turkas*, which in England wee call a pair of pincers, and under every nail there was thrust in two needles over even up to the heads... neither would he then confess it the sooner for all the tortures inflicted upon him.

Then was he with all convenient speed, by commandment, continued again to the torment of the boots... and did abide so many blows in them, that his legs were crushed and beaten together as small as might be, and the bones and flesh so bruised, that the blood and marrow spouted forth in great abundance, whereby they were made unserviceable forever. And notwithstanding all these grievous pains and cruel torments he would not confess anything, so deeply had the devil entered into his heart....

Upon great consideration therefore taken by the King's majesty and his Counsel, as well for the due execution of justice upon such detestable malefactors, as also for example... to all others hereafter, that shall attempt to deal in the like wicked and ungodly actions, as witchcraft, sorcery [and] conjuration,... the said Doctor *Fian* was soon after arraigned, condemned, and adjudged by the law to die, and then to be burned according to the law of that land... he was put into a carte, and being first strangled, he was immediately... burned in the Castle hill of Edinburgh.

A Level Exam-Style Question Section A

Read Source 4 before you answer this question.

Assess the value of the source for revealing the part played by torture and the organisation of witch-hunts in the late 16th century.

Explain your answer, using the source, the information given about its origin and your own knowledge about the historical context. (20 marks)

Tip
It is important to take note of the provenance of the source in order to assess any insights the author may have had, or what the agenda of the author may have been when compiling the source.

ACTIVITY
KNOWLEDGE CHECK

Agnes Sampson and John Fian

1 In what ways is the case of Agnes Sampson unique among the suspected witches?

2 Why was John Fian accused? Why do you think he faced so many charges?

The role of the king and torture

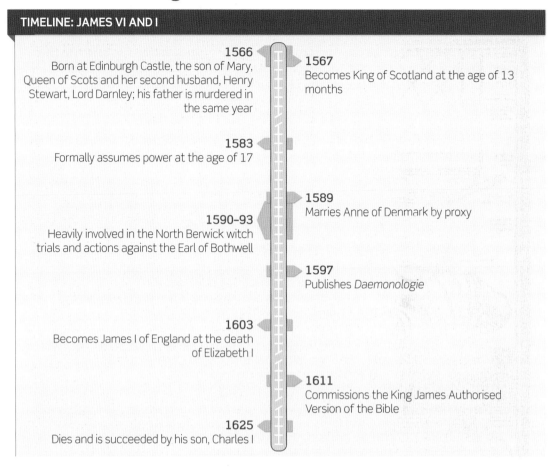

1566
Born at Edinburgh Castle, the son of Mary, Queen of Scots and her second husband, Henry Stewart, Lord Darnley; his father is murdered in the same year

1567
Becomes King of Scotland at the age of 13 months

1583
Formally assumes power at the age of 17

1589
Marries Anne of Denmark by proxy

1590–93
Heavily involved in the North Berwick witch trials and actions against the Earl of Bothwell

1597
Publishes *Daemonologie*

1603
Becomes James I of England at the death of Elizabeth I

1611
Commissions the King James Authorised Version of the Bible

1625
Dies and is succeeded by his son, Charles I

The role of James

As we have seen, James took a personal interest in the North Berwick witches, and was at the centre of events. As the accused had been charged with attempting to harm him and his new queen, he took a leading role in interrogating and prosecuting the suspects.

It should be noted that James was still relatively inexperienced. He formally came of age and assumed power in 1583, at the age of 17, and was 24 in 1590 when the events at North Berwick began to unfold. There were two influences that made him particularly suspicious and likely to take an interest in witch-hunting.

- Firstly, his childhood and years as a young adult were marked by political crisis. His father, Lord Darnley, was murdered when James was eight months old. His mother, Mary, Queen of Scots, then married James Hepburn, 4th Earl of Bothwell, who was assumed to be responsible for Darnley's death. Following an uprising against her, Mary was forced to abdicate in favour of her infant son and fled to England, hoping that Queen Elizabeth, her first cousin once removed, would welcome her. Instead, Elizabeth viewed Mary with suspicion and had her imprisoned. She was executed for plotting to overthrow Elizabeth in 1587. Dangerous conspiracies were part of his make-up, and there was a long history of violence among the nobility well before Mary came to the throne. James was always conscious that plots against him could begin at any time.

- Secondly, he grew up in a highly charged religious environment. Concern about his mother's Catholicism was countered by the Calvinism of his tutors, and he inherited a country struggling to define its religious identity, as the nobility were divided on the issue. In February 1589, he discovered that an influential Catholic, George Gordon, was plotting to assist Spain in an invasion of Scotland; however, James appeased his Catholic Lords as they provided a degree of balance against the radically Protestant Kirk. In this context, it is easy to see why James was attracted to ideas of the (Catholic) antichrist at work in Scotland.

King James interrogates Agnes Sampson, John Fian and others. Taken from an illustration in the contemporary pamphlet, *Newes from Scotland* (1591).

The confession of Agnes Sampson caught James' attention because it provided an explanation for the storms faced by his and Anne's fleets. Sampson also referenced the king directly when she stated that the Devil had told her the king and all of Scotland would be destroyed. James certainly approved the torture of suspects, and interviewed many himself, both before and after torture had been inflicted, as well as advising the legal authorities on methods of interrogation. He also promoted the idea that the suspected witches were actively worshipping the Devil. Given his concern with plots against his person, as well as his genuine belief in the **divine right of kings**, his enthusiasm can be more easily understood. James could also use the trials to assist his political cause. He had long coveted the English throne, and was keen to promote himself on the other side of the border. *Newes from Scotland*, published in England, presented him as a godly Protestant who was concerned with defending his people from the same threats faced by the English.

At the end of *Newes from Scotland*, the author concludes that James was protected from the witches because he was a devout Christian. By making a clear connection between James and the trials, the author sought to justify the deaths of the witches. *Newes from Scotland*, although it was almost certainly not written by James as suggested by some early historians, provided justification and acted as a guide for further witch-hunts in Scotland because it showed that the king agreed that the witches should be eliminated. His passion for the cause was underlined in the case of Barbara Napier, who was initially acquitted. James personally arranged for the jurors to be themselves tried for their error.

KEY TERM

Divine right of kings
The notion that kings are appointed by God.

Use of torture

By all accounts, James approved of the torture that was carried out on the accused. Gilly Duncan was subject to horrendous torture by David Seaton. Agnes Sampson was placed in the witch's bridle, and the use of thumb screws, 'boots' and cords tied around the head were all recorded. In Scotland, torture could only be used if officially sanctioned by the Privy Council, but James' personal involvement ensured that it was used widely.

The North Berwick witch-hunt is rare in that a detailed account of the torture inflicted on suspected witches survives, in the form of the pamphlet *Newes from Scotland*. It is difficult to ascertain whether the level of torture found at North Berwick is typical of witch-hunting in Scotland as a whole, but it seems that torture was frequently used without official permission.

ACTIVITY
KNOWLEDGE CHECK

The role of James and torture

1 Why was James interested in witches?

2 Why was torture used so extensively in North Berwick?

The involvement of the Earl of Bothwell

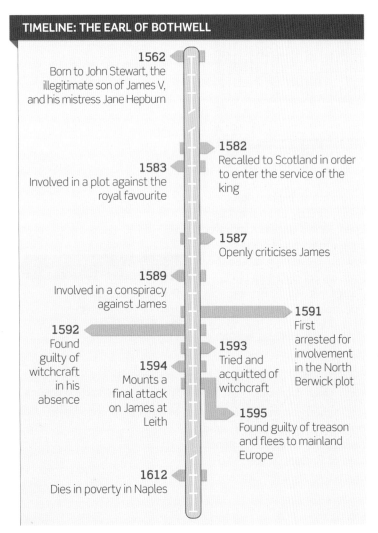

TIMELINE: THE EARL OF BOTHWELL

1562
Born to John Stewart, the illegitimate son of James V, and his mistress Jane Hepburn

1582
Recalled to Scotland in order to enter the service of the king

1583
Involved in a plot against the royal favourite

1587
Openly criticises James

1589
Involved in a conspiracy against James

1591
First arrested for involvement in the North Berwick plot

1592
Found guilty of witchcraft in his absence

1593
Tried and acquitted of witchcraft

1594
Mounts a final attack on James at Leith

1595
Found guilty of treason and flees to mainland Europe

1612
Dies in poverty in Naples

Bothwell's early career

Francis Stewart, 5th Earl of Bothwell (1562–1612) moved in the highest circles of Scottish society. He was the first cousin of James, as they were both grandsons of King James V. He studied at the University of St Andrews, and travelled widely on the continent before being recalled by James in 1582. Trusted by James at first, he became a military commander and joined the Privy Council, rising to the office of Lord High Admiral of Scotland. His career took a downward trajectory and he became involved in a number of criminal cases and plots.

- In 1583 he was involved in a plot to oust the **royal favourite**, the Earl of Arran, and spent time under house arrest.

- In 1587 he openly criticised James for failing to prevent the execution of his mother (and Bothwell's aunt), Mary, Queen of Scots.

- In 1589 he was accused and found guilty of treason as part of a group who were believed to be conspiring to seize the king. His sentence was deferred.

KEY TERM

Royal favourite
A close adviser given significant power and influence by a monarch.

SOURCE

The witches meet and plot with the Devil to raise storms. Some historians have claimed that the Earl of Bothwell played the role of the Devil. Right and bottom right: a witch-hunter is magically transported from Scotland to the wine cellar of a merchant in Bordeaux. Taken from an illustration in the contemporary pamphlet, *Newes from Scotland* (1591).

Involvement in North Berwick

It is unlikely that Agnes Sampson knew Bothwell, but she confessed that he had asked her to divine how long James would live, and requested that she predict what would happen after James' death. She also claimed that he had encouraged her to send her familiar to kill the king. Another of the accused, Richard Graham, confessed that Bothwell was part of the conspiracy. Bothwell was arrested on 15 April 1591 and held at Edinburgh Castle.

James had a clear dislike for Bothwell, but he may have had genuine reason to believe that he was involved. As admiral, Bothwell had suggested that James make the journey to collect Anne himself, which automatically implicated him in the eyes of James because it appeared that Bothwell had foreknowledge of the storms that would disrupt the journey. James also seems to have been in fear of Bothwell. Later, when Bothwell was seeking a pardon from James, he entered Holyrood Palace in person with a number of associates. On 24 July 1593 they entered James' chamber, and James attempted to flee into the queen's bedroom, but found the door was locked. James was supposed to have remarked that they could kill him, but they could never take his soul. His fear of Bothwell lay not in his power as an assassin, but in his power as a magician.

Attempts to punish Bothwell

In April 1591, Bothwell was summoned before the Privy Council to explain himself. He strongly denied any involvement, but was held at Edinburgh Castle to await trial. He escaped in June, believing that the accusations were a plot to diminish his political influence, and it was reported that he entered Holyrood Palace a few days later to reconcile with James. Before he did this, a royal proclamation had been issued, publicly accusing Bothwell of being in league with the Devil, depriving him of all titles and declaring him an outlaw.

Bothwell spent the next few months in hiding, assembling a force in an attempt to attack Edinburgh. On 27 December he attacked Holyrood Palace, but he was repelled by James' guards. Bothwell escaped, and although James made attempts to capture him, he was able to go into hiding once more. In April 1592, James attempted to pursue him again after hearing that he was residing in Dundee, and the Privy Council found him guilty of witchcraft in his absence. In June, Bothwell made another attempt to capture the king, accompanied by more armed supporters. Another pursuit took place, but James failed to capture him; however, a number of Bothwell's supporters were arrested and imprisoned.

Between July and October 1592, more of Bothwell's supporters were charged but Bothwell himself continued to evade capture. As the net closed around him, Bothwell took the extraordinary decision on 24 July 1593 to enter Holyrood and plead with the king in person, and although James was left shaken by the incident, he seems to have been convinced of Bothwell's innocence. Bothwell received an official pardon and in August a farcical trial was held to clear Bothwell of the original witchcraft charges.

Bothwell's trial, 1593

Bothwell seems to have had the upper hand during his trial. He had persuaded James of his innocence and he now filled Edinburgh with his armed supporters as a show of strength. He defended himself, and presented the accusations as a deliberate attempt to politically undermine him (fitting the modern definition of a 'witch-hunt' – in reality nothing to do with witches). He claimed to have witnesses who could testify that they were threatened with torture if they did not implicate him in the plot against James. The jury acquitted Bothwell unanimously.

The next month, fearful of Bothwell's growing political influence, James withdrew his pardon and proclaimed that Bothwell would effectively have to go into exile and he was forbidden from approaching the king again. Bothwell then attempted one last uprising and joined a group of rebels in Linlithgow, who attacked the king's forces at Leith in March 1594. This was unsuccessful, and he withdrew to the English border. James again proclaimed that Bothwell was guilty of treason in early 1595, and he eventually departed for mainland Europe, where he spent time in France, Spain and Italy before dying in Naples in 1612.

EXTEND YOUR KNOWLEDGE

Bothwell in exile

After Bothwell's failed attempt at rebellion James revoked his pardon and Bothwell escaped and found his way to Italy, via France and Spain. He was reported to have visited London and a half-hearted attempt was made to have him arrested. He eventually settled in Naples where he lived in poverty.

Visitors to Bothwell during his exile in Naples noted that he maintained a reputation as a powerful magician. In 1826, Sir Walter Scott wrote that while abroad Bothwell embraced the Catholic faith and while he was in Spain he was held in high regard as a fortune teller, but fell under the suspicions of the Inquisition who believed him to be a sorcerer.

George Sandys, a contemporary traveller, wrote in 1627 that he found Bothwell living in Italy. He records that in conversation with a local resident from the south of Italy he was told that Bothwell had a reputation as a sorcerer. Documents have also surfaced suggesting that shortly before his death, Bothwell may have written letters to a French witch-hunter, admitting his involvement in occult practices, although they may be forgeries.

The impact of the confessions, trials and executions

The judicial proceedings against the suspected witches began in 1590 and lasted for three years, including the trial of the Earl of Bothwell in August 1593. In total, 70 people were implicated, although not all were arrested. The total number arrested is not known, although the initial arrests took place in November 1590 and the trials began in January 1591.

A number of the accused fled to England, and James instructed David Seaton, the former employer of Gilly Duncan, to recapture them. At least one woman was tracked down and extradited to Scotland, where she was tortured and confessed more names. The fate of the most high-profile witches is known, and includes the following.

- Gilly Duncan, the original accused witch, was hanged.

- John Fian was executed by strangulation and his body burned.

- John Grierson died in custody.

- Agnes Sampson suffered the same fate as Fian – strangulation followed by burning on Castle Hill in Edinburgh.

- Another of the accused, Barbara Napier, was due to be executed on 11 May 1591, but when her friends claimed that she was pregnant, her execution was delayed. Although James demanded a retrial, there is no evidence that she was ever executed.

- Effie McCalyan also attempted to feign pregnancy, but with less success. She was due to be burned alive on 19 June 1591, but this was delayed after her claims. She was ultimately executed less than a week later, on 25 June. The severity of her punishment was reduced, as she was not burned alive, but first strangled like Fian and Sampson. Before her execution, she spoke to the crowd that had assembled, declaring that she was innocent.

As well as the above, there were countless others accused as a result of torture and confessions, about whom little is known. Many were likely executed. Some of the individuals mentioned in confessions include:

- Margaret Acheson, who was accused by Napier and Sampson of meeting the Devil and plotting against King James

- Meg Bogtoun, who was implicated by others in plotting to destroy James' and Anne's ships

- Bessie Broune, who was accused by Sampson of dismembering a corpse at Halloween

- Michael Clark, who was mentioned in Fian's confession as someone who was present at meetings at the North Berwick Kirk.

The Earl of Bothwell and the impact of the legal process

1 If Bothwell was involved with the North Berwick witches, what might his motivation have been?

2 Do you think James genuinely believed that Bothwell was involved in witchcraft? Explain your answer.

3 Create a flow chart to explain the stages by which Bothwell was pursued by both James and the courts.

4 From the information above, why do you think so many suspects were caught up in the witch-hunt?

5 Why were some of the accused strangled before being burned?

WHY WERE PERSECUTIONS WIDESPREAD IN THE YEARS TO 1597?

Two of the major witch-hunts in Scottish history took place in the 1590s: the North Berwick hunt of 1590–91 and the witch-hunt of 1597. Between 1591 and 1597 a number of other trials took place. In 1595, three suspected witches were sent to Edinburgh from Caithness after apparently fraternising with the Earl of Bothwell. In the same year, a number of witches were reported to have been burned in the Scottish border region of Merse. In 1596, the trial of Alison Jollie was held at Edinburgh. She had been accused of hiring a witch to kill her neighbour and found not guilty. In the same year, James once again appeared in person at the trial of Cristian Stewart, who was accused of murder through witchcraft. All cases between 1592 and 1596 are relatively isolated, but in 1597 a national hunt began in earnest.

Judicial procedures

The 'general commission', 1591–97

The historian Christina Larner has suggested that a general commission for the trying of witches was established in the closing stages of the North Berwick panic, but eventually miscarriages of justice caused it to be revoked. Other historians, such as Jenny Wormald, have suggested that this commission began later, around 1592. Julian Goodare, however, has questioned whether a formal commission into witchcraft existed at all between 1591 and 1597. He argues instead that procedures for trying witches did not change in the 1590s, with trials either taking place in Edinburgh or, with permission, in the localities. This situation had not changed since the Witchcraft Act was passed in 1563. It is known that the Scottish parliament discussed legislation regarding procedures against witches in 1597, but any details have been lost.

Either way, the judicial procedures in place in the years 1591–97 made witch trials easy to arrange and convictions likely. A variety of cases were heard and commissions were created.

- In October 1591, five judges were named on a commission with no specified subjects. They were given commission to torture at will.

- Commissions were given by the king in mid-1592 to nobles and magistrates for the investigation and trial of witches.

- In 1596, James proclaimed that all requests for commissions into cases of witchcraft should be submitted to the Privy Council for discussion, rather than to the king personally. In the same year, the Privy Council gave a commission to Sir William Steward to investigate accusations of sorcery and witchcraft, as well as other crimes such as murder and theft, in the Highlands and Islands region.

- In 1595, authorities in Edinburgh tortured a suspected witch, Alison Balfour, for two days, without a warrant from the king. She was initially accused of being hired by Patrick Stewart to poison his brother. Her 81-year-old husband was tortured by having iron bars pressed on his body, her son was tortured with 'boots' and her seven-year-old daughter was tortured with thumbscrews. She was executed despite the fact that she recanted the confession that was made under torture. This case goes some way to explaining why the Privy Council reduced the number of commissions after 1597.

The witch-hunt of 1597

The next great hunt after North Berwick took place in 1597. In March, a large trial took place in Aberdeen against an accused witch named Janet Wishart. In echoes of the events of 1590, Wishart was accused of raising storms, as well as causing injury and death to victims with several accomplices. She was executed with one of her accused accomplices. Although the hunt was over by October, it had spread beyond Aberdeenshire as far as Fife, Perthshire and Stirlingshire, leading to around 400 accusations. Many of these were accused by Margaret Aitken, who was arrested as a witch in April and agreed to assist the authorities in identifying further offenders, possibly after being interrogated by James himself. She travelled around Scotland with the king's agents and was asked to identify witches for trial. The authorities became suspicious in August, however, when she began to identify people as witches who she had previously claimed were innocent. The hunt ended shortly afterwards, and it would be 30 years before such intense witch-hunting would take place again in Scotland.

The hunt of 1597 was not officially documented by the central government of Scotland because many of the interrogations and trials were carried out at a local level, and therefore it is not as well known as the North Berwick hunt. It came at a time of poor harvest and widespread plague and disease, often cited by historians as ideal conditions for witch-hunts. The judicial procedures in use also contributed to increased executions, as they were again under the instruction of local officials, who would rely on disgruntled local witnesses.

Lack of strong central control

James always had problems maintaining central control. There are reports of him growing dissatisfied with the Kirk for not doing enough to deal with witchcraft, and the Kirk had a vested interest in ensuring that James failed. Between 1585 and 1592, there was relative peace between monarch and Kirk, but relations broke down after 1592, and the two sides were in open conflict in 1596. Friction was caused by James' unwillingness to take action against Catholics in Scotland, and as a believer in divine right, the more extreme Presbyterians in the Kirk believed he should be subject to their authority as they believed he was not appointed by God.

Although the 1590–91 and 1597 hunts may have taken place under the authority of a royal commission, trials were often carried out by local officials and there were no instructions from central government on how to carry out trials. It was also difficult for the government to maintain control over judicial proceedings far from Edinburgh, in the Highlands and Islands. In these areas, most trials took place on the estates of large landowners, and reports back to the Privy Council were limited.

Bothwell's role was a threat when there was limited central control. As long as James remained without an heir, Bothwell could make a claim to the Scottish throne. If James married Anne and had children, Bothwell no longer had a claim. Indeed, Agnes Sampson confessed that she had constructed a wax image of James at the behest of Bothwell, and historian Margaret Murray and the author Montague Summers have even suggested that Bothwell played the part of the Devil at the meetings of the North Berwick coven. The historian Donald Tyson, however, refutes this (Extract 3).

EXTRACT 1

From Margaret Murray, 'The "Devil" of North Berwick' in *The Scottish Historical Review* (1918).

The man who instigated the meetings, and to whom, consequentially, suspicion points, was Francis, afterwards Earl of Bothwell... James's own opinion on the matter is shown in his speech to his parliament in 1592, when he denounced Bothwell as an aspirant to the throne, although he was 'but a bastard, and could claim no title to the crown.'... the significance of the witches' attempt, as well as the identity of the chief personage at their meeting, is given in Barbara Napier's evidence as to the reason for the attempted murder of the King, 'that another might have ruled in his Majesty's place, and the government might have gone to the Devil.' By changing the title 'the Devil,' by which he was known to the witches, to the 'Earl of Bothwell,' by which he was known outside the community, the man and the motive seem manifest. This hypothesis is borne out by the contemporary accounts.

EXTRACT

2   From Montague Summers, *Witchcraft and Black Magic* (1946, reprinted 2000).

Under the direction of Francis Stewart, Earl of Bothwell, who was aiming at the throne, the whole body of witches combined to attempt by any possible means they could the life of King James VI. On All Hallows Eve, 31 October, 1590, a full assembly of more than two hundred witches was convened at midnight at the old haunted church of North Berwick, where the Grand Master, Bothwell himself, harangued them from the pulpit.

EXTRACT

3   From Donald Tyson, *The Demonology of King James* (2011).

This fanciful theory [that Bothwell was involved] depends on a rather startling presupposition – that prior to the exposure of the plots of the witches, Bothwell was the active head of a large coven of witches accustomed to meet at the North Berwick Kirk and elsewhere in the dead of night, where he dressed up in costume and played the part of Satan. If such nocturnal meetings took place, they must have been executed with a mastery of stealth and guile since this considerable undertaking of manpower and resources passed unnoticed in the small, closely knit communities near the church, where the members of the coven lived.

THINKING HISTORICALLY   Evidence (6c)

Comparing and evaluating historians' arguments
Extracts 1, 2 and 3 relate the role of the Earl of Bothwell in the North Berwick witch-hunt, but come to different conclusions.

1 Extract 1 supports the idea that Bothwell played the role of the Devil and Extract 3 rejects this idea.

   a) Which has the better supported claim?

   b) How could you add something to Extract 1 to make the claim stronger?

2 What is particularly strong about the claim in Extract 3 compared to the others?

3 How does Extract 2 challenge the argument in Extract 3?

4 What is weak about the argument in Extract 2?

5 Consider all the extracts. Which do you think is the best argument? Explain your answer.

ACTIVITY
KNOWLEDGE CHECK

Persecution to 1597
1 Why were so many commissions created to investigate witchcraft after 1591?

2 Why did trials peak again in 1597?

3 Was a lack of central control the most important factor in explaining why witch-hunts were so widespread in the 1590s? Explain your answer.

The role of King James and *Daemonologie*

The publication of *Daemonologie*

James saw himself as an intellectual, and endeavoured to gain expert knowledge of a variety of subjects, taking a personal interest in the occult. It is not clear when James began work on his guide to witchcraft, *Daemonologie*, published in 1597, but it was certainly published following the witch-hunt of that year. It is presented as a dialogue between Philomathes, a sceptic of magic and witchcraft, and Epistemon, who enlightens Philomathes on the subject. He outlines his reasons for writing the book, stating that Reginald Scot's sceptical work in particular had caused him to clarify his stance on witches.

SOURCE 7

Adapted from King James VI, *Daemonologie* (1597). Here, James is explaining why he has written his book and its contents.

The fearful abounding at this time in this country, of these detestable slaves of the Devil, the Witches or enchanters, hath moved me (beloved reader) to dispatch in post, this following treatise of mine, not in any way (as I protest) to serve for a show of my learning and ingine, but only (moved of conscience) to press thereby, so far as I can, to resolve the doubting hearts of many; both that such assaults of Satan are most certainly practised, and that the instruments thereof, merits most severely to be punished: against the damnable opinions of two principally in our age, whereof the one called SCOT an Englishman, is not ashamed in public print to deny, that there can be such a thing as Witch-craft: and so maintains the old error of the Sadducees, in denying of spirits... And for to make this treatise the more pleasant and facile, I have put it in form of dialogue, which I have divided into three books: The first speaking of Magic in general, and Necromancy in special. The second of Sorcery and Witch-craft: and the third, contains a discourse of all these kinds of spirits, and Spectres that appears and troubles persons: together with a conclusion of the whole work. My intention in this labour, is only to prove two things, as I have already said: the one, that such devilish arts have been and are. The other, what exact trial and severe punishment they merit: and therefore reason, what kind of things are possible to be performed in these arts, and by what natural causes they may be, not that I touch every particular thing of the Devil's power, for that were infinite: but only, to speak scholastically, (since this cannot be spoken in our language) I reason upon kind (genius) leaving appearance (species), and differences (differentia) to be comprehended therein.

In general, the key points made by James in *Daemonologie* are as follows.

- In the first part, the two characters discuss the reality of witchcraft, and agree that the Devil is extremely powerful and is a danger on Earth.

- James also attempted to prove that both necromancers (people who attempted to communicate with the dead) and witches have a close association and allegiance to the Devil.

- He described the practices witches engage in, including initiation ceremonies and making a pact with the Devil.

- He explained the gathering of covens as inverted Protestant rituals. At covens, the witches would renounce their Christian baptism.

- He does admit that witches and the Devil only have certain powers. This is because God had limited the Devil's power at the beginning of time.

As well as discussing the nature of witchcraft and magic, James provides a guide to identifying witches.

- He held the search for the Devil's mark in high regard, as this would be something acquired by a witch when they renounced their baptism. This led the way for the widespread searching of witches in the 17th century.

- He suggested that the swimming test would be an effective way of identifying witches. Although this was used overwhelmingly in England rather than Scotland, it was used once during the panic of 1597.

- He believed in demonic possession and claimed that this was easy to identify. The cure consists of fasting and prayer.

- The two characters also discuss the vulnerability of women to the deceptions of the Devil. They are more likely to be witches because they are easily led astray, ever since Eve was deceived by the serpent in the Garden of Eden.

SOURCE 8

Adapted from King James VI, *Daemonologie* (1597). Here, James discusses the ability of witches to travel by using supernatural powers.

The Devil will be ready to imitate God, as well in that as in other things: which is much more possible to him to do, being a Spirit, then to a mighty wind, being but a natural meteor, to transport from one place to another a solid body, as is commonly and daily seen in practise... And in this transporting they say themselves, that they are invisible to any other, except amongst themselves; which may also be possible in my opinion. For if the devil may form what kind of impressions he pleases in the air, as I have said before, speaking of Magic, why may he not far easily thicken & obscure so the air, that is next about them by contracting it strait together, that the beams of any other mans eyes, cannot pierce thorough the same, to see them? But the third way of their coming to their conventions, is, that wherein I think them deluded: for some of them sayeth, that being transformed in the likeness of a little beast or foul, they will come and pierce through whatsoever house or Church, though all ordinary passages be closed, by whatsoever open, the air may enter in at. And some sayeth, that their bodies lying still as in an ecstasy, their spirits will be ravished out of their bodies, & carried to such places... for this form of journeying, they affirm to use most, when they are transported from one Country to another.

SOURCE 9 The original cover of *Daemonologie* (1597). The book was reprinted several times, both before and after James' death.

DAEMONOLO-
GIE, IN FORME
of a Dialogue,
Diuided into three Bookes.

EDINBVRGH

Printed by Robert Walde-graue,
Printer to the Kings Majeftie. An. 1597.

Cum Privilegio Regio.

The concluding argument that James puts across is that witches exist, and they should be prosecuted by the authorities. If people deny that this is the case they have been led astray, and are perhaps in league with the witches themselves. The most obvious targets of James' attack appear to be the ministers and laymen who had criticised his support of the 1597 witch trials.

How far was James responsible for the persecutions of the 1590s?

There is no doubt that *Daemonologie* was conceived at least in part as a reaction to the trials of 1590–91, and the fact that it was published towards the end of 1597 has led some historians to suggest that its publication was an immediate reaction to the trials of that year. James talks of witch-hunts as something that had recently been happening, and there was a plan to publish the 1597 witches' confessions at the same time.

The historian Jenny Wormald has questioned James' role in the 1597 panic. She agrees that James had a role in actively promoting the North Berwick hunt, but claims that his role in 1597 was as a sceptic rather than someone who encouraged the persecutions. She argues that in 1592, James was content to pass on much of the responsibility for dealing with witchcraft when he sent an order to the church to that effect. The church then established a system for dealing with witchcraft accusations that they exercised to the full in 1597. Julian Goodare has argued against this, claiming that the 1592 order does not set out a mechanism for dealing with witchcraft. As always, the only mechanisms for dealing with cases were commissions issued by the crown to investigate witchcraft and trials at the Edinburgh court of justiciary.

James' interest in the Stirlingshire panic, 1597

There is definitive evidence that James still wanted to interrogate witches personally in 1597, and he took an active interest in events in Stirlingshire in that year. On 16 September, he ordered the magistrates of Stirling to send an unnamed suspected witch to him, who had recently been subject to having her skin pricked as part of the magistrates' investigations. Patrick Heron and his wife were accused by the unnamed witch, and it is no coincidence that they were in a property dispute with Sir William Menteith and his son. The Menteith family probably arrested the suspected witch with the intention of forcing her to confess and accuse the Herons. Heron fled, and was subject to a prosecution for witchcraft from the Menteith family. The case came close to being quashed, but was reignited in response to a letter from the king.

Later scepticism

The apparent miscarriages of justice in 1597 greatly affected James, and he became sceptical of witchcraft by the turn of the next decade. He seemed more concerned with discovering fraudulent witches than those using real supernatural powers, and wrote a letter to his eldest son, Prince Henry, congratulating him on uncovering a false witch. He reminded Henry that what people often think are miracles or mystic occurrences are actually illusions, and that accusations – especially those made in a court of law – should be treated with caution.

ACTIVITY
KNOWLEDGE CHECK

James VI and witchcraft

1 Why did James publish *Daemonologie* in 1597?

2 Look at the key points James made in *Daemonologie*. In which English and Scottish trials have you seen these elements of witchcraft?

3 Would the persecutions of the 1590s have been widespread without the personal role of James?

4 Why do you think James was later sceptical of witchcraft?

Conclusion: Why was witch-hunting so widespread between 1590 and 1597?

Why did North Berwick become the first truly widespread witch-hunt in Scottish history, and why did its repercussions last for so long? A number of reasons have been put forward by historians to explain this.

- The role of James is key in explaining the extent of the hunt. If a less superstitious monarch was on the throne, local officials may not have been given such a free hand to carry out torture, trials and executions.

- The fact that the monarchy was relatively weak, and that Scotland had a long history of royal and clan rivalry also played a part. It is impossible to ascertain just how involved the Earl of Bothwell was, but he clearly had designs on the throne.

- Weather and natural disasters played a part. The initial 1590–91 accusations were associated with storms and 1597 with famine and disease.

- As with all subsequent Scottish hunts, social factors played a role. Scotland was a more patriarchal society, and men were perhaps quicker to accuse women of witchcraft than their English counterparts. Scotland also had a well-entrenched belief in folk magic, fairies and witches.

- The judicial system, which included majority verdicts in jury trials and less control from central government, meant that miscarriages of justice were more likely to take place.

A Level Exam-Style Question Section B

How accurate is it to say that it was the interest taken by James VI that accounts for the extent of witchcraft persecutions in Scotland in the years 1590–97? (20 marks)

Tip
The role of James should be balanced against other factors, such as the judicial situation in Scotland and social factors.

ACTIVITY
SUMMARY

Why was the witch-hunt so widespread, 1590–97?

1 Look at the statements in the conclusion.

   a) Create a table in order to assess which factor is most important in explaining the extent of the witch-hunt. Your headings should be: 'The role of James', 'Lack of central control', 'Weather and natural causes', 'Social factors', 'Judicial system'.

   b) For each, find two or three examples from the North Berwick hunt and its aftermath and include them in the table under their respective headings.

   c) Produce a paragraph explaining which factor you feel is the most significant in explaining the extent of the witch-hunt and why.

The role of the individual

2 Although many people were implicated in accusations and trials in the years 1590–97, four of the accused made a significant impact: Gilly Duncan, John Fian, the Earl of Bothwell and Agnes Sampson. For each, explain:

   a) how they became embroiled in the witch-hunt

   b) the extent of their involvement

   c) why the authorities were particularly interested in them

   d) their punishment or the outcome of their involvement.

WIDER READING

Goodare, J. (ed.) *The Scottish Witch-Hunt in Context*, Manchester University Press (2002). Contains a number of essays that deal with wider issues around Scottish witch-hunting, including a detailed discussion of the 1597 panic.

Normand, L. and Roberts, G. (eds) *Witchcraft in Early Modern Scotland: James VI's Demonology and the North Berwick Witches*, University of Exeter Press (2000). Includes the key documents, including *Newes from Scotland*.

Pavlac, B.A. *Witch Hunts in the Western World*, University of Nebraska Press (2010). Provides information on the Scottish context, the North Berwick trials and the role of James.

The Survey of Scottish Witchcraft at the University of Edinburgh provides a database of all known witch trials in Scotland – www.shca.ed.ac.uk/Research/witches/

3.3

The Lancashire witches of 1604–13

4

KEY QUESTIONS

- What was the significance of the social, economic and religious context of the Pendle witch trials?
- Why, and with what effect, were Lancashire families accused of witchcraft?
- In what ways were the outcomes of the trial significant?

INTRODUCTION

The importance of the Lancashire witches

Just seven years after the Gunpowder Plot to blow up parliament was exposed, another danger from within threatened to result in turmoil in James I's England. Like the events of 1605, the Lancashire witch trials were held in the context of anti-Catholic hysteria and suspicion; it was even alleged that the witches were plotting to blow up Lancaster Castle with gunpowder. The clerk of the court, Thomas Potts, published a detailed record which acts as a key primary source for the events, *The Wonderfull Discoverie of Witches in the Countie of Lancaster* in 1613. It is no coincidence that he dedicated his work to Thomas Knyvet, who had been credited with apprehending Guy Fawkes in the cellar of the Houses of Parliament.

The events that took place in and around the Pendle Forest shared many of the same features as other 17th-century witch trials.

- At their heart was a feud between neighbours and rival families.
- Interrogations and trials were of questionable legitimacy.
- Evidence of pacts with the Devil was sought in all cases.

James had effectively written the guidebook for the authorities to use in the trial when he published *Daemonologie* in 1597, but even he had reservations about witch-hunting after he became King of England on the death of Elizabeth I in 1603.

There is one element of the Pendle case that makes it truly groundbreaking: the use of child witnesses. In modern Britain, it is quite normal for young children to give evidence in court cases, but before the nine-year-old Jennet Device gave evidence in the 1612 trial, children under 14 were viewed as unreliable witnesses. Her evidence led to the execution of ten people, including her entire family.

1604 - New witchcraft statute in England modifies the law of 1563

April 1612 - Old Demdike, Old Chattox and others are implicated

10 April 1612 - The meeting at Malkin Tower, leading to further accusations

| 1604 | 1612 January | 1612 February | 1612 March | 1612 April | 1612 May | 1612 June | 1612 July |

March 1612 - Alizon Device meets pedlar John Law and is accused of bewitching him

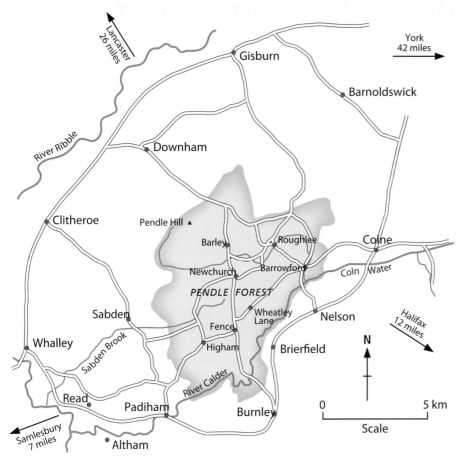

Figure 4.1 Pendle Forest and the surrounding area.

In 1618, the writings of Thomas Potts and the evidence presented by Jennet Device were included in a new handbook for Justices of the Peace called *The Country Justice*. The book covered all types of crime from minor thefts to murder, and included witchcraft as another serious breach of the law. This book became incredibly significant for a number of reasons.

- The book went through more than 20 editions before 1746 and was used by all subsequent magistrates investigating cases of witchcraft. Its popularity was based on the wide range of examples and precedents that magistrates could refer to.

- It made allowances for the testimony of children, because of the events at Pendle.

- The book was used at the notorious Salem witch trials in Massachusetts in 1692, where most of the evidence was given by children.

1613 - Thomas Potts publishes *The Wonderfull Discoverie of Witches in the Countie of Lancaster*

| 1612 August | 1612 September | 1612 October | 1612 November | 1612 December | 1613 | 1614 | 1615 |

August 1612 - The majority of defendants are found guilty at the Lancaster assizes and executed on Gallows Hill, Lancaster

WHAT WAS THE SIGNIFICANCE OF THE SOCIAL, ECONOMIC AND RELIGIOUS CONTEXT OF THE PENDLE WITCH TRIALS?

During the 1960s and 1970s, a new approach to explaining witchcraft developed among historians: the 'village tensions' approach. Instead of focusing on the narrative of prosecution and detailed analysis of trials, the social and economic pressures of the 16th and 17th centuries were explored. Disputes between neighbours, whether rich or poor, in the context of population pressure, inflation and poor harvests were investigated in order to ascertain why witch trials took place. These tensions and disputes are as relevant in Pendle as in any other European witch-hunt.

More recently, historians have focused on religion as a key factor in explaining witch trials. As we will see, the argument first put forward by Hugh Trevor-Roper in 1967 – that witch-hunts were more likely to occur in areas where there was a clash between Reformation Protestantism and Catholicism – has been revisited by historians.

The economic and social context

The economy of Pendle

Pendle Forest was originally set aside for deer hunting, but by 1296 over 900 cattle were kept on farms there. In 1327, there were at least four water-powered mills for finishing cloth in Lancashire, with two close to Pendle Forest. In the early 17th century, Pendle could be categorised as an upland **pastoral** economy. There was limited **arable** farming, which mainly centred on the production of oats, and there was also a thriving cloth industry. Most cloth was worked in the homes of farmers, and entire families would assist with the process of cloth production. Heavy industry, such as coal mining and quarrying for building materials existed in Lancashire, but the vast majority of people were engaged in pastoral farming. Colne, less than six miles from Pendle Hill, held cattle markets three times a year, in February, May and September.

Probate inventories from Lancashire show that many families were engaged in both cattle rearing and the manufacture of cloth. The inventories of 17th-century houses in Pendle show that 70 percent contained the tools required for cloth production, such as spinning wheels and looms. Many families had no choice but to take on this work as revenue from agriculture could be unpredictable. Evidence presented at the trials shows that Anne Whittle, known as Old Chattox, was still carding wool for the wife of James Robinson in 1606, when she was well into her seventies. Another witch tried in 1612, Katherine Hewit, also known as Mouldheels, was the wife of a **clothier** from Colne.

Cattle and the witch trials

As with many other witch trials, suspects were accused of damaging livestock as well as people, which demonstrates the importance of cattle to the economy of Pendle. Cows were valuable, and could fetch nearly £3 at market, which a skilled manual worker could expect to earn in around six months. Old Chattox was accused of bewitching cattle belonging to Hugh Moore, as well as a cow belonging to Anthony Nutter after he appeared to favour the friendship of her rival, Old Demdike. Old Chattox and her daughter, Elizabeth, were also accused of killing a cow belonging to John Nutter after Elizabeth begged him for a dish of milk. Interestingly, this may have been the same cow that John Nutter had asked Old Demdike to cure.

Inflation

Pendle Forest passed into Crown ownership in 1399 when Henry, Duke of Lancaster, took the throne to become Henry IV. Cattle farms continued to be leased to tenants on an informal basis until 1507, when arrangements were formalised with fixed rents and **entry fines** introduced. As a result of the new arrangements, rents increased by 39 percent, and more general price inflation in the 16th century, especially for agricultural goods, meant that **copyholders** benefited through increased profits. Those who did not have rights as copyholders and had to pay forest entry fines and rents found that their economic situation became strained. As well as this, the increase in **enclosure** meant that many tenants faced the constant threat of eviction.

KEY TERMS

Pastoral
Land used for the rearing of sheep and cattle.

Arable
Arable farmers concentrate on growing crops rather than keeping animals.

Probate inventories
Lists of items belonging to a person drawn up after their death in order to establish the value of their estate.

Clothier
A person who makes or sells clothing or cloth.

Entry fines
A fixed sum paid to the owner by a tenant of a property to renew a tenancy.

Copyholder
Originally someone who laboured on the land of a lord with some privileges to use land for him/herself. They eventually gained more rights and were able to occupy smaller landholdings within manors. Although still technically owned by the Lord of the Manor, copyhold land could be bought and sold, rented out, inherited and left in a will, with certain fees paid to the lord.

Enclosure
The process of fencing off common land. The land would then be let out or farmed by the individual who paid for the enclosure.

The impact of population growth

Mortality (death) rates in England were lower in the 17th century than in the preceding three centuries, primarily because of a decline in incidences of the plague, although epidemics such as the one in 1665 killed 100,000 people in London alone. The infamous bubonic plague, or Black Death, that reached England in 1348 had a dramatic impact on the population, which was just 1.5 million in the 1450s compared with five million before the plague struck. By the 1520s, the population was around 2.5 million and it continued to increase rapidly. In the mid-16th century, short-lived epidemics of other viral diseases hampered growth, but these had reduced greatly by 1612.

In 1443 there were just 24 tenants in Pendle Forest, rising to 100 in 1527. As each tenant brought with him a family consisting of at least three others, the population must have been at least 400 in 1527. It was, however, common for families to sublet land and there were inevitably a number of families who remained landless, so the true population would have been higher than this. We know that the population had risen to about 1,620 in 1650. As the population increased, food needed to be produced more efficiently and the religious needs of the population catered for.

- In 1546, a new corn mill was built.

- Another corn mill was constructed in 1598.

- The church of Newchurch, to the south-east of Pendle Hill, was consecrated in 1544.

Year	Population
1443	96
1527	400
1563	580
1650	1,620

Figure 4.2 Population growth in Pendle.

Clashes with the duchy of Lancaster

Despite their relatively sheltered position in the community, the copyholders came to blows with the **duchy of Lancaster** in 1607, when lawyers for the duchy questioned the validity of the copyholders' estates. In reality the duchy hoped to gain money for the Crown from the copyholders. The copyholders of Pendle petitioned the duchy of Lancaster in 1608, explaining that they had limited resources with which to pay further fees (Source 1). All of this added to the economic tensions that already existed in the community.

KEY TERM

Duchy of Lancaster
The territory controlled by the duke of Lancaster. Since 1399, the duchy has been in the hands of the reigning monarch, who draws much of their income from the estate.

SOURCE 1

From the petition of the copyholders of Pendle to the duchy of Lancaster (1608).

> The soil thereabouts [is] extremely barren and unprofitable and as yet capable of no other corn but oats and that but only in dry years and not without the continual charge of every third year's new manuring, but also in the building of their houses and habitations thereon having no timber there nor within many miles thereof and having from time to time ever since enjoyed the same and therefore paid a rent and fine at the first as much or more and now very near the value thereof, have nearly disposed, employed and placed all the fruit and increase of their ancestors and their own labourers and industries.

From their petition, the copyholders appear to have been leading a difficult life of subsistence farming. Although they were probably exaggerating in order to avoid further fees, there is some truth to the petition. Their subtenants must have been in an even poorer state. In 1609, an agreement was made with the duchy whereby the copyholders were expected to pay a lump sum of 12 years' rent in order to confirm their rights and privileges. With economic ruin on the horizon, many copyholders were forced to sell or mortgage part of the land. In this context, it is easy to understand why residents of Pendle would be less inclined to offer charity to the vulnerable women who would be accused of witchcraft.

Copyholders, subtenants and squatters

The relatively wealthy copyholders had to pay rent to the duchy of Lancaster, but subtenants who rented from the copyholders had to pay rents that were on average 25 times higher than the rent paid by the copyholders in the first decade of the 17th century. A feeling of insecurity was increased by the lengths of contracts given to subtenants, which were often only a year or less. Evidence from the Pendle trials shows that a number of the suspected witches were subtenants: Old Chattox's daughter, Anne Redferne, was a tenant of Robert Nutter, who old Chattox was accused of murdering.

Illegal squatting and unrecorded tenancies were also commonplace, and although the law prohibited houses with fewer than four acres of land from being let, landlords ignored it as small holdings could be lucrative. It is likely that many of the suspected witches lived in properties acquired by this arrangement, and with no legal contracts they were exposing themselves even more to economic difficulties.

The economic and social context

1 Explain why the economy around Pendle was vulnerable to crises.

2 How could it be argued that inflation and population growth made a witch-hunt more likely?

3 Why do you think the more wealthy copyholders were more likely to support witch trials in the early 17th century?

The religious context

The Reformation in Lancashire

On the surface, it seems that the area around Pendle did not suffer as much as other communities that went through the Protestant Reformation. Despite Lancashire's reputation as a refuge for **recusant** Catholics, the records from Pendle are quite unremarkable.

The local clergy occasionally came to blows with their superiors. Christopher Nuttall, a minister in Pendle, came to the attention of the authorities when he married a couple in an alehouse, and had married a couple without a licence in 1592. The curate of Newchurch in Pendle, John Horrocks, gained a reputation later in the century for heavy drinking and immoral behaviour.

There are some limited examples of the residents of Pendle troubling the church courts in the early 17th century. In 1611, two Catholics were found living in the house of Henry Standen in secret and not attending their parish church, a fact that was reported to the church courts but not acted upon. In 1626, Richard Moore was charged for claiming that God did more harm than good, and a constable was charged in 1622 for being absent from church. These examples are isolated and sporadic, which perhaps makes the sudden zeal for witch-hunting a surprise.

The fact that the older witches were charged with using spells based on corrupted versions of old Catholic prayers indicates that the Protestant (and the more extreme Puritan) Reformation may have only had a limited impact on many people.

KEY TERM

Recusant
A person who refused to comply with the authority of the Church of England and remained loyal to the Catholic faith.

SOURCE

2 A Catholic priest is branded. From an 1826 copy of a late-16th century original included in an anti-Catholic pamphlet.

Church organisation and the witch-hunt

Newchurch in Pendle was a **dependent chapelry** of the parish of Whalley, which also included the chapelries of Colne, Clitheroe, Padiham, Burnley, Holme and Whitewell. In total the parish of Whalley covered 180 square miles and comprised a population of 10,000 people. Some historians have suggested that this was too large to effectively manage the population, and the authorities in London viewed Lancashire as an ignorant corner of England where Catholicism and superstition could easily be fostered.

The region was without a cathedral or bishop until Chester cathedral was established in 1541, and on Henry VIII's dissolution of the monasteries (1536–41) Whalley Abbey was closed down. For centuries, the abbey had provided charity and education to the local population, and when it closed the Pendle Forest lost an irreplaceable resource. The abbey owned vast swathes of land, and received a healthy income from rents. This inflow of wealth enabled the abbey to provide cloth, grain and money to the poor of Pendle Forest, as well as providing for the upkeep of chapels and parish churches across Lancashire.

In the absence of a Catholic abbey, a group of Puritan clergy and their associates amongst the gentry were able to wield more influence. The abbey and its lands automatically became the property of the Crown, who then instructed two members of the local gentry to manage the estate, and so the landed gentry were now able to exercise more power than they had done before. Some of these gentry were Puritan, and many were certainly anti-Catholic Protestants. Around the turn of the 17th century, attempts were made to clamp down on drunkenness and reduce the strength of the beer sold in the many alehouses around the Pendle Forest, and in 1594 a rare case of witchcraft was recorded that hints at the influence of more godly Puritans in religious matters. The case centred on the household of Nicholas Starkie of Huntroyd, within Whalley parish, and resulted in the publication of George More's *A Discourse Concerning the Possession and Dispossession of 7 Persons of one Family in Lancashire* in 1600. More explained that it was Puritan ministers that were to thank for ending the possession, and his work was used as a guide to influence the 1612 witch-hunt.

'White' magic

It seems that in Lancashire, the notion that a witch entered into a pact with the Devil was a relatively recent one. Historian Kirsteen Macpherson Bardell has investigated the wider witch-hunting landscape in Lancashire and has found evidence of nearly 100 other cases from the **Lancashire Quarter Sessions**. In these cases, magic is accepted as a familiar part of religious life, and there are blurred boundaries between witchcraft and the work of village healers, who used helpful, or 'white' magic. The evidence from Pendle seems to suggest that the senior witches, Old Demdike and Old Chattox, were involved in the 'white' magic as well as *maleficium*.

> **KEY TERM**
>
> **Dependent chapelry**
> A district served by a chapel rather than a larger parish church.

> **KEY TERM**
>
> **Lancashire Quarter Sessions**
> A local court that met four times a year in order to try criminal cases deemed too serious to be dealt with by JPs.

ACTIVITY
KNOWLEDGE CHECK

The religious context

1 Do you think the Protestant Reformation made the witch-hunt more likely?

2 What impact did the closure of Whalley Abbey have on Pendle Forest?

The significance of the new witchcraft statute of 1604

Attitudes to witchcraft before 1604

Before 1604, English courts had tended to work within a more traditional framework when investigating witchcraft. Unlike the continental system (in particular that of Germany, as discussed in Chapter 5), English law required members of the local community to make accusations, rather than clergy or professional inquisitors, and juries were drawn from the community. The crimes that witches were charged with had not changed for centuries because they were based on accepted, popular beliefs that affected the community. *Maleficium*, particularly in the form of harm done to grain or livestock, was the overwhelming accusation in the 15th and 16th centuries. Until the statute was amended in 1604, English courts required tangible evidence of *maleficium*, such as death or injury, and treated suspects in a similar way to other criminals, such as robbers and murderers.

The impact of the 1604 statute

Historians have been quick to identify the accession of James VI and I to the throne in England in 1603 as an important catalyst in reforming witchcraft legislation. As we saw in Chapter 3, he took a close interest in witchcraft and interrogated suspected witches in person. What made the 1604 statute significant was its inclusion of the conjuring of spirits as a capital offence. In the Act, James was promoting the continental view that the most damaging aspect of witchcraft was that it originated from a pact with the Devil. This pact was a threat to the social order, and the 1612 trial, as recorded by Potts, was the first evidence that the law was working. The historian Stephen Pumfrey has argued that the Lancashire trials represent a fusion of the continental focus on the diabolical pact and more traditional popular beliefs (Extract 1).

EXTRACT 1

From Stephen Pumfrey, 'Potts, plots and politics: James I's *Daemonologie* and *The Wonderfull Discoverie of Witches*' in Robert Poole (ed.), *The Lancashire Witches: Histories and Stories* (2002).

Late-twentieth-century historians... have shown that trial records such as those accurately reproduced by Potts are the result of complex interactions between the elite culture of demonology and the popular one of instrumental *maleficium*. In his book *The Night Battles*, Ginsberg convincingly showed how popular non-diabolic beliefs could be transformed by elite inquisitors into stories of Satanism that could even come to be accepted by the accused themselves. There is no reason to assume that the testimony concerning Chattox, Demdike, Alice Nutter and the rest was not fashioned in this way. *The Wonderfull Discoverie* therefore represents the first successful intrusion of elite demonology into an English trial... Local, popular beliefs shaped local versions of elite witchcraft discourse. English elites accepted the popular (English) belief that witches kept familiars, or companion animals. Continental demonology and trials had no place for familiars.

> **ACTIVITY**
> **KNOWLEDGE CHECK**
>
> **The 1604 statute**
> Read Extract 1. According to Pumfrey, what was the impact of the 1604 statute?

A Level Exam-Style Question Section B

How far do you agree that the Witchcraft Act of 1604 caused an intense interest in witch-hunting that resulted in the Pendle trials of 1612? (20 marks)

Tip
Assess a number of other contextual factors, including the economic and social environment around Pendle.

WHY, AND WITH WHAT EFFECT, WERE LANCASHIRE FAMILIES ACCUSED OF WITCHCRAFT?

Alizon Device and John Law

Initial encounter

The case has its immediate origins in an accusation made by a **pedlar** from Halifax, John Law, who encountered Alizon Device on his travels. As Thomas Potts (who acted as clerk of the court) recounts in Source 3, Law was travelling with his wares on 18 March 1612 when he encountered Alizon, who was begging outside of Pendle Forest on the road to Colne, and asked him for some pins. When he refused to give her any, she reacted angrily and he immediately suffered great pain, becoming paralysed down one side (presumably from a stroke) and unable to speak. He then encountered her familiar in the shape of a black dog, and Alizon briefly appeared to him. He remained in pain, tormented by the *maleficium* caused by Alizon.

KEY TERM

Pedlar
A person who travels from place to place selling small goods.

Accounts of the confrontation

According to Alizon's own testimony, her familiar spirit (the black dog) had appeared to her immediately after the encounter and asked if she would like to harm Law. As a relative novice at witchcraft, she told the dog to harm Law and was apparently surprised when the curse worked immediately.

There are some contradictions in the story of Alizon and Law's encounter. She later confessed to laming Law because he would not sell her any pins, and at her trial Law stated that she had begged him for pins and he had refused her, after which he became ill. His son Abraham, however, told the court that not only had Alizon no money to pay for the pins but that his father had actually given her some. Naturally, Potts presents the encounter as the typical story of a witch being refused help by a member of the community and retaliating in revenge.

SOURCE

3 From Thomas Potts, *The Wonderfull Discoverie of Witches in the Countie of Lancaster* (1613).

He [John Law] deposeth and saith, That about the eighteenth of March last past, hee being a Pedler, went with his Packe of wares at his backe through Colne-field: where unluckily he met with *Alizon Device*, now Prisoner at the Bar, who was very earnest with him for pins, but he would give her none: whereupon she seemed to be very angry; and when he was past her, he fell downe lame in great extremitie; and afterwards by meanes got into an Ale-house in Colne, near unto the place where hee was first bewitched: and as hee lay there in great paine, not able to stir either hand or foote; he saw a great Black-Dogge stand by him, with very fearefull fiery eyes, great teeth, and a terrible countenance, looking him in the face; whereat he was very sore afraid: and immediately after came in the said *Alizon Device*, who staid not long there, but looked on him, and went away.

After which time hee was tormented both day and night with the said *Alizon Device*; and so continued lame, not able to travel or take paines ever since that time: which with weeping teares in great passion turned to the Prisoner [Alizon Device]; in the hearing of all the Court hee said to her, *This thou knowest to be too true*: and thereupon she humblie acknowledged the same, and cried out to God to forgive her; and upon her knees with weeping teares, humbly prayed him to forgive her that wicked offence; which he very freely and voluntarily did.

Hereupon Master *Nowell* standing up, humbly prayed the favour of the Court, in respect this Fact of Witchcraft was more eminent and apparant than the rest, that for the better satisfaction of the Audience, the Examination of *Abraham Law* might be read in Court.

The role of Abraham Law

Immediately after he became aware of his father's condition via a letter sent to him in Halifax, Abraham Law came to see his father at Colne. He went in search of Alizon and brought her to his father on 29 March. Alizon begged for his forgiveness, which he gave her, but Abraham was incensed and reported the matter to a local magistrate, Roger Nowell. From there, the witch-hunt snowballed quickly and by the end of April, 19 people were in custody at Lancaster Castle awaiting trial at the August assizes.

ACTIVITY
KNOWLEDGE CHECK

Alizon Device and John Law

Why do you think John Law was prepared to forgive Alizon Device? Why was his son so keen to follow up on the accusations?

Old Demdike and Old Chattox and their witchcraft families

Family rivalry

The chain of events that led to the 1612 trial can be traced to around 1601, when the senior members of two rival families – Anne Whittle, known as Old Chattox, and Elizabeth Southerns, known as Old Demdike – fell out.

The source of the disagreement between the women was the theft of some clothing and grain from Alizon Device (granddaughter of Old Demdike) worth 20 shillings. The next Sunday, Alizon claimed that she had seen Anne Redferne, daughter of Old Chattox and wife of Thomas Redferne, wearing a stolen cap and band. It was not long before the two families were trading various accusations of theft and slander, and Old Chattox, who seems to have been the more powerful of the two women, was offered a settlement from John Device, the father of Alizon. He promised to pay her a yearly tribute of grain, which seems to have settled the situation until John Device's death a few years later.

In his account of the trials, Potts commented on the rivalry between the two families, stating that Old Chattox was 'always opposite to Old Demdike, for whom the one favoured, the other hated deadly, and how they envy and accuse one another in their examinations may appears'. The historian John Swain believes that there was more to the family rivalry than one incident of theft (Extract 2).

EXTRACT

2 From John Swain, 'Witchcraft, economy and society in the forest of Pendle' in Robert Poole (ed.), *The Lancashire Witches: Histories and Stories* (2002).

It is possible that the two families were bitter enemies for reasons other than the break-in, because they were competing against each other for a limited market, making a living by healing, begging and extortion. Alizon Device said that although she did not have the power to cure the pedlar John Law, her grandmother, Old Demdike, could have done it if she had lived. John Nutter had apparently asked Demdike to cure a sick cow, but it died. Some of those indicted were probably wise women or men, practitioners of herbal or folk medicine, and inevitably sometimes things went wrong and they got the blame. They certainly obtained some income from begging. Alizon Device said that she had been on several begging expeditions with her grandmother, Old Demdike... A reputation for witchcraft, and being more successful than rivals, was therefore all-important.

Earlier reputation

Even before the family rivalry became heated, accusations of witchcraft were being made. In about 1595, Christopher Nutter was travelling home from Burnley with his sons, Robert and John. They lived at Greenhead, an impressive residence within the boundary of Pendle Forest. At the time, Old Chattox was living as a tenant on their land with Anne and Thomas Redferne and other members of the family. According to Potts' account, Robert was unwell and insisted to his father that he had been bewitched by Chattox and her daughter. His father did not believe him, and Robert threatened Thomas Redferne that he would have him removed from his house, before leaving for Chester. Robert died on his return from Chester, and soon his father became ill and died after three months. Although initially sceptical about witchcraft, Christopher insisted on his deathbed that he had been bewitched, but did not name any individuals. John, the surviving son, would later give evidence against Old Chattox.

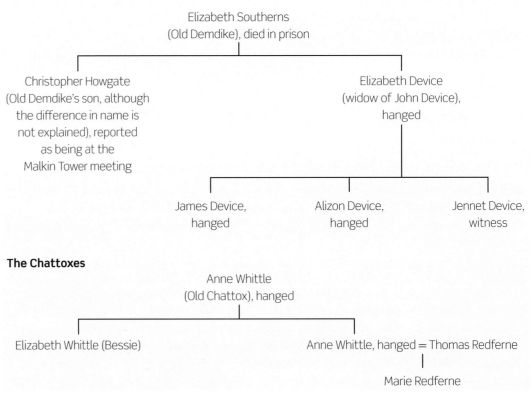

Figure 4.3 The Demdike and Chattox family trees. Adapted from Edgar Peel and Pat Southern, *The Trials of the Lancashire Witches* (1994).

Earlier cases of witchcraft in Lancashire

Although the Pendle trials are the most well known, Lancashire was not unfamiliar with witches in the 16th and 17th centuries.

In a very early English witchcraft case in 1546, William Walker of Yealand was accused by James Standisshe of using magic to convey a silver spoon to Wigan.

In 1594, known conjurer and faith healer Edmund Hartlay was accused of witchcraft when two children he was caring for and treating with herbs for illness showed signs of getting worse. Others in the same household fell ill and the events in the house were interpreted as demonic possession. The case was recorded by two notable authors on witchcraft, John Darrell and George More.

ACTIVITY
KNOWLEDGE CHECK

Witchcraft families

1 List as many reasons for the rivalry between the two families as you can think of.

2 Rank them in order of importance and explain your first choice.

The investigations of Roger Nowell

Roger Nowell's background

Thomas Potts' account includes a number of examinations and confessions conducted in the presence of Roger Nowell, a local magistrate who was central to compiling the case and conducting the witch-hunt.

Nowell was 62 in 1612, and was an experienced JP and local landowner. He had been High Sheriff of Lancashire and had strong connections with high-profile Protestants. The half-brother of his grandfather was Alexander Nowell, Dean of St Paul's Cathedral throughout Elizabeth's reign, and his second cousin was John Wolton, Bishop of Exeter. He was related by marriage to Nicholas Starkie, who led the family that experienced possession in Lancashire in the mid-1590s.

Although we know little about his knowledge or attitude towards witchcraft, it has been speculated that Nowell was familiar with William Perkins' *Discourse of the Damned Art of Witches* (1608), which promoted the notion that witchcraft consisted of a pact with the Devil, and with King James' *Daemonologie*. It is unclear whether he was determined from the beginning to investigate witches or whether he was convinced to take action by the succession of witnesses put before him.

The investigation – Alizon Device's confession

The investigations began in earnest when Abraham Law – son of the supposedly bewitched John Law – told Nowell of his being called to Colne by the letter that reached him on about 21 March. After he had accused Alizon Device, she was interrogated by Nowell and confessed that she had lamed Law senior. It is not known by what means Nowell interrogated her, but it is likely the usual methods (sleep deprivation, pricking, watching, etc.) recommended in the 17th century were utilised. She described in some detail what had occurred, including a conversation with a black dog that triggered the curse which injured Law.

Nowell was now in a position to charge Alizon, but she did not stop with her confession. She elaborated on her story and Nowell's investigation became more widespread:

Alizon described her initiation into witchcraft and explained that her grandmother (Old Demdike) had attempted to persuade her to take a familiar one day when they were begging together. As is so common in witchcraft confessions, she was promised that the familiar would give her anything she desired if she allowed it to suckle from her. The black dog had first approached her around two years before the encounter with Law, and she recounted three further examples of Demdike's witchcraft.

- The first related to a local farmer, John Nutter, whose cow became sick. As she had a reputation as a folk-healer, Nutter asked Demdike to heal the cow. As Demdike was blind, Alizon led her from her house, and her younger sister Jennet helped her to return. Alizon heard the next morning that the cow had died, and concluded that Demdike had bewitched it.

- The second example concerned some milk Alizon acquired through begging and brought into the house she shared with her family. When Alizon arrived home, Demdike was lying in bed. Alizon left the milk, and when she returned half an hour later there was a quarter of a pound of butter in it, despite the fact that Demdike had not left her bed.

- The third incident related to a feud between Demdike and a local farmer, Richard Baldwin. Alizon again explained that Demdike asked for assistance leaving the house at night, and the next morning Baldwin's daughter became ill. His daughter died after a year, and Alizon admitted to Nowell that she had heard her grandmother cursing Baldwin.

These incidents were recorded in the account of Thomas Potts (Source 4).

SOURCE 4
From Thomas Potts, *The Wonderfull Discoverie of Witches in the Countie of Lancaster* (1613).

And upon her examination, she [Old Demdike] further confesseth, and saith. That a little before Christmas last, this Examinates Daughter having been to help Richard Baldwyns at the Mill: This Examinates Daughter did bid her this Examinate goe to the sayd Baldwyns house, and aske him some thing for her helping of his Folkes at the Mill, (as aforesaid:) and in this Examinates going to the said Baldwyns house, and neere to the sayd house, she met with the said Richard Baldwyn; Which Baldwyn sayd to this Examinate, and the said Alizon Device (who at that time ledde this Examinate, being blinde) get out of my ground Whores and Witches, I will burne the one of you, and hang the other. To whom this Examinate answered: I care not for thee, hang thy selfe: Presently whereupon, at this Examinates going over the next hedge, the said Spirit or Devil called Tibb, appeared unto this Examinat, and sayd, Revenge thee of him. To whom, this Examinate sayd againe to the said Spirit. Revenge thee either of him, or his. And so the said Spirit vanished out of her sight, and she never saw him since.

And further this Examinate confesseth, and sayth, that the speediest way to take a mans life away by Witchcraft, is to make a Picture of Clay, like unto the shape of the person whom they meane to kill, & dry it thorowly: and when they would have them to be ill in any one place more then an other; then take a Thorne or Pinne, and pricke it in that part of the Picture you would so have to be ill: and when you would have any part of the Body to consume away, then take that part of the Picture, and burne it. And when they would have the whole body to consume away, then take the remnant of the sayd Picture, and burne it: and so thereupon by that meanes, the body shall die.

Alizon then went on to explain the rivalry between her grandmother and Anne Whittle (Old Chattox). They were both witches, Alizon said, but Chattox had committed particularly heinous crimes, including the following.

- She claimed that Chattox was guilty of murder through witchcraft. She recalled a story of Chattox cursing her and her friend, Anne Nutter, for apparently laughing at her. Three weeks later, Anne Nutter died, a victim of Chattox's magic.

- Alizon spoke of a rivalry between Chattox and a gentleman, John Moore of Higham. Moore had accused Chattox of turning his ale sour, after which she made threats against him and his son became ill and died. Alizon witnessed Chattox holding the clay image of a child, who she assumed to represent Moore's son.

- Another man, Hugh Moore of Pendle, died after accusing Chattox of bewitching his cattle.

- The same John Nutter who had requested Demdike to heal his cow, also came into contact with Chattox's family. One of her daughters, Elizabeth, had requested some milk from Nutter for her mother. Chattox began to use the milk to recite a charm, and on witnessing this, Nutter's son kicked over the can containing the milk. The next day, one of John Nutter's cows became ill and died.

Apart from this very fruitful questioning, Alizon was searched for the Devil's mark. Potts also records that her mother Elizabeth was searched, and she admitted to having a mark on her left side that had been present for 40 years. Despite this admission, and for seemingly unknown reasons, she was allowed to go free, along with her son, James.

SOURCE

In 1621, the playwrights William Rowley, Thomas Dekker and John Ford produced *The Witch of Edmonton*. Although it was based on another case of witchcraft, it was clearly influenced by the Lancashire trials and Potts' account, and includes similar descriptions of the witches and that of a black dog. The front cover below is from a 1658 edition.

Further arrests

Although only Alizon Device was detained at first, three days later both Old Demdike and Old Chattox were called in for questioning along with Anne Redferne (the daughter of Old Chattox). Nowell also found several neighbours prepared to testify against the women, and examined them on 2 April at the village of Fence. The village was close to where the women lived, and Nowell presumably chose it because the women's infirmities prevented them from travelling far. Nowell was concerned with hearing testimonies that corroborated that of Alizon, and although she died before she could be brought to trial, Potts' account gives us much detail in particular about the interrogation and confession of Demdike (Source 6).

SOURCE 6

From the confession of Old Demdike in Thomas Potts, *The Wonderfull Discoverie of Witches in the Countie of Lancaster* (1613). Potts was Clerk of the Court during the trials.

The said Elizabeth Sowtherns [Old Demdike] confesseth, and sayth; That about twentie yeares past, as she was comming homeward from begging, there met her this Examinate near unto a Stonepit in Gouldshey, in the sayd Forrest of Pendle, a Spirit or Devil in the shape of a Boy, the one halfe of his Coate blacke, and the other browne, who bade this Examinate stay, saying to her, that if she would give him her Soule, she should have any thing that she would request. Whereupon this Examinat demanded his name? and the Spirit answered, his name was Tibb: and so this Examinate in hope of such gaine as was promised by the sayd Devil or Tibb, was contented to give her Soule to the said Spirit: And for the space of five or sixe yeares next after, the sayd Spirit or Devil appeared at sundry times unto her this Examinate about Day-light always bidding her stay, and asking her this Examinate what she would have or doe? To whom this Examinate replyed, Nay nothing: for she this Examinate said, she wanted nothing yet. And so about the end of the said sixe yeares, upon a Sabbath day in the morning, this Examinate having a little Child upon her knee, and she being in a slumber, the sayd Spirit appeared unto her in the likeness of a browne Dogg, forcing himselfe to her knee, to get blood under her left Arm: and she being without any apparrell saving her Smocke, the said Devil did get blood under her left arme. And this Examinate awaking, sayd, Jesus save my Child; but had no power, nor could not say, Jesus save her selfe: whereupon the Browne Dogge vanished out of this Examinats sight: after which, this Examinate was almost stark mad for the space of eight weekes.

And further this Examinate confesseth, and sayth, that the speediest way to take a mans life away by Witchcraft, is to make a Picture of Clay, like vnto the shape of the person whom they meane to kill, & dry it thoroughly: and when they would haue them to be ill in any one place more then an other; then take a Thorne or Pinne, and pricke it in that part of the Picture you would so haue to be ill.

A Level Exam-Style Question Section A

Read Source 6 before you answer this question.

Assess the value of the source for revealing beliefs in witchcraft and the organisation of witch-hunts in the late 17th century.

Explain your answer, using the source, the information given about its origin and your own knowledge about the historical context. (20 marks)

Tip

Make use of both the text and the provenance of the source when writing your answer. Remember that this extract comes from a wide-reaching work that incorporates the entire witch-hunt.

Her confession contained many of the familiar traits of witchcraft confessions. She referred to an inability to invoke the name of Jesus to protect herself after meeting with her familiar, Tibb. This echoes stories of witches being unable to recite the Lord's Prayer. She also described making an effigy of a person in order to bewitch them, and of course, the suckling of a familiar. Old Demdike's confession, like that of the other suspected witches, may have been made under torture or threats. As she already had a reputation locally, Nowell may have convinced her that she was a genuine witch, and that the animals she had encountered in her daily life were in fact the Devil in disguise.

After her own confession, Demdike turned her attention to her old rival, Old Chattox. She told of a time when she saw Chattox and her daughter Anne sitting outside making figures from clay. Her familiar, Tibb, who was now in the shape of a cat, told her that they were effigies of Christopher Nutter, Robert Nutter and Robert's wife, Marie. Tibb suggested that she could help the other women in making the effigies, and when she refused Tibb pushed her into a ditch.

After Demdike's interrogation came Chattox's. She admitted – according to Potts, voluntarily – that around 15 years earlier she had been pestered by a man who wanted her to give him her soul. Eventually she consented, and was promised that from that moment she would want for nothing and be able to take revenge on any people who had wronged her. She was told to call her spirit 'Fancie', and when she did not call on her spirit for some time, it became restless and began to encourage her to harm people.

A number of witnesses were also present on 2 April, and Nowell took statements from them.

- Margaret Crook, Robert Nutter's sister, spoke about her brother's quarrel with Anne Redferne and his belief that she had bewitched him.

- John Nutter relayed the events of 18 years previously, when his father was apparently killed as a result of witchcraft.

- James Robinson, who was probably a servant of the Nutters, gave evidence that Old Chattox and Anne Redferne were well-known witches. Unusually, Robinson had hired Chattox to card wool at his house six years earlier. While working at Robinson's house, Chattox had accidently soured some casks of drink and claimed to have a charm to reverse what she had done.

Nowell had now received full confessions from the old women, but from the account left to us by Potts it seems that Anne Redferne said nothing, although she was now implicated by confessions and witness statements. As a JP, Nowell now had the authority to decide whether to deal with the cases himself or send the women to a high court for trial. Because the charges were so serious he decided to keep the women detained until he could send them to the Lancaster assizes in August.

Four women were now being prepared to be committed to Lancaster Castle: Alizon Device, Anne Redferne, Old Demdike and Old Chattox. This could easily have ended Nowell's investigations, but a week later, a meeting was held at Malkin Tower, the home of Old Demdike, that would result in a number of other suspected witches being brought under suspicion.

Roger Nowell's investigations

1 Do you think Nowell was eager to hunt witches? Explain your answer.

2 Why was Alizon Device's confession so important to the outcome of the investigations?

3 Why do you think many of the confessions and witness statements related to events that took place many years earlier?

The meeting at Malkin Tower

Figure 4.4 No contemporary depictions of the meeting at Malkin Tower exist. This illustration is from an 1849 book *The Lancashire Witches* by William Harrison Ainsworth and is highly sensationalised, depicting the witches carrying out a ritual around their cauldron while their familiars watch over them.

Discovery of the coven

When knowledge of the meeting reached Roger Nowell, he resumed his investigations immediately. Historians Edgar Peel and Pat Southern believe that the meeting bore little resemblance to the typical depiction of a **witches' sabbat** (Extract 3).

EXTRACT

From Edgar Peel and Pat Southern, *The Trials of the Lancashire Witches* (1994).

This meeting is often instanced as the only recorded example of a witches' sabbat in England at that time. Compared with the satanic midnight orgies reputedly taking place on the Continent, this noon gathering, consisting mostly of worried and helpless peasants, was a tame affair. They were unable to depend on the Devil to find them something to eat, and their hunger was appeased by a meal of beef, bacon and mutton, the last from a sheep stolen the night before by James Device.

Another JP, Henry Hargreaves, visited Malkin Tower in mid or late April, and, with the help of James Device (Alizon's brother), discovered a clay image and some teeth from the graveyard at Newchurch. James was now under suspicion, but was assisting the authorities with their enquiries. The two men then crossed the county border into Yorkshire and visited another suspect, Jennet Preston, in Gisburn, in order for James to identify her as someone present at the infamous meeting at Malkin Tower.

Nowell then sought the help of another magistrate, Nicholas Bannister, on 27 April, and together they examined Elizabeth, James and Jennet Device in order to ascertain what happened at the Malkin Tower meeting. Jennet, who was only nine years old, would become Nowell's star witness at the trial of her family.

Contents of the meeting

Young Jennet's evidence proved to be crucial in unravelling the supposed coven. She explained to Nowell that James had stolen a sheep to be eaten at the meeting, and he had killed it at their house in front of her. She said that around 20 witches were present at the meeting, but she could name only six. When James was interrogated, he was able to reveal more names. Potts collated the names given by the Device family and came up with a list of those present at what he called the Great Assembly and Feast (Source 7).

SOURCE

From the list of those present at the 'Great Assembly and Feast' at Malkin Tower, according to Thomas Potts and transcribed with additional commentary in Edgar Peel and Pat Southern, *The Trials of the Lancashire Witches* (1994).

Elizabeth Device, daughter of Old Demdike, whose house it now was;

James Device, son of Elizabeth, who provided the mutton;

Jennet Device, nine-year-old sister to James, who later played a very important role in the trial;

Christopher Howgate (or Holgate) of Pendle, Demdike's son;

Elizabeth Howgate, his wife;

Jennet Hargreaves, wife of Hugh Hargreaves, of Under Pendle, a farm on the Pendle Hill side of Barley;

Alice Nutter: Jennet Device described her as Dick Myles' wife, of Roughlee; James spoke of the mother of Myles Nutter;

Christopher Hargreaves (nicknamed Christopher Jackes) of Thorneyholme;

Elizabeth Hargreaves, his wife;

John Bulcock, of Moss End, a farm near Newchurch;

Jane Bulcock, his mother;

Alice Gray, of Colne;

Katherine Hewitt, of Colne, nicknamed Mouldheels;

Anne Cronkshaw of Marsden;

Grace Hay of Padiham;

Jennet Preston, of Gisburn in Craven, recently released after a trial at York.

Two women from Burnley were also recorded as being present, but their names were not given, and according to Potts, more were present but had fled in order to avoid justice. Nowell discovered that the meeting had three objectives.

- First, they planned to secure the release of the four women imprisoned at Lancaster Castle by blowing it up and murdering the gaoler. This seems to be an unrealistic objective, and in reality may not have been planned at all.

- Second, they met in order to carry out a ritual that would give a name to Alizon Device's spirit. As she was detained and could not be present, this ritual was not carried out.

- Third, they intended to provide protection to Jennet Preston, the woman identified as a witch by James Device and the JP, Henry Hargreaves. She had been accused by the Lister family and recently released after being on trial at York.

Questionable evidence

Much of the evidence relating to the meeting is suspect, as it came from a young girl, Jennet, and her deceitful brother James. A great deal of the evidence given by James about his own experience as a witch was also suspect. It included a number of clichés, including a brown dog pestering him to give up his soul and a black cat visiting him in his bedroom at midnight. He claimed that he eventually took on a familiar in the shape of a black dog that he called Dandie. He also admitted to murdering two people who mysteriously died within a week of meeting him. There is a strong chance that a meeting of some sort did take place, but it is more likely that it was between neighbours and friends worried that they might be implicated through association with those already arrested.

Jennet and James had both implicated their mother, Elizabeth, who, according to Potts, made a voluntary confession. Her confession included the admission that she was responsible for the murder of John Robinson with the help of her familiar, Ball. Robinson had accused her of having an illegitimate child. She also admitted that she was responsible for the death of Robinson's brother, James, but the reason is not clear.

Despite the large number of people accused as a result of the Malkin Tower confessions, only Alice Nutter, John and Jane Bulcock, Katherine Hewitt and Alice Grey were sent with James and Elizabeth to Lancaster. In total, 11 people were now detained as result of Nowell's investigations.

ACTIVITY
KNOWLEDGE CHECK

The meeting at Malkin Tower

1 How was the meeting at Malkin Tower discovered?

2 Why were the objectives at the supposed meeting unrealistic?

3 What was the impact of James and Jennet Device's confessions?

A Level Exam-Style Question Section B

How far do you agree that Roger Nowell's enthusiasm for investigating witchcraft was the primary cause of the Pendle trials of 1612? (20 marks)

Tip

Think about the wider context, as well as established factors such as the rivalry between the main witchcraft families.

IN WHAT WAYS WERE THE OUTCOMES OF THE TRIAL SIGNIFICANT?

Judges Bromley and Altham

The death of Old Demdike

With the trial set for August, the suspects were held in the dungeon of Lancaster Castle. Old Demdike survived the journey but died shortly afterwards. It is assumed that she died before 19 May, as on this date Old Chattox was examined and there is no mention in the record of her cellmate, Old Demdike, being present. In this examination, Chattox changed her story and laid much more blame on Demdike. She changed the place of her conversion from her home to Malkin Tower, the home of Demdike, and blamed Demdike for her conversion. She also claimed that she had heard Demdike confess to several murders, perhaps in a final attempt to secure her own release or preferential treatment. She was examined by Thomas Covell, a coroner; William Sandes, Mayor of Lancaster; and James Anderton, a JP.

SOURCE 8

A contemporary woodcut illustration of the execution of the Pendle witches at Lancaster Castle. A condemned witch looks on from inside the cell while her associates are hanged.

The judges

The 11 men and women arrested by Roger Nowell were joined by other suspects. A woman from Padiham was detained by Nicolas Bannister, the magistrate who assisted Nowell in his interrogation of the Device family. Another five women and two men came from Samlesbury, and one from St Helens. Very little is known about the Samlesbury witches, as their trials are not recorded in any detail. Potts gives their names as Jennet Bierley, Ellen Bierley, Jane Southworth, John Ramsden, Elizabeth Astley, Isabel Sidegraves and Lawrence Haye.

The practice of judges travelling across the country to hear cases had been established for centuries, and it worked relatively well in order to reduce the bias associated with local magistrates overseeing local cases. Lancaster would have been visited three or four times a year, and on 16 August the judges arrived. They were immediately presented with a list of prisoners awaiting trial and the prisoners were called to the bar one by one.

Sir James Altham (died 1617) was coming to the end of a distinguished legal career. He was from an established gentry family, and his father had been Sheriff of both London and Essex. He was educated at Trinity College, Cambridge, and was called to the bar after entering Gray's Inn. He was elected as MP for Bramber in 1589 and knighted by James I in 1605. He was appointed **Baron of the Exchequer** in 1606. By all accounts, he was well respected and had a reputation as an orthodox Protestant, resulting in him rising quickly in the reign of James I. He probably held similar views on witch-hunting to the king, and may well have carried with him and consulted a copy of *Daemonologie* during the trial.

Sir Edward Bromley (1563–1626) came from a similar background to Altham, also rising to become a Baron of the Exchequer. He came from a Shropshire gentry family, and was educated in the Calvinist tradition. As his father was a high-profile lawyer he was able to receive his legal training without charge and entered the Inner Temple. From 1603 he was given a number of important legal responsibilities and he was returned as MP for Bridgenorth six times between 1586 and 1604, with the final parliament lasting until 1611. King James gave him the role of mediator with the House of Lords over proposals for a union between England and Scotland, demonstrating the trust placed in him by the king.

KEY TERM

Baron of the Exchequer
One of the most senior judges in England. The Barons of the Exchequer presided over the English Exchequer of Pleas.

In 1610, Bromley was made a **Serjeant-at-law** and Baron of the Exchequer. He was knighted in the same year. Both Altham and Bromley worked as assize judges alongside their work in London, and it seems Bromley was hoping to be promoted to a circuit closer to London. There is no doubt that they were both concerned with gaining the king's favour, and positive convictions for witchcraft may have been a way of achieving this.

> **KEY TERM**
>
> Serjeant-at-law
> A senior barrister in the English legal system.

The conduct and outcomes of the trial

The structure of the trial

The main trial at Lancaster (Jennet Preston was tried at York on 27 July and found guilty) was held on 18–19 August. Each suspected witch was asked in turn whether they believed themselves to be guilty. All but one pleaded 'not guilty', and a jury was sworn in. Although on the surface the assize courts seemed relatively fair, the defendants were not allowed to prepare a defence, and it is likely that many did not know the exact charges against them until they were read out in court. Both judges were renowned as rational and wise men, but as was so common in witch trials, they were prepared to accept dubious evidence and confessions that were probably made under torture. Altham had only recently been accused of sending an innocent woman to the gallows for witchcraft at the York assize on the evidence of nine-year-old Jennet Device.

The two judges divided the cases between them, and in the first session, Bromley announced that all JPs involved and all witnesses should be in attendance. Roger Nowell acted as prosecutor.

Old Chattox

With Old Demdike now dead, Old Chattox was clearly the most senior witch on trial. From Potts' account, we know that she spoke plainly and with a measure of truth in court. She was formally charged with the murder, 18 years earlier, of Robert Nutter. Despite Alizon Device claiming that she was responsible for the deaths of her father, John Device, Anne Nutter and Hugh Moore, she was not charged with these murders. She formally pleaded not guilty to the murder of Robert Nutter, and the statement she had given to Roger Nowell was read out, along with Demdike's statement that suggested Chattox and Anne Redferne had been seen with clay images of people they were intending to bewitch.

It is unlikely that any other statements were required, as the confession of a witch was held in high regard as evidence. Despite her last-ditch attempt to divert attention away from her and towards the now deceased Demdike, Chattox knew that she had no hope of being reprieved. She broke down, and acknowledged that the evidence presented was true. In front of the court, she asked for God's forgiveness, and asked for his mercy on her daughter, Anne Redferne. She would not be sentenced immediately, as time was limited and the judge was in a rush to hear from Elizabeth Device.

Elizabeth Device

Old Demdike's daughter, Elizabeth Device, is presented by Potts as an extremely ugly and confrontational woman. In contrast to the meekness of Chattox, she had to be taken from the courtroom kicking and screaming before the trial could begin. She was charged with three murders: that of John and James Barley and Henry Mitton. When the star witness, her daughter Jennet, was brought into court, Elizabeth cursed angrily to her and caused her to cry. It was only when Elizabeth was led away that Jennet was led up to a table to give her evidence so that all the court could see her.

Jennet's evidence was well rehearsed and confident. She said that her mother had been a witch for three or four years, and that she had seen her familiar, Ball, on several occasions. The familiar had even spoken to her at their house. To back this evidence up, part of James Device's testimony was read out, demonstrating that Elizabeth had been instrumental in organising the meeting at Malkin Tower. When Elizabeth was finally allowed back in the court, she denied her previous confession and spoke against her children.

James Device

According to Potts, James Device was showing signs of severe illness or weakness at the trial, and he was unable to speak or stand. This may explain why it was only he and Chattox that were examined for a final time on 19 May, as there was a chance that either or both of them could die before their trial. He had to be held up in court, and was charged with the murders of Anne Towneley and John Duckworth. Anne Towneley's husband was called to give evidence, but unusually Potts omits this from his account of the trial. James had effectively signalled his own execution when he made his detailed confession on 27 April, and when it was read out in court he acknowledged that it was true. To make doubly sure, his sister Jennet was once again called to give evidence, which she did, according to Potts, with great eloquence.

He was also charged with the murders of John Hargreaves and Blaze Hargreaves, crimes which he had never admitted to previously. He pleaded not guilty, but his sister was brought out once again and stated that she was aware that her brother had killed them both. Before each murder, she said, James' familiar, Dandie, had appeared at Malkin Tower as a black dog.

At the end of James' brief trial, Judge Bromley called the jury to consider verdicts on Chattox, Elizabeth Device and James Device. They were quick to find all three guilty.

Anne Redferne

Old Chattox's daughter, Anne Redferne, was tried on the evening of 18 August, for her role in the death of Robert Nutter. Surprisingly, she was found not guilty, and it seems the evidence against her was weak. She was the only one of the original four women detained who did not confess to witchcraft. On the Wednesday, she was presented with a further charge of murdering Robert's father, Christopher Nutter. Exactly the same evidence used against her mother was presented in Anne's trial, including Demdike's account of seeing them with three clay figures. Chattox was brought into the court, where she appeared to make a final effort to save her daughter's life by stating that she made the clay figures, and fell to her knees, begging the court to spare Anne. Unfortunately for Anne, her mother's efforts were to no avail.

Alice Nutter

Alice Nutter is unusual among the accused because she was from a relatively high-status family. Potts explained that although most witches were poor women who desired riches, the Devil could seduce wealthier women with promises of revenge against their enemies. She was charged with the murder of Henry Mitton, together with Old Demdike and Elizabeth Device. The statements of Elizabeth and James Device, as well as the evidence presented by Jennet Device, all agreed that she was at the meeting at Malkin Tower.

Her fate was sealed when Judge Bromley arranged for an identity parade, whereby Jennet Device was expected to pick out witches from a line-up that included other prisoners and women brought in from the street. She identified Alice Nutter and took her by the hand, even identifying where she sat at the sabbat. Alice still refused to confess, perhaps expecting her status and connections to be beneficial in securing a last minute reprieve. She was found guilty, and historians have long struggled to explain why she made it all the way to the gallows without her influential family and associates intervening.

Katherine Hewitt

Katherine Hewitt was accused of being present at the Malkin Tower meeting. She was charged with the murder of a child at Colne. The statement of James Device was again read out, which included a reference to Hewitt and Alice Gray's confession at Malkin Tower to the murder. After Elizabeth Device's statement was read out, an identity parade was again used, according to Potts, although this may be the same one used during Alice Nutter's trial.

The jury were asked to give verdicts on Katherine Hewitt, Anne Redferne and Alice Nutter. All were found guilty.

John and Jane Bulcock

Mother and son, Jane and John Bulcock, were accused of bewitching Jennet Deane, causing her to go mad. Potts makes reference again to the identity parade, and although Jennet Device had been unable to name the Bulcocks previously, she identified both Jane and John in the line-up. Once again, the questionable evidence of James Device was used.

Alizon Device

Next came the trial of the suspect who had begun the entire affair, Alizon Device. Her victim, John Law, was present at the trial and upon seeing him in court, Alizon repeated her original confession, including her initiation into witchcraft and her bewitching of Law. He was asked to give evidence, and presented a similar account of the events of 18 March. Alizon asked for his forgiveness and when asked if she could restore him to health, stated that she was unable to. She also stated that if Old Demdike was still alive she would be able to help him. She was found guilty, along with the Bulcocks.

Margaret Pearson

The witches investigated by Roger Nowell had now been tried, and it was now the turn for Nicholas Bannister to present the case of Margaret Pearson. This was the third time she had been on trial, as she had been previously accused of both murder and witchcraft. On this occasion she was accused of killing a horse belonging to a Mr Dodgson. Old Chattox was brought out as a witness against her, and she stated that she had seen Pearson's familiar in the shape of a cloven-footed man. She recalled Pearson telling her in their shared cell that she had killed the horse by climbing into its stable and sitting on it until it died. She was found guilty and sentenced to four days of public humiliation in the pillory. This lenient sentence reflects the lingering doubts associated with trying a woman who had been through the courts twice before.

The Samlesbury Witches

Potts dedicates 24 pages to a trial completely unconnected to events in Pendle, known as the trial of three of the Samlesbury Witches: Jennet Bierley, Ellen Bierley and Jane Southworth. They had been accused by a 14-year-old girl of practising witchcraft. Judge Bromley had already ordered the release of the other defendants from Samlesbury. The case was thrown out of court because the girl who made the accusations, Grace Sowerbutts, was exposed by Bromley to be unreliable, and apparently under the influence of a Catholic priest.

A final witch called Isobel Roby was brought to trial, although she appears to be an outsider who had no connection with Pendle, and at the end of the proceedings all of those who had been found guilty were brought back into court. The judge informed them that they were to be executed by hanging. Those found not guilty (Elizabeth Astley, John Ramsden, Alice Gray, Lawrence Hay and Isabel Sidegraves) were briefly addressed by the judge. Potts omits their trials from his account, so little is known of their crimes.

ACTIVITY
KNOWLEDGE CHECK

The 1612 trial

1 Why were Altham and Bromley unlikely to give the witches a fair trial?

2 Which evidence presented at the trial seems to be particularly weak?

3 The evidence of James and Jennet Device was used heavily. Explain why the prosecution were so keen to utilise their statements.

The impact of Thomas Potts' account

The production of Potts' account

As Clerk of the Court, Thomas Potts had a unique insight into the trial, and his account is entirely first-hand. The two judges ordered him to write an account of the trials that could be made public, and it was completed on 16 November 1612, just three months after the trials. Judge Bromley checked and corrected the manuscript before it was published in 1613. Both judges seem to have taken a very close interest in the production of the account, and may have even written sections themselves.

Potts' background

Potts was brought up in the home of the man he ultimately dedicated his account to, Thomas Knyvet, who had been credited with apprehending Guy Fawkes in 1605. He did not go to university, thus making a career in law out of reach. He took a number of positions as clerk in various courts, and later in his career he appears to have become a well-regarded civil servant.

The impact of *The Wonderfull Discoverie of Witches*

In the introduction to his work (Source 9), Potts states that the judges placed their respect in him by asking him to publish an account of the trial, and his aim is to hold up the trials as an example to others.

SOURCE

9

Thomas Potts, *The Wonderfull Discoverie of Witches in the Countie of Lancaster* (1613).

It hath pleased them [the judges] out of their respect to mee to impose this worke upon mee, and according to my understanding, I have taken paines to finish, and now confirmed by their judgement to publish the same, for the benefit of my Countrie. That the example of these convicted upon their owne Examinations, Confessions, and Evidence at the Bar, may worke good in others, Rather by with-holding them from, then emboldening them to, the Achieving such desperate actes as these or the like.

From the point of view of its author and editors, the *The Wonderfull Discoverie of Witches* fulfilled two objectives.

- Firstly, it provided an account that justified the trials and could be read as a true version of events that had a scholarly air to it.

- Secondly, it protected the reputations of Potts, Bromley and Altham and could enable them to advance their careers.

In order to achieve these objectives, Potts is selective in the details that he includes in his account. Although it is an important and unique work, Potts presents written witness statements as if they were spoken in court in order to add to the drama of the proceedings. He also edited the speeches of Bromley and Altham in order to improve them, and fails to include any of the build-up to the trials and the legal processes involved in bringing the cases to court. Instead of presenting a word-for-word transcript of the trials, his work is very much an overview of what happened.

ACTIVITY
KNOWLEDGE CHECK

Thomas Potts

Why can Potts' account not be completely trusted?

ACTIVITY
SUMMARY

Explaining the Pendle witch-hunt

1 The Pendle witch trials stand out as particularly widespread in a county where witch-hunts were relatively rare. In order to ascertain why this was the case, complete the following activities.

a) Produce a list of as many accused witches as you can find in the text.

b) For each, record the basic information surrounding their accusation in a table. Include their background, alleged crimes and evidence against them.

c) Do you notice any repetition in the table? Is any of the same evidence being used repeatedly? Are any of the crimes similar? Are the witches from similar backgrounds?

d) What is it about this particular group that made them likely to be embroiled in witchcraft accusations?

e) Finally, do you believe that any of the suspects were genuinely involved in activities that the authorities would deem inappropriate? Explain your answer.

Change (8a, b & c) (II)

Judgements about change

The attitudes in the table below are generalisations for the benefit of the exercise. They may represent a view, but this does not necessarily mean that it was the prevalent view of the time.

Attitude A	Attitude B	Attitude C	Attitude D
At the time of the event	*Halfway between the event and the present*	*The present*	*200 years into the future*
Commentators at the time of the event believed that the great figures that initiated much of what happened were the key drivers. These men of ability and power shaped the history around them. It was their thoughts and deeds that were largely responsible for what happened and how people reacted to it. However, they also believed strongly in supernatural causes.	Historians at this time were beginning to see the history of witch-hunts as being driven by the conditions brought about by changes in the attitudes of the masses. Any important decisions were only taken because the agent who made them believed they were permissible and in line with the feelings of a large body of people.	Historians see the inter-relationship between the great men and the masses and how both interacted with each other to make events happen. It is widely assumed that western democracy, rationalism and science are valid and, in some cases, the inevitable result of historical events.	?

1 Work in small groups. Answer the following question:

Let us assume that 200 years into the future western democracies have collapsed in a series of brutal civil wars. They have been replaced by loose coalitions of tribal groups based on race and led by very powerful warlords. What do you think are the possible attitudes that could be written in the box for attitude D? Write down at least three ideas. Which do you think are the most likely?

2 Think about the causes and outcome of the Pendle witch trials and answer the following questions individually. When you have completed them, compare them with your group.

a) Imagine that you lived at the time of the Pendle witch trials and just after. How would you have answered the following question? 'How significant is the role of Roger Nowell in causing the trials?'

b) Imagine that you lived halfway between 1612 and the present. How would you have answered the previous question?

c) Imagine that you lived now and held attitude C. How would you have answered the previous question?

d) Which of the three answers would be 'correct'?

e) Sometimes the question changes slightly and the answer has to be adapted. If we change the question to: 'In what ways did Roger Nowell contribute to the events of 1612?', which of the answers (a–c) would have to change the least? Explain why this is.

3 Constructed history is a view of the past. It can often reveal things about the time that it was made. Answer the following question:

An academic historian once said that 'the future will change the past'. What do you think he meant by that?

WIDER READING

Goodier, C. *1612: The Lancashire Witch Trial*, Palatine Books (2011). An entertaining and accessible introduction to the trials.

Peel, E. and Southern, P. *The Trials of the Lancashire Witches*, Hendon (1994). Provides a clear narrative account of the investigations and trials.

Poole, R. (ed.) *The Lancashire Witches: Histories and Stories*, Manchester University Press (2002). Includes a number of essays on various aspects of the trials, including the economic, religious and social context and the shaping of Potts' account.

3.5

The Great Witch-Hunt in Bamberg, Germany, 1623–32

KEY QUESTIONS

- What was the significance of the economic, political and religious context of the witch-hunt?
- Why, and with what effect, were specific individuals and groups targeted in the Great Witch-Hunt?
- Why did the witch craze come to an end?

INTRODUCTION

The extent of witch-hunting in the Holy Roman Empire

Over the course of nine years, as many as 900 accused witches were executed in the small state of Bamberg. A variety of people, both low-born and of high social standing, were caught up in the craze, and there were complicated social, economic and religious causes. The craze in Bamberg was part of a wider trend of witch-hunting in Germany in the 16th and 17th centuries.

In the 17th century, Germany was not a unified state. The territory that we would call Germany today was part of the **Holy Roman Empire** (Figure 5.1), a patchwork of political entities of varying size and influence. Geographical and religious boundaries were overlapped, with Catholics living alongside Calvinists and Lutherans. Some towns and cities could enjoy relative freedom if they had the status of an Imperial City, with only the Holy Roman Emperor to report to. Town and village courts were given a remarkable amount of freedom to make their own judgements, with jurors selected from the locality. Cases could be referred to the governor of a particular territory, and sometimes appeals to higher courts were possible, but not always.

Across the German-speaking world, witch-hunts followed different patterns. In some areas, no witches were executed at all. In others, a handful of witches would be executed each decade, but in some regions, mass witch-hunts took place with hundreds, and in some cases thousands, losing their lives.

The religious context

As well as complex geographical boundaries, religious passion made the situation even more dangerous. As the Protestant faith gradually gained support in the early 16th century, German towns became divided. After the Catholic Emperor Charles V gained victory over a Protestant confederacy in 1548, a new principle was established: that the religion of a ruler should be the religion of a region. There then developed a complicated arrangement whereby a town with a Protestant majority could be ruled by a minority Catholic clique, and vice versa. Catholics, Calvinists and Lutherans lived side-by-side, and although they could live harmoniously together, the balance could be easily upset.

1609 – Frederick Förner becomes Vicar General of Bamberg

1617 – Ferdinand II becomes king of Bohemia

1623 – John George II Fuchs von Dornheim becomes Prince-Bishop of Bamberg

1605	1610	1615	1620

1616–19 – First wave of witch-hunting under Johann Gottfried von Aschhausen

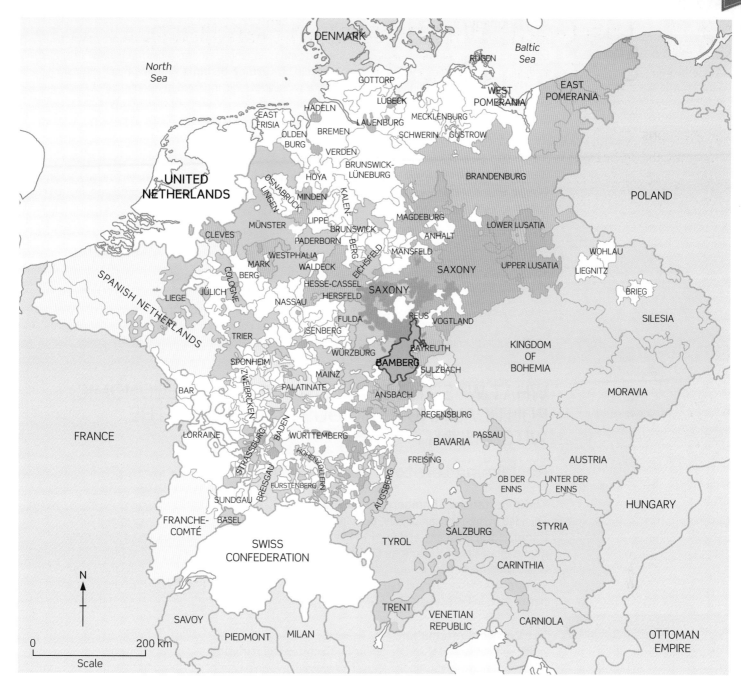

Figure 5.1 The location of Bamberg within the Holy Roman Empire, 1618.

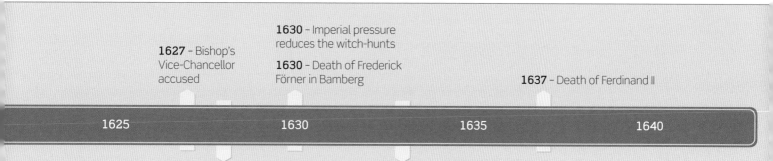

1627 – Bishop's Vice-Chancellor accused

1630 – Imperial pressure reduces the witch-hunts

1630 – Death of Frederick Förner in Bamberg

1637 – Death of Ferdinand II

1628 – Mayor of Bamberg accused and tortured

1633 – John George II Fuchs von Dornheim dies

1625   1630   1635   1640

Why Germany?

As we have seen, Germany was not the only region in Europe to experience widespread witch-hunts, but the hunts here were often brutal and with many more victims. Historians have struggled to explain this: in Germany, Catholic regions ruled by **prince-bishops** were the most extensive witch-hunters, but in Catholic Spain, where the Inquisition was involved in hunting witches, relatively small numbers were executed. Anti-Catholic Scotland suffered a number of high-profile witch-hunts and Lutheran Sweden experienced a witch-hunt in 1675 that resulted in 71 people being executed in a single day. It seems, therefore, that Catholics were no more inclined to horrific witch-hunts than Protestants.

Across Europe, the image of the witch was very similar. To most Europeans, a witch was a poor old woman who cavorted with the Devil and caused harm. In Germany, a number of factors led to more panics spreading and becoming widespread.

- The fact that political and judicial authority was fragmented meant that panics could easily take hold.

- The context of the Reformation and Counter-Reformation is important because it led to Germans fearing the Devil's work all around them.

- Germany also had a limited legal framework to use against witches. A law code created under Charles V in 1532 known as The Carolina specified that justice should remain a local matter. Although it contained little to guide witch-hunters, they cited it regularly in order to justify their work.

WHAT WAS THE SIGNIFICANCE OF THE ECONOMIC, POLITICAL AND RELIGIOUS CONTEXT OF THE WITCH-HUNT?

Reclaiming territory for the Catholic Church

The importance of Bamberg

Founded in the 11th century, the principality of Bamberg was created to aid the spread of Christianity in Germany, and from 1242 its bishops became prince-bishops, and it became an important centre of the Roman Catholic Church. A confused picture emerged in prince-bishoprics, as a bishop might have complete judicial control over one geographical area, but lack the power to set up courts in others. The extensive lands ruled by the Catholic prince-bishops saw most witch persecution in Germany in the 17th century.

The Counter-Reformation

In the second half of the 16th century, a **Counter-Reformation** began, which gained territory and followers back for the Catholic faith. This was led by zealous prince-bishops from across the Holy Roman Empire and gained momentum through the influence of the recently established **Jesuit** order. Jesuit churches were founded in cities like Munich, and the message from the clergy was fiercely anti-Protestant. In return, Protestants believed that Catholics were in league with the Devil and that the pope was the Antichrist.

Catholic emperors were keen to promote the Jesuit cause, and they were settled across modern Germany and in Vienna, Graz, Innsbruck and Linz in Austria. Traditional forms of Catholic devotion were encouraged, and new shrines dedicated to saints were established. The Catholic faith became an essential component of the prince-bishopric, and the elites who governed these states supported the **Habsburgs** and enabled them to cement their overall control.

Bamberg and the Counter-Reformation

In the parish church of St Michael in the small town of Zeil (which was within the bishopric of Bamberg) an important ceiling painting can be found. It shows the Catholic Church victorious over the Protestant heretics. Mary holds high a chalice while Protestant clergy in black robes crouch with snakes in their mouths. In purgatory, women are seen chained as they languish as witches. The connection between Protestantism and witchcraft is clear for all to see.

The Counter-Reformation did suffer resistance. In the small Lutheran commune of Marktzeuln, which was officially controlled by the bishop of Bamberg, the parishioners of the local Protestant church refused to renounce their faith, despite enormous pressure to do so. When the Catholic authorities attempted to place new ministers in office, they were faced with threats and weapons and chased out of the area. When Johann Gottfried von Aschhausen was appointed prince-bishop of Bamberg in 1609, he prioritised the conversion of his Protestant parishes to Catholicism. A number of methods were employed that caused further resentment between followers of the two denominations.

- Fines were imposed on parishes that insisted on remaining Protestant.

- Supplies of wood to Protestant parishes were restricted.

- Catholic troops were quartered in Protestant villages.

- Dissidents (those who actively opposed official policy) were sent into exile.

- On a number of occasions, Lutherans were rounded up and arrested.

As well as these persecutions, Protestants could also face imprisonment in Bamberg tower, in a room twelve feet wide and infested with vermin. Despite this, Protestant communities in Bamberg remained stubborn and in 1619, some parishioners in Marktzeuln were still refusing to convert to Catholicism.

Johann Gottfried von Aschhausen and the first witch trials

Von Aschhausen invited the Jesuits to settle in Bamberg, and founded Catholic schools. He also sent unco-operative priests to their own prison, known as the 'Priests' Vaults'. Although his persecution of Protestants and, as a result, suspected witches, was not as widespread as that of his successor, John George II Fuchs von Dornheim, he had around 300 suspected witches executed. Even before von Aschhausen took office, anti-Protestant witch trials had taken place. His predecessor, Neytard von Thungen, initiated the first persecutions in 1595 (see Figure 5.2). Margarethe Pemmerin was charged with witchcraft in this year, and she admitted worshipping the Devil for a period of ten years. She was sentenced to being burned at the stake, but in a last-minute change of heart Bishop Neytard allowed her to be executed by the sword, a punishment viewed as less brutal.

In 1610, von Aschhausen issued a new ordinance concerning witchcraft. In it, he ordered an investigation, whereby any person found practising magic would be severely punished. It is no coincidence that this ordinance coincided with Protestant rebellions in nearby Bohemia. He also stated that contrary to the laws of the Catholic Church and the Empire, sorcerers and fortune tellers were at work in Bamberg.

Despite the ordinance, the bishop's visitation report of 1611 stated that blasphemous practices were still being carried out in Bamberg, including fortune-telling and spell casting. Pre-Christian activities were reported at an old pagan shrine. In the same regions where evidence of occult practices were found, Protestant preachers were being harboured, thus enhancing the connection between Protestantism and witchcraft in the eyes of the Catholic authorities. When one woman, Lena Pantzerin, was accused in 1612, no one seemed to know how to examine a witch, so an outsider named Trill was called in. As with so many other witch-hunts across Europe, the accusation against Pantzerin led to many more being accused and ultimately executed. The years 1616–19 saw an intensity of witch-hunting not seen before in Bamberg, although trials were brought to an end in 1619 by a group of moderates on the local council. They claimed that with war breaking out in neighbouring Bohemia, the authorities could not afford the luxury of chasing phantoms. With the election of George II Fuchs von Dornheim as prince-bishop in 1623, any opposition to witch-hunting was effectively removed and the hunts were able to begin again.

Year	Number of trials
1595	2
1598	2
1601	1
1604	1
1612	4
1613	10
1616	15
1617	107
1618	30
1619	20
1620	1
1621	1
1622	2
1623	1
1625	12
1626	65
1627	133
1628	121
1629	192
1630	63

Figure 5.2 Number of witch trials in Bamberg, by year. From J.R. Palframan, 'Frost Witches: The Spark of the Bamberg Witch Craze' in *Oglethorpe Journal of Undergraduate Research (OJUR)* (2013).

ACTIVITY
KNOWLEDGE CHECK

The Counter-Reformation in Bamberg

1 Why do you think the Counter-Reformation led to the number of witch-hunts in Germany increasing?

2 Why was Bamberg a likely place for large-scale witch-hunting to take place?

The impact of the Thirty Years' War on Bamberg

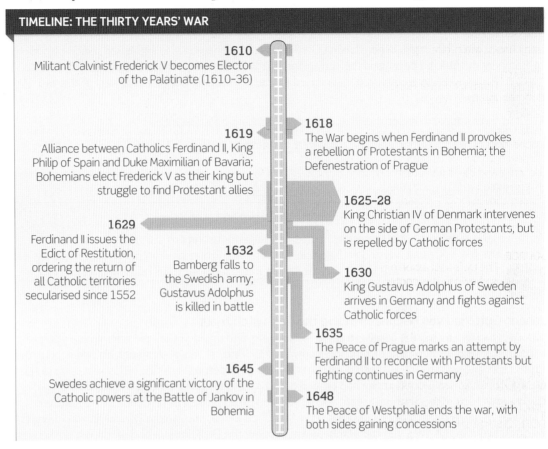

TIMELINE: THE THIRTY YEARS' WAR

1610
Militant Calvinist Frederick V becomes Elector of the Palatinate (1610–36)

1618
The War begins when Ferdinand II provokes a rebellion of Protestants in Bohemia; the Defenestration of Prague

1619
Alliance between Catholics Ferdinand II, King Philip of Spain and Duke Maximilian of Bavaria; Bohemians elect Frederick V as their king but struggle to find Protestant allies

1625–28
King Christian IV of Denmark intervenes on the side of German Protestants, but is repelled by Catholic forces

1629
Ferdinand II issues the Edict of Restitution, ordering the return of all Catholic territories secularised since 1552

1632
Bamberg falls to the Swedish army; Gustavus Adolphus is killed in battle

1630
King Gustavus Adolphus of Sweden arrives in Germany and fights against Catholic forces

1635
The Peace of Prague marks an attempt by Ferdinand II to reconcile with Protestants but fighting continues in Germany

1645
Swedes achieve a significant victory of the Catholic powers at the Battle of Jankov in Bohemia

1648
The Peace of Westphalia ends the war, with both sides gaining concessions

The origins of the Thirty Years' War

Witch-hunting developed to become extensive across Germany during the Thirty Years' War (1618–48), and Bamberg was affected significantly by the conflict. The origins of the war lay in both the religious divisions found in Northern Europe and the ambitions of the Habsburg monarchy.

The role of Holy Roman Emperor was still a powerful one, but by the 17th century the office was declining in authority. The Habsburg Emperors were historically concerned with enhancing their territory, usually through marriage. This would often cause resentment, as was the case in both Moravia and Bohemia, where Protestants became bitter as a result of Counter-Reformation policies. In Prague, defenestration (the act of throwing someone out of a window) was carried out on representatives of the emperor. The Protestants of Bohemia then raised armies in support of Frederick V, Elector Palatine, the son-in-law of James VI and I of Scotland and England.

EXTEND YOUR KNOWLEDGE

The Defenestration of Prague

A major catalyst for conflict in the Holy Roman Empire came in May 1618 when four Catholic representatives of the Holy Roman Emperor arrived in Prague to meet with the recently dissolved assembly of the Bohemian Protestant estates.

Bohemia, a neighbouring state of Bamberg, had been under the control of the Habsburgs since 1526, although they did not generally act to force their Protestant subjects to convert to Catholicism. Under Rudolf III (Emperor and King of Bohemia 1576-1612), Protestants enjoyed increased rights and more autonomy over religious matters.

Rudolf was succeeded by his younger brother, Matthias, in 1612. Under pressure over his lack of

enthusiasm for the Counter-Reformation, Matthias gave way to his cousin, Ferdinand, who became King of Bohemia in 1617 and Holy Roman Emperor in 1619. As a staunch proponent of the Counter-Reformation, conflict between Ferdinand and the Protestant authorities in Bohemia was inevitable.

Ferdinand sent four noble representatives to Prague to meet with the Protestant authorities. Angered that the four nobles may have been responsible for an order to halt the construction of Protestant churches, Count Thurn, the leader of the Protestants, did not allow the two most hard-line nobles, along with their secretary, to leave the meeting. All three were thrown out of a window, and survived the 70-foot fall.

Many of the German states ultimately became embroiled in the war, and a number of historians have argued that this led to an increase in witch-hunting across the Empire (Extract 1). This view has been criticised (Extract 2) by some historians who point to the fact that in many areas, witch-hunting ceased with the arrival of war.

EXTRACT

1 From H.R. Trevor-Roper, *The Crisis of the Seventeenth Century: Religion, the Reformation and Social Change* (1967).

When religious war returned to Europe the witches were suddenly found, once again, to have increased alarmingly during the years of peace. In the 1620s, with the destruction of Protestantism in Bohemia and the Palatinate, the Catholic reconquest of Germany was resumed. In 1629, with the Edict of Restitution [which authorised forced conversion of Protestants], its basis seemed complete. Those same years saw, in central Europe at least, the worst of all witch-persecutions, the climax of the European craze.

EXTRACT

2 From Bengt Ankerloo, William Monter and Stuart Clark, *Witchcraft and Magic in Europe, Volume 4: The Period of the Witch Trials* (2002).

The majority of Europe's witch trials and executions took place in the century after 1560, coinciding with Europe's wars of religion in France and the Low Countries, and frequently rose to a crescendo during the Thirty Years' War. It has therefore been tempting to conclude that Europe's great witch-hunt was simply one tragic social consequence of its religious conflicts. However, any correlation between these two phenomena is far from direct. In the first place, the outbreak of warfare, whether or not religiously motivated, temporarily ended witch trials whenever and wherever it occurred. War disrupted all normal government activity. In the Saarland, for example, witch-hunting ended abruptly in the mid-1630s and did not resume for 30 years, because the region was so badly devastated that it lost up to four-fifths of its population. Subtler connection must be found.

SOURCE

1 The Defenestration of Prague, which acted as a catalyst for the Thirty Years' War, is shown in this contemporary news sheet (1618).

Impact on Bamberg

Foreign armies became involved in the war, with nearly 150,000 Swedes and 100,000 Danes fighting for the Protestant cause, as well as Dutch, Scottish and English involvement. From 1635, France joined the anti-Habsburg alliance and the war became less a war of religion and more a continuation of the existing rivalry between the French and the Habsburgs in Spain and Germany.

The presence of large armies had a devastating impact on Bamberg and the wider Empire. Famine was caused as a result of soldiers requisitioning food, villages and towns were plundered for supplies, and young men and boys were forcibly conscripted by both sides. This, combined with crop failures and inflation (discussed below and on page 115) led to an increased fear of witches as misfortune was seen to be present everywhere.

In this context, those Catholics in Bamberg who had fought for the Counter-Reformation became more fanatical than ever. People who deviated from orthodox Catholic practices were labelled as heretics, and inevitably suspicion was laid upon the Devil. Those who were targeted in the context of war usually fell into one of the following categories:

- women whose sexual behaviour deviated from that expected from the Catholic Church. This fear originated from the Protestant belief that priests should not necessarily live lives of celibacy

- people (both women and men) whose political views or attitude to the war deviated from those of the Catholic authorities

- people who had an existing reputation for healing, fortune-telling or sorcery, who became easy scapegoats for the destruction that was taking place everywhere

- members of the upper class. Under Prince-Bishop von Dornheim (1623–32) a law that allowed for the confiscation of witches' property was exploited, resulting in the upper classes being disproportionately targeted.

ACTIVITY
KNOWLEDGE CHECK

The Thirty Years' War

1 Why have some historians argued that the Thirty Years' War increased witch trials in Germany?

2 Why have other historians argued that this was not the main reason for an increase in witch trials?

3 What impact did the war have on Bamberg specifically?

Economic crises

The impact of weather and crop failures

A number of witch trials between 1623 and 1632 made reference to weather and poor harvests.

- In the trial of Lorentz Kempffen Seebauer's wife in 1629, she was accused of suggesting that a frost should ruin the fruit harvest, and recent freezing conditions were mentioned throughout the trial.

- The confession of Katharina Merckhlerin, made in November 1626, contained the admission that she had been part of a plot to freeze and destroy all of Bamberg's crops.

Witch trials peaked in Bamberg in 1629, and it was also the year that frost destroyed the wine crop. The 1620s were generally cold and wet, and in trial records 1628 is remembered as a year without a summer. The early 17th century coincided with the so-called 'Little Ice Age', which was a period of significantly colder and unsettled weather in Europe, peaking between 1560 and 1660. Combined with debt from the Thirty Years' War, crop failure amounted to a crisis for the state. Debts from war increased to 800,000 florins by its end, and during the war the authorities had little choice but to levy high taxes. It was in the interest of the prince-bishop to carry out witch-hunts in order to ensure that the frost did not return.

Although the vast majority of suspects in Bamberg were arrested after they were named by others under torture as accomplices, petitions from subjects to their overlords were also a regular feature of witch trials. These petitions demanded the eradication of witches in a particular village, parish or town, and evidence from a contemporary, Hans Langhans, who was mayor of the town of Zeil and was himself executed for sorcery in 1628, indicates that a petition produced after the frost of May 1626 triggered some of the trials.

SOURCE

From the diary of Hans Langhans, Mayor of Zeil (1626).

Then there was much supplication and petition among the common rabble, why should they simply stand by while the sorcerers and witches destroy even the crops.

Inflation and economic crisis

As well as crop failures, the supply of money in general was an issue. Silver from America had been relatively well supplied until around 1610, when imports started to decline. Across the Empire, non-silver (especially copper) currency was utilised. The gold florin, which was used across Europe as a **reserve currency**, had reduced in gold content from 79 percent in the early 15th century to 77 percent in 1626. As money lost its real value and poor weather resulted in crop failures, the price of goods increased (known as inflation). The people of Bamberg had little understanding of economics, and if they did they lacked the data with which to make an informed interpretation. The only possible explanation for many was to place the crisis within a framework that they understood to be rational: that of magic and witchcraft. It is no coincidence that those accused of witchcraft in Bamberg and beyond were more likely to live along trade routes. This meant they were more likely to engage in financial conflict with their neighbours and others.

Maria Anna Junius, nun and daughter of the Mayor of Bamberg, John Junius (who was accused of witchcraft himself), attempted to explain the causes of the witch-hunt in her memoirs. The primary reason she puts forward is inflation, and the reduction in the value of currency. In confessions, economic causes are also mentioned.

- Margaretha Eissmennin admitted that after extensive **coin clipping**, money had lost its value, and she was forced to turn to the Devil. The familiar tale told in witch trials across Europe – that of the poverty-stricken turning to the Devil – became more and more common in Bamberg.

- Kunigudta Rindterin confessed that she entered into a relationship with a rich man in order to avoid poverty. This was interpreted by her accusers as a pact with the Devil.

- Margaretha Gussbacherin prostituted herself to a man in a black feather hat to free herself of poverty and suffering. This was again interpreted as a diabolical pact.

ACTIVITY
KNOWLEDGE CHECK

Economic crises

1 Why were witches blamed for crop failures?

2 How was inflation caused? What were the consequences of this?

A Level Exam-Style Question Section B

How accurate is it to say that it was the impact of the Thirty Years' War that accounts for the extent of witch-hunting in Bamberg in the years 1623–32? (20 marks)

Tip
This is a question on causation, which should account for other factors such as economic crisis and the impact of the Counter-Reformation.

WHY, AND WITH WHAT EFFECT, WERE SPECIFIC INDIVIDUALS AND GROUPS TARGETED IN THE GREAT WITCH-HUNT?

Numbers and social groups affected by the witch-hunts

Numbers and gender affected by the witch-hunt

Estimates of the number of people implicated and executed in Bamberg between 1623 and 1632 vary from 600 to 900. As with all major witch-hunts, women were significantly more likely to be accused. Women made up 72.7 percent of those brought to trial from 1623 to 1631, which is slightly lower than the 81.1 percent of those brought to trial in the major wave of 1616 to 1622.

The election of John George II Fuchs von Dornheim – who was a keen supporter of witch trials – as prince-bishop in 1623 allowed for the craze to become widespread. After a few isolated trials in the years 1623–25, mass trials took place from 1626. The initial epicentre of the hunt was in Zeil, a town under the authority of Bamberg, where 59 people were charged in 1626. At least 30 of these were executed or died in custody. In 1627, 130 suspects from Zeil were called before the court in Bamberg, and in 1628 the trials spread to Bamberg itself. According to contemporary records, at least 642 individuals were brought to trial between 1623 and 1631. Of these 45 were released or escaped, with the remainder being executed.

Social groups

Closer examination of the evidence shows that few victims meet the usual criteria for those accused of witchcraft. The stereotype of the witch as old and poor is rarely found in Bamberg. In Zeil, the small town that produced many of the victims for trials held in Bamberg itself, only seven older women were sent for execution, and just two of these were identified in trial records as 'wisewomen'. The majority of women across the region of Bamberg who were brought to trial were of marriageable age, and the number of widows was small. The average age of the 300 women for whom this can be determined is 33½.

Most of the men accused were middle-aged, although a case is recorded of a nine-year-old boy tried for witchcraft. His name is not recorded, although he was interrogated for a number of weeks. Unusually, he confessed without being tortured to a wildly exaggerated story about an encounter he had with a demon he named as George. He claimed that the demon appeared to him with horns and goat feet, and after initially threatening the boy, encouraged him to learn witchcraft. His story related to various acts of *maleficium*, including destroying crops, stealing wine and causing livestock to be killed by freezing conditions. He also stated that his demon was able to visit him while he was in prison, and that it even assisted him in escaping for a short time through a gap in the wall. There is no record of his execution, but his crimes are comparable with those of other suspects who were burned in Bamberg.

High-status individuals

Those from higher social groups were extensively targeted, with the most notable individual being John Junius, Mayor of Bamberg, who is discussed at length below. Other high-status individuals included the following.

- Hans Langhans, the mayor of Zeil, kept an accurate diary of the witches and sorcerers put on trial. He confessed after torture in 1628 that he had been baptised by the Devil in 1611. He also admitted to being responsible for the frost that destroyed the wine crop in 1615–16.

- Along the Lange Gasse, the main street through the centre of Bamberg, 17 different households became victims, all of them from well-respected backgrounds.

- The leading citizens of both Bamberg and Zeil suffered. As well as Langhans, 10 other members of the town council or mayor's office were executed. At least 20 relatives of town councillors were also found guilty. In total, around half of those accused in Zeil were either local officials or their relatives.

The reason so many high-status individuals were accused – as well as the obvious financial advantages for the prince-bishop from property confiscations – lies in their opposition to the trials. Even Georg Eder, the son of a well-known Catholic reformer at the imperial court, was executed. As a passionate supporter of the Counter-Reformation, Eder could not comprehend why he was accused of witchcraft and used this fact as part of his defence. For the Catholic authorities in Bamberg, however, this was no surprise, because in opposing the trials, Eder and the other officials were aiding the Devil, and there was a widespread belief that public officials who failed to persecute witches effectively were themselves witches. This belief is echoed in an anonymous pamphlet that was found under the door of an official in Bamberg in September 1629. The pamphlet is written as a dialogue between two labourers, who are concerned at the number of witches in the town of Forchheim (Source 3).

SOURCE 3

From an anonymous pamphlet written in Bamberg and intended for distribution in the Catholic prince-bishoprics, September 1629.

> Many folk say that the bishop just doesn't have the heart to fight with the councillors... In all of Forchheim there are only two honourable officials, the rest are all witches... [the council is filled with] witches, thieves and scoundrels.

Interestingly, Forchheim was almost untouched by the witch trials, despite being under the jurisdiction of the prince-bishop.

As we have seen, there was a clear anti-Protestant theme that ran through the craze at Bamberg, and from 1628 officials began examining parish records for individuals who failed to receive Catholic communion. They were then reported to the official commission on witchcraft. Many of these individuals had either refused to convert to Catholicism or had only reluctantly converted, and a number of them fled Bamberg.

- Albert Pfersmann, whose wife, mother-in-law and sister-in-law had all been executed, sought protection in Hungary.

- Two brothers, Johann and Georg Kauwer, fled to Rome where they presented the Vatican with a complaint against the prince-bishop. Both of their parents had been executed.

- Margarethe Weltzin, whose friends and relatives had been burned, escaped to Vienna where she petitioned the imperial court.

Hereditary guilt

Although women still outnumbered men, they were often not the focus of trials. In a number of cases, a pattern emerges whereby a father was initially accused and was executed along with his wife or daughter. Sometimes the opposite pattern can be seen: the cathedral chancellor, Georg Hann, who had made the mistake of questioning the trials, was arrested following the execution of his wife and daughter in 1628. Hann came under suspicion after he petitioned the imperial high court to intervene in the cases of accused women in Bamberg. The execution of his wife and daughter was beneficial to the authorities because it helped to convince others of his guilt. His son and daughter-in-law were then condemned after they in turn protested at the treatment of Hann and his wife.

Hereditary guilt can also be seen in the cases of Conrad Merklein and Conrad Orter, who both held senior positions on the town council in Zeil. They were both executed on 10 November 1626, and two months later Orter's wife and daughter were arrested. In April 1627 Merklein's daughter Christina was arrested and four days later Orter's son-in-law was detained. Christina was executed, and both of her sons, together with two servant girls from her house in Bamberg, were arrested. The eldest of her sons, Hans, was 14 years old, and claimed that he had been persuaded into witchcraft by one of the servant girls, who was in fact the Devil in disguise. He was burned shortly after his fifteenth birthday. By 1629 the Merklein and Orter families had been virtually wiped out.

ACTIVITY
KNOWLEDGE CHECK

Groups affected by the witch-hunt

1 Why was the proportion of women involved in the trials lower than in many other European witch-hunts?

2 Why were so many high-status individuals accused in the witch-hunt?

3 What evidence can you use to identify anti-Protestant feeling during the trials?

4 Why was George Hann accused of witchcraft?

The use of torture and property confiscations

The use of torture

As with many German witch-hunts, torture was used extensively. The Carolina Law Code of 1532 allowed for an extensive range of torture devices to be used on suspects (see Source 4), and with the judicial freedom that the prince-bishop enjoyed, numerous confessions were extracted in this way.

A network of informers was created and a witch-prison was built in order to carry out torture. Confessions obtained under torture were permissible in court and defendants were denied many basic legal rights. A number of torture methods were utilised.

- A common device used at Bamberg was the thumbscrews. The thumbs of the accused were placed in a vice-like contraption, which would be gradually tightened if the suspect refused to confess. Toes were also crushed in a similar manner.

SOURCE
4

Some of the torture devices used in Bamberg, including the thumbscrews (lower middle) and strappado (lower right), that would be used to suspend a victim in the air by their wrists. From the *Constitutio Criminalis Carolina*, or Carolina Law Code (1532).

- The strappado, a device that was used to suspend a victim in the air by their wrists, was used extensively. Victims at Bamberg were left elevated for several hours at a time. This would often result in the dislocation of the wrists. Heavy weights could be attached to the bodies of victims in order to cause further pain.

- Recorded examples from Bamberg also include the burning of a woman's hair.

- Whipping was also common, but it is usually recorded only in conjunction with the other methods of torture.

- Some prisoners were forced to kneel on a piece of wood covered with metal spikes for several hours.

- Food containing excessive salt and pepper was given to some victims, who were then deprived of water.

- A small room with spikes on the floor was used in order to prevent the suspects from sleeping.

The case of John Junius

One of the most high-profile, and best recorded cases from Bamberg is that of John Junius, who experienced some of the most brutal torture documented. By the time of his arrest in June 1628 Junius had served as mayor for 20 years, and shortly before his arrest his wife had been executed as a witch, thus implicating him by association. He was also implicated by Georg Hann and his family, who named Junius and many others, including priests and councillors, before they were executed. Hann swore on his life that he witnessed Junius a year and a half earlier at a witch-gathering in the electoral council room.

The court records contain a detailed account of his interrogation (Source 5).

SOURCE 5

The official court account of John Junius' interrogation at Bamberg, June 1628.

On Wednesday, June 28, 1628, was examined without torture Johannes Junius, Burgomaster at Bamberg.

Says he is wholly innocent... has never in his life renounced God; says that he is wronged before God and the world, would like to hear a single human being who has seen him at such gatherings.

Hereupon he was told that his accomplices had confessed against him and was given time for thought...

Thumb-screws were applied. Says he has never denied God his saviour nor suffered himself to be otherwise baptized [initiated by the Devil]; will again stake his life on it; feels no pain in the thumb-screws.

Leg-screws. Will confess absolutely nothing; knows nothing about it... feels likewise no pain.

Is stripped and examined; on his right side is found a bluish mark, like a clover leaf, is thrice pricked therein, but feels no pain and no blood flows out.

Strappado. He has never renounced God; God will not forsake him... He knows nothing about witchcraft.

On July 5, the above named Junius is without torture, but with urgent persuasions, exhorted to confess, and at last begins and confesses.

When in the year 1624 his law-suit at Rothweil cost him some six hundred florins, he had gone out... into his orchard... there had come to him a woman like a grass-maid, who had asked him why he sat there so sorrowful... she had led him by seductive speeches to yield him to her will... and thereafter the wench had changed into the form of a goat... the transformed spirit had seized him by the throat and demanded that he should renounce God Almighty.

He was then named Krix. His paramour he had to call Vixen... At this time his paramour had promised to provide him with money, and from time to time to take him to other witch-gatherings...

Of crimes. His paramour had immediately after his seduction demanded that he should make away with his young son Hans Georg, and had given him for this purpose a gray powder; this, however, being too hard for him, he had made away with his horse instead.

His paramour had also often spurred him on to kill his daughter,... because he would not do this he had been maltreated with blows by the evil spirit.

Once at the suggestion of his paramour he had taken the holy wafer out of his mouth and given it to her...

Read Source 5 before you answer the question.

Assess the value of the source for revealing the role of torture and contemporary beliefs in witchcraft in the 17th century.

Explain your answer, using the source, the information given about its origin and your own knowledge about the historical context. (20 marks)

Tip
It should be noted that this source is from the official account of the interrogation and trial, and although it does not have a named author, there are valuable implications in understanding the provenance of the work.

Junius was able to smuggle a letter out of prison to his daughter, which serves as one of the most powerful accounts of torture and persecution from the period (Source 6). In the letter, he explains that he was entirely innocent, and that it was only torture that compelled him to confess.

SOURCE
6   From a letter sent by John Junius to his daughter from prison, 24 July 1628.

Many hundred thousand good-nights, dearly beloved daughter Veronica. Innocent have I come into prison, innocent have I been tortured, innocent must I die. For whoever comes into the witch prison must become a witch or be tortured until he invents something out of his head and – God pity him – bethinks him of something. I will tell you how it has gone with me. When I was the first time put to the torture, Dr Braun, Dr Kotzendorffer, and two strange doctors were there. Then Dr Braun asks me, 'Kinsman, how come you here?' I answer, 'Through falsehood, through misfortune.' 'Hear, you,' he says, 'you are a witch; will you confess it voluntarily? If not, we'll bring in witnesses and the executioner for you.' I said 'I am no witch, I have a pure conscience in the matter; if there are a thousand witnesses, I am not anxious, but I'll gladly hear the witnesses.'... And then came also... the executioner, and put the thumb-screws on me, both hands bound together, so that the blood ran out at the nails and everywhere, so that for four weeks I could not use my hands, as you can see from the writing... Thereafter they first stripped me, bound my hands behind me, and drew me up in the torture. Then I thought heaven and earth were at an end; eight times did they draw me up and let me fall again, so that I suffered terrible agony.

When at last the executioner led me back into the prison, he said to me: 'Sir, I beg you, for God's sake confess something, whether it be true or not. Invent something, for you cannot endure the torture which you will be put to; and, even if you bear it all, yet you will not escape, not even if you were an earl, but one torture will follow after another until you say you are a witch.'

In his letter, Junius goes on to explain that he begged for an extra day to consider his situation and speak with a priest. The chance to consult a priest was denied, but he was allowed a day of reflection, after which he decided to confess to being a witch, and he was pressed for the names of his accomplices (Source 7).

SOURCE
7   From a letter sent by John Junius to his daughter from prison, 24 July 1628.

Then I had to tell what people I had seen [at the witch-sabbat]. I said that I had not recognised them. 'You old rascal, I must set the executioner at you. Say – was the Chancellor [Georg Hann] there?' So I said yes. 'Who besides?' I had not recognised anybody. So he said: 'Take one street after another; begin at the market, go out on one street and back on the next.' I had to name several persons there. Then came the long street. I knew nobody. Had to name eight persons there.

Then I had to tell what crimes I had committed. I said nothing... 'Draw the rascal up!' So I said that I was to kill my children, but I had killed a horse instead. It did not help. I had also taken a sacred wafer, and had desecrated it. When I had said this, they left me in peace.

Now, dear child, here you have all my confession, for which I must die. And they are sheer lies and made-up things, so help me God. For all this I was forced to say through fear of the torture which was threatened beyond what I had already endured. For they never leave off with the torture till one confesses something; be he never so good, he must be a witch. Nobody escapes, though he were an earl.

ACTIVITY
KNOWLEDGE CHECK

John Junius

Why did Junius ultimately confess? What role did torture play in his confession?

The content of confessions

The authorities in Bamberg established a schedule of 101 questions to be asked during interrogation, some of which are listed in Source 8.

SOURCE 8

Some of the questions used by the Bamberg torturers during interrogation.

What did the Devil promise her (the witch) in return for her soul, and did he keep his promise?

Where was it that she first pledged herself to the Devil, with which words did they address each other?

What was the intention of her words, did she not think that it was against God and Morality to submit to the Devil and denounce God and all his saints?

In which locality was the devil's pact concluded and who attended the ceremony?

What evil deeds did they commit after the devil's baptism, and which ones after the second and third?

Who were the accomplices of the black art, what did they do, and where did they commit their crimes?

The historian Hans Sebald (1990) has identified a number of typical elements that can be found in the records of Bamberg confessions.

- The first part of a confession usually involved recounting how the accused became involved with the Devil.

- In the second part of the confession the accused usually described a death threat given to them by their demon or familiar in order to force co-operation.

- An oath of loyalty or mock baptism in the presence of demons or other initiates normally followed next. The initiate would be given a new name by the Devil.

- All confessions describing a baptism with the Devil reported the receipt of a gift. A common example was a piece of gold that turned into a slice of turnip or a worthless piece of pottery.

- Additional demons or conspirators were an important part of confessions, and naturally names of fellow witches were sought by torturers.

- Confessions of night-flight were common, whereby the witch would travel through the sky to a sabbat with others.

- In order for the confession to be acceptable, the accused was asked to provide a list of evil deeds committed, such as damage to crops, harming people or harming animals.

- Sacrilege and blasphemy were the most abhorrent of witches' deeds, and accounts of witches stealing the wafer (representing the body of Christ) from communion and desecrating it occur on more than one occasion.

Property confiscations

The law in Bamberg allowed for the confiscation of witches' property, which encouraged the persecution of the upper classes. The victims were also responsible for all of their court costs, thus reducing any financial liability that the state had.

- They were responsible for the travel expenses of interrogators and torturers.

- They were also responsible for paying any extra staff or horses required by the authorities.

- At the execution itself, the families of the victims were charged for every element of the process, from the raw materials such as wood, rope and nails to a fee for the executioner and removal of the body.

As the witch-hunt paid for itself, there developed a witch-hunting industry in Bamberg. The local economy benefited, and the profits of lawyers, coachmen, rope-makers, blacksmiths and tavern owners among others all increased as their services were required to support the process.

Towards the end of the persecution, in April 1631, 22 inmates were still being held on charges of witchcraft, including the prince-bishop's treasurer. Their property was confiscated when they were first admitted to prison, and this totalled 220,000 florins. Around 500,000 florins was confiscated in total, with 100,000 coming from Georg Neudecker, who had been Mayor of Bamberg and was one of its richest citizens. He was kept imprisoned for three years, presumably in order to squeeze as much money from him as possible. Wolfgang Hoffmeister, Treasurer of Bamberg, had 50,000 florins confiscated.

ACTIVITY
KNOWLEDGE CHECK

Property confiscations
How did property confiscations enable the witch-hunt to expand?

The roles of Prince-Bishop von Dornheim and Frederick Förner

Prince-Bishop von Dornheim

There is no doubt that the extensive nature of the witch-hunt between 1623 and 1632 was due largely to the actions of the prince-bishop, John George II Fuchs von Dornheim (died 1633), known as the *Hexenbischof* (witch-bishop). He was a champion of the Counter-Reformation, and like his predecessor, von Aschhausen, believed that tackling witchcraft was of utmost importance. He took personal responsibility for the investigation, and hired a number of people to assist him. His vicar general, Frederick Förner (discussed on page 123) was indispensable to him, and his legal adviser, Dr Ernst Vasolt, acted as an interrogator. Property confiscations helped to ensure that the Treasury, and as a result, von Dornheim's own wealth, increased dramatically.

In 1627, von Dornheim had a *Drudenhaus*, or witch-prison, built to contain 30 to 40 suspects at a time. The walls of the prison were covered in biblical texts, where those suspected of witchcraft could be tortured with his personal consent. Other smaller prisons were constructed in smaller towns within the bishopric.

SOURCE
9 'Malefiz House', or witch-prison, constructed in 1627 on the orders of Prince-Bishop von Dornheim.

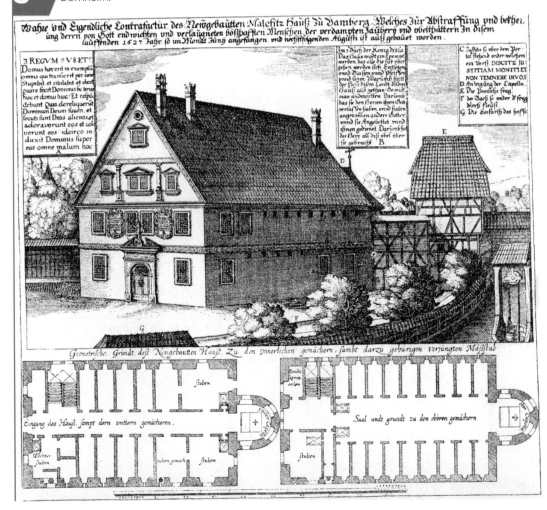

Frederick Förner

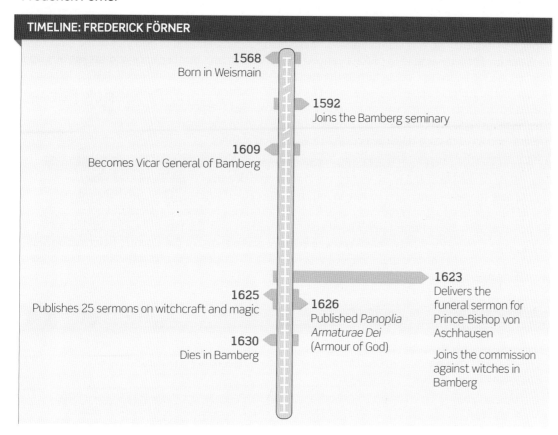

TIMELINE: FREDERICK FÖRNER

1568
Born in Weismain

1592
Joins the Bamberg seminary

1609
Becomes Vicar General of Bamberg

1623
Delivers the funeral sermon for Prince-Bishop von Aschhausen

Joins the commission against witches in Bamberg

1625
Publishes 25 sermons on witchcraft and magic

1626
Published *Panoplia Armaturae Dei* (Armour of God)

1630
Dies in Bamberg

As vicar general, Frederick Förner (1568–1630) acted as deputy to von Dornheim. Like von Dornheim, he was a strong advocate of the Counter-Reformation and relentlessly pursued suspected witches. He studied initially at the University of Würzburg and took up a position at the newly founded seminary in Bamberg in 1592. He continued his studies in Rome and after being ordained, he returned to Bamberg in 1598 and held a number of positions in churches and in the administration of the city.

He seems to have been involved in witch-hunting before Johann Gottfried von Aschhausen became prince-bishop in 1609, and became vicar general in the same year. He gave the funeral sermon of von Aschhausen in 1623, and in it he blamed the rise of Protestantism for the outbreak of the Thirty Years' War. He published 25 sermons on witchcraft and magic in 1625, and his output continued unabated for several years. Overall, his arguments for the Counter-Reformation and witch-hunting can be summarised up as follows.

- Calvinism was detestable because its preachers were false prophets who taught lies about the Catholic clergy and were no different to magicians. Förner illustrated this point by reporting the result of a successful exorcism, whereby the demon that was encountered stated that it had no fear of Calvinist ministers because they were allies.

- In his role as vicar general, he reported that in the areas of Bamberg where occult practices were being carried out, Protestant preachers were also being harboured.

- Both witches and Protestants undermine the entire social and political order by failing to respect the sacraments, relics and festivals of the Catholic Church.

- The defeat of one demonic force leads to the rise of another, more lethal force. He claimed that witchcraft only emerged in Bamberg once the influence of Lutheran clergy, whom he considered to be a demonic force, had been extinguished.

- His writings suggest that more than anything else, the outbreak of the Thirty Years' War caused cases of witchcraft to increase. He believed that the Protestant rebellion that caused the war, and increased incidences of *maleficia* both represent the final stage in the struggle between God and the Devil.

How did von Dornheim and Förner justify their actions?

Förner provided an intellectual framework for the witch-hunts that von Dornheim could not grasp as easily, and he was therefore indispensible to the prince-bishop. Both he and von Dornheim believed strongly that obedience was central to a well-functioning society, and found evidence in the Bible to back this up. Förner was able to make a connection between man's disobedience and sin, idolatry and witchcraft. Obedience to God, in turn, is the source of faith and order. His interest in history led him to present the struggle between God and the Devil as a historical one, where the Devil had always preyed on man's disobedience in order to offer false promises – especially to would-be witches – and false religions. This disobedience had existed from the days of the pharaohs of Ancient Egypt to the present, and as each false religion died, the Devil created another.

An important belief that both von Dornheim and Förner held was that the closer one came to the final defeat of the Devil, the more violent the Devil would become. If the Devil uses violence, it is justifiable to use violence and torture in return on suspected witches. They also believed that it should be expected to find more witches in Catholic territories because the Devil did not need to use his power against those Protestants who already believed his lies. The fact that more witches were being discovered as the Thirty Years' War gained pace was a sign that the Counter-Reformation was a success because it showed that the Devil was resorting to desperate tactics as his Protestant allies were flagging on the battlefield.

EXTEND YOUR KNOWLEDGE

The writings of Frederick Förner

Förner was well known as an author on theology and witchcraft, and his works all point towards his obsession with suppressing Protestant heresy.

He is especially remembered for his 1626 work on witchcraft, *Panoplia Armaturae Dei* (Armour of God), but he wrote widely on a number of subjects. He was especially interested in history, and in *Relatio Historico-Parenetica* he shows himself to be a strong supporter of the Counter-Reformation by describing church properties converted to secular use after the Reformation. This work was intended to encourage Ferdinand II to enforce the Edict of Restitution, authorising the forced conversion of Protestants, in the city of Nuremberg.

ACTIVITY
KNOWLEDGE CHECK

Prince-bishop and vicar general

1 What do you think motivated von Dornheim to pursue witches with such zeal?

2 Why was Förner so instrumental in the witch-hunt?

3 What was their biblical justification for the witch-hunt?

A Level Exam-Style Question Section B

To what extent do you agree that the extensive use of torture explains why the witch-hunt in Bamberg lasted for so long? (20 marks)

Tip

Think about both short- and long-term factors. It may be appropriate to discuss the Counter-Reformation and the preconditions that existed in Bamberg, as well as the actions of witch-hunters such as Frederick Förner.

WHY DID THE WITCH CRAZE COME TO AN END?

The influence of Emperor Ferdinand II and the Imperial Chamber Court

Scepticism before 1630

The witch-hunt fell into a steep decline with the involvement of Emperor Ferdinand II in 1630, but there was growing scepticism about the trials before this. In early 1627, complaints about innocent people being executed for witchcraft began to be made at both religious and imperial courts. In July 1627, von Dornheim issued a proclamation stating that those who give false testimony at witch trials should be flogged, and a whipping post was erected for this purpose. The authorities must have been aware that not all accusations were genuine, as they renewed von Dornheim's proclamation in 1628. As always, however, it seems that von Dornheim's decision was simply reactionary and only concerned with protecting his inner circle. A series of accusations of witchcraft had actually been made against Frederick Förner and others in his administration. Von Dornheim was shocked that men who had served Bamberg in hunting witches should be accused themselves, and issued the proclamation as a warning against further slander.

Ferdinand's involvement: the case of Dorothea Flock

The emperor finally became directly involved in 1630, when a Bamberg councillor, Georg Heinrich Flock, was accused. Flock soon fled to Nuremberg, but his wife Dorothea was arrested. Her husband and family initially appealed to Ferdinand, stating their particular concern for her health and that of her newborn child, and the legitimacy of the legal process. Von Dornheim despatched a letter to the emperor stating that there were no concerns over the health of mother or baby, and that the trials he had been undertaking were simply following standards already set in other parts of Germany. He also accused Flock of being dishonest in his own account of the facts, and compelled the emperor to ignore his complaints. He added that he had only initiated the trials in order to honour God and turn people away from ungodly behaviour.

Renewed proceedings against Dorothea Flock in April 1630 led her relatives to appeal directly to the pope and the emperor again. Both Ferdinand and the pope requested that von Dornheim stop the trial, and wrote in a letter that all documents related to the trial should be sent to the imperial **Holfrat** for review, and that if he did not obey their orders he would be punished.

On hearing that letters were on the way from Ferdinand and the pope, von Dornheim rushed the trial through and had Dorothea executed before they could arrive on 17 May (Source 10). She was sentenced to be burned alive, but von Dornheim permitted her to be beheaded first. The sentence was carried out in secret at 6 a.m.

KEY TERM

Holfrat
A high-ranking adviser to the Holy Roman Emperor, similar to an English Privy Councillor.

SOURCE 10

The judgement against Dorothea Flock, 17 May 1630.

On account of her evil deeds, done with sorcery, wherein she first denied almighty God and the all-holy Trinity in a shocking and unchristian manner, then gave herself bodily to Satan, and did much other evil, in particular, desecrated the most holy Host and gave herself to Satan as a lover.

The execution of Dorothea Flock led to renewed protests from her relatives, who sent a bitter letter to Ferdinand claiming that her trial was illegal and contrary to religious law. They questioned the proceedings on a number of grounds.

- Flock was not able to question the testimony of her accusers or hire a lawyer, because the trial was conducted in secret.
- The Carolina Law Code of 1532, which witch trials were based on, specifically required judges to establish the credibility of witnesses. The nature of the proceedings against Flock meant that it was impossible to determine which witnesses were credible.
- The Carolina Law Code also stated that confessions taken through torture should only be permissible in court if they were supported by other evidence. This had not been the case.

The involvement of the Imperial Chamber Court

Complaints started reaching the **Imperial Chamber Court** in Speyer, where von Dornheim's representative reported back that two other escapees from the witch-prison in Bamberg had sent complaints directly to the emperor, and compelled von Dornheim to take immediate action to preserve his reputation.

Von Dornheim decided to send two of his witch-commissioners, Dr Harsee and Dr Schwartzkonz, to the **Diet of Regensburg** in order to present a defence of the witch trials. They were able to present their case to the Aulic Council, another of the high courts. Although they felt their audience with the court went well, high-profile members, such as William Lamormaini and Count von Fürstenberg, were already sceptical about the witch-hunt and felt that Ferdinand's position would be jeopardised if he tolerated the persecutions.

KEY TERMS

Imperial Chamber Court
The highest judicial court in the Holy Roman Empire, with judges appointed directly by the emperor. It acted as an appeals court, and the emperor could become directly involved in cases.

Diet of Regensburg
A meeting of the senior leaders of the Holy Roman Empire, held between July and November 1630.

On 15 August, Ferdinand wrote to von Dornheim in an even more forceful tone than in his previous letters. He criticised von Dornheim for continuing the trials in defiance of his earlier instructions, and he complained about the case of Barbara Schwarz, who had fled to Vienna after escaping from the witch-prison in Bamberg (Source 11). After Schwarz had petitioned Ferdinand, he ordered von Dornheim to send the original trial documents for review. When these documents arrived, Ferdinand sent a strongly worded letter to the prince-bishop criticising him and his commissioners for the over-zealous use of torture and the blatant disregard of imperial decrees.

SOURCE

11 The petition of Barbara Schwarz, 20 September 1630.

I, a poor citizen of Bamberg, a wretched, sick woman whom even the coldest heart would surely pity, appeal to your royal majesty with the greatest subservience. For almost three full years now I have been held in the Bamberg witch-prison, kept in fetters and surviving on a scant supply of bread and water. All this is because a feckless man named Stefan Bayer accused me of witchcraft and reported me after there had been a quarrel between us.

They brought me to Zeil where they tormented me with thumb screws, leg screws, canes and whips. I nevertheless endured this torture, the weak woman that I am, and insisted upon my innocence. And although the law states that anyone who denies the charge but has withstood the punishment should be set free, I was still detained in bonds and irons alongside many others who protested their innocence in spite of the torture suffered.

Until I finally was able to flee in order to escape death by starvation. I used a stone to file through the bonds which kept me pinned to the wall. I travelled through Bamberg to get here.

Please provide me with a letter of protection; I ask that you order the bishop, the prince and his commissioners to allow me to return to my husband that I might once again tend to my home and look after my children.

Further trial documents were demanded by Ferdinand, and when it was discovered that they were in fact copies, he demanded that the originals be sent. Von Dornheim refused and instead sent transcripts that he claimed were copied verbatim from the original trial records. Attached to these transcripts was a letter from the witch-commissioners of Bamberg, stating that no one had been arrested for witchcraft since June 1630. Meanwhile, children were learning magic and witchcraft in the street and the trials must continue in order for their teachers to be punished.

Despite the claim that arrests had stopped in Bamberg, Ferdinand discovered in March 1631 that a minimum of 25 people had been arrested in the meantime. The relatives of the victims of Zeil informed him that the commissioners continued to grow in riches through property confiscations, while the cost of trials was causing the town to go bankrupt.

Georg Wilhelm Dümler's letter and the end of the trials

A powerfully written letter by Georg Wilhelm Dümler, a former administrator of St Martin's Church in Bamberg, may have been the final piece of evidence needed to convince the emperor once and for all that the trials needed to be stopped. In his letter, he stated the following.

- Several hundred respectable people had suffered as a result of torture and the leaders of the witch-commission were easily led by false accusations.

- There was never sufficient proof in the trials to legitimately find suspects guilty.

- In August 1628, his pregnant wife had been taken from their house to the witch-prison, where she was tortured and miscarried. She was executed, and now he had been accused of witchcraft. Both he and his wife were entirely innocent and were raised as pious Catholics.

- The Carolina Law Code permitted the accused an advocate or lawyer to represent them in court, but this had been denied at the Bamberg trials.

- Cases of witchcraft should be heard in the civil courts, but in Bamberg they were being heard behind closed doors by the commissioners.

On 12 June 1631, Ferdinand announced that he was to punish those responsible for the Bamberg trials. He appointed a new director of the witch-commission, Dr Anton Winter, and decreed that all future trials be conducted according to the Carolina Law Code. The confiscation of property was forbidden. Von Dornheim stubbornly remained in Bamberg, and gave little support to Winter. He sent a final letter to the emperor, reiterating his view that those who had accused him of malpractice were involved in witchcraft themselves. He refused to release those still held in custody, and it was only the advance of the Swedish army that encouraged him to flee and end the persecutions.

ACTIVITY
KNOWLEDGE CHECK

The role of Ferdinand II

1 Why was the case of Dorothea Flock an important turning point in the development of the trials?

2 Read Source 11. Why do you think this petition was particularly convincing to the imperial court?

3 Why did the involvement of Ferdinand II never completely extinguish witch persecutions in Bamberg?

The arrival of the Swedish army

Swedish involvement in the Thirty Years' War

With the Protestant Swedish army, led by King Gustavus Adolphus, entering the war in 1630 and achieving important victories in 1631, it looked as though the tide of the Thirty Years' War was turning. Much of the territory lost by the Protestants was regained between 1630 and 1634, and Adolphus' dream of a Swedish empire became a reality. The Swedish army swelled in size, from approximately 40,000 in 1630 to 150,000 in 1632. An army of this size required huge amounts of resources and food, and the army took to plundering the countryside in order to maintain itself.

The arrival of the Swedish army in Bamberg

Despite the emperor's direct involvement in the hunts, as long as von Dornheim remained as prince-bishop, the persecutions would continue. When the Swedish army invaded and took over the administration of Bamberg, von Dornheim was forced to flee.

Bamberg was already tired of the fighting, as it was on one of the main routes that troops took when traversing Germany. The population that would decline by around 40 percent during the war was already in decline when the Swedish army arrived.

The Swedish army were outside Bamberg by February 1632, which led to the downfall of von Dornheim as prince-bishop. He looted the cathedral's treasure, which included 12 chests of gold and valuable documents, and fled to Austria. He died there, of a stroke, on 19 March 1633. Despite Bamberg being occupied by

Protestants, it seemed that Catholic nuns were able to continue with their ordinary way of life with little interference, and were even able to organise a nativity scene at Christmas. Jesuits were also allowed to continue their work. Counter-attacks by Catholic forces contributed to the feeling of panic and chaos across the region.

SOURCE **12**
A Protestant news-sheet showing the arrival of the Swedish king, Gustavus Adolphus and his army in Germany. Adolphus is assisted by an angel, and on the left, Johann Tserclaes, one of the Catholic commanders, is in chains (1631).

With a declining population, decimated farms and constant fighting, combined with the flight of the prince-bishop, witch-hunting was no longer seen as a priority by the authorities. Any trials that could take place had to follow the Carolina Law Code, and there was no longer a use for the witch-prison and its torture chambers.

ACTIVITY
KNOWLEDGE CHECK

Swedish involvement

Why did the arrival of the Swedish army result in witchcraft persecutions coming to an end?

Conclusion: Why were the Bamberg witch trials so extensive?

A number of reasons have been put forward by historians to explain the extent of the witch-hunt.

- Personalities were important. Frederick Förner was perhaps the single most significant individual, as an instigator of the trials and influential author on witchcraft. However, without the consent of Prince-Bishop von Aschhausen, the initial wave of trials between 1616 and 1619 would not have taken place. Prince-Bishop von Dornheim also acted with passion to ensure that the trials became extensive and horrific.

- In addition to the three personalities mentioned above, a host of others enabled the trials to spread quickly. The members of the witchcraft commission, particularly von Dornheim's legal adviser Dr Ernst Vasolt, as well as the torture masters, were essential in moving the hunt forward. Vasolt often demanded of the suspects 100 names of their accomplices or those seen at meetings. With so many names being put forward under torture, it was not long before men and women of quality were suggested.

- The judicial environment in which the trials took place also meant that it was able to continue unchecked for a relatively long period of time. The group that carried out the investigations were able to operate outside of ordinary judicial structures, because the judges were obliged to follow the lead of the witch-hunters, who were held in high regard and were not questioned.

- A number of high-profile individuals were executed in both Bamberg and Zeil. Clearly the property confiscated from this group added much to the Treasury, but there were other reasons why they were targeted. A generation earlier, a large proportion of officials in Bamberg were Protestant. The witch-hunts provided an opportunity for many newly converted Catholics to prove their loyalty to the regime, but it also resulted in an increased number being accused by their colleagues.

- It is no coincidence that the most intense phase of witch-hunting coincides with the Edict of Restitution of 1629, in which Ferdinand II called for the conversion of Protestants to Catholicism. As Förner pointed out in *Panoplia Armaturae Dei*, the bishop had the opportunity to destroy the two demonic threats of heresy and sorcery. By the end of the craze, von Dornheim was willing to defy even the emperor.

- The witch-hunts can be seen as the culmination of a long process whereby increasing power was centralised in the hands of the prince-bishop. Gradually, old structures that kept the bishop in check, such as the local council and cathedral chapter, were neutralised and placed under the control of the bishop and his agents. By the time von Aschhausen became bishop, there was virtually no organised opposition within Bamberg.

A Level Exam-Style Question Section B

How far do you agree that the persecutions in Bamberg came to an end because of the arrival of the Swedish army? (20 marks)

Tip
Try to assess two or three other factors to compare to that of the arrival of the Swedish army. These could include the role of Ferdinand II and the importance of sceptical cases.

ACTIVITY
SUMMARY

Accusers and accused

1 Hundreds of people were executed in the course of the witch-hunt. There are many for whom we will never know their story, but the trial records of a small number are recorded in detail. In order to assess the motivations of the authorities, complete the following tasks.

a) Look back through the chapter and look for as many individual examples of suspected witches as you can find.

b) Create a table with the following headings and fill in the information about each suspect: social background, circumstances of arrest (if known), use of torture, main elements of confession.

c) Based on the information you have collected, what kind of people were most likely to be accused by the authorities? What do the accused have in common?

2 A number of individuals were involved in carrying out the persecutions in Bamberg. For each of the following individuals, answer the questions that follow: Prince-Bishop von Aschhausen, Prince-Bishop von Dornheim, Frederick Förner, Dr Ernst Vasolt.

a) What was their role in the persecutions?

b) What was their educational/social background?

c) What was their ideological motivation for carrying out the persecutions?

THINKING HISTORICALLY   Interpretations (6a)

Ever-changing history

Our interpretations of the past change as we change. This may be because our social attitudes have changed over time or perhaps a historian has constructed a new theory or perhaps technology has allowed archaeologists to discover something new.

Work in pairs.

1 Make a timeline that starts with the Bamberg witch trials and ends 50 years in the future. Construct reactions that illustrate the point that time changes history. In the future box you can speculate how people might react to the event in 50 years' time.

You might wish to start with attitudes towards the witch trials when they began in 1623, followed by attitudes when Prince-Bishop von Dornheim left Bamberg in 1632. You could then include 1660, when the Royal Society had been founded, and then a date in the mid-20th century. An example is shown below.

1914	1917	1932	1968	2066
Event: The outbreak of the First World War	German patriot: 'The start of Germany's greatest war' Farmer from Northern France: 'A disaster'	British diplomat: 'The start of Britain's greatest colonial era'. Unemployed German: 'A disaster'	Farmer in Northern France: 'The start of the war. I keep finding bullets' British diplomat: 'The beginning of the end of the British Empire' An Indian historian: 'A major step on the road to Indian independence'.	?

2 Answer the following questions.

a) Identify three factors that have affected the way the Bamberg witch trials have been interpreted over time, or might affect it in the future.

b) If a historian was to write a book proposing a radically new interpretation of the Bamberg witch trials, how might other historians react? What would affect their reaction?

c) How will the future change the past?

WIDER READING

Bradford Smith, W. *Reformation and the German Territorial State: Upper Franconia, 1300–1630,* University of Rochester Press (2008). The final chapter includes a wide-ranging discussion of Bamberg, including the nature of those accused and the use of torture.

Levack, B.P. *The Witch-hunt in Early Modern Europe,* Pearson (2006). Light in detail on Bamberg, but important in understanding the motivations for the witch-hunt in Germany.

Pavlac, B.A. *Witch Hunts in the Western World,* University of Nebraska Press (2010). Provides information on the wider German context, Bamberg and the case of John Junius.

Sebald, H. 'Witches' confessions: Stereotypical structure and local color, the case of the Prince-Bishopric of Bamberg', *Southern Humanities Review,* 24 (1990). Provides a detailed discussion of the types of confessions that were made at Bamberg.

3.6 Matthew Hopkins and the East Anglian witch craze, 1645–47

KEY QUESTIONS

- How far were economic and political issues responsible for the East Anglian witch craze?
- How far were Matthew Hopkins and John Stearne responsible for the extent of the witch craze?
- Why did the witch craze come to an end in 1647?

INTRODUCTION

The story of the East Anglian witch craze, and Matthew Hopkins in particular, has passed into legend. Figure 6.1 shows Vincent Price playing Hopkins in the film *Witchfinder General* (1968). In the film, Hopkins is presented as a vicious torturer who is eventually axed to death in order to end his brief but prolific career as a witch-hunter. In reality Hopkins died of natural causes just two years after his career started and was no older than 28 when he died, significantly younger than the 57-year-old Price. Despite the inaccuracies of the film, it demonstrates the fear and confusion that existed in East Anglia in the context of the English Civil War, which would manifest itself in the largest witch-hunt in English history.

Figure 6.1 Vincent Price as Matthew Hopkins in *Witchfinder General* (1968).

1642 – Start of the Civil War

1645 – Hopkins and Stearne begin their careers as witch-hunters

| 1641 | 1642 | 1643 | 1644 | 1645 |

1644 – Hopkins first becomes suspicious of suspected witches in Manningtree

Hopkins and his older colleague, John Stearne, made a lucrative trade from witch-hunting across East Anglia and beyond as a result of the payments made by town and parish councils, and were responsible for the deaths of as many as 400 people. This is more than twice as many as had been executed for witchcraft in England in the preceding century. The true motivations of the witch-hunters may never be known, but it is most likely that they were encouraged in their work by one or both of the following factors.

- The lucrative fee that could be charged by the witchfinders could be as much as £23 from one town – an enormous sum considering their work in each town would only take a few days.

- They may have been motivated by genuine religious conviction. On the cover of Hopkins' *The Discovery of Witches*, he includes the famous line from Exodus (22.18) used in so many witch-hunts across Europe: 'Thou shalt not suffer a witch to live'. Here, Hopkins was clearly using Biblical justification to carry out his investigations.

Both Hopkins and Stearne wrote their own defence of the witch-hunt, and claimed that they only charged 20 shillings per town for their work. Although his father was a Puritan minister, there is no evidence to suggest that Hopkins was particularly fanatical before the witch-hunt began.

The story of Hopkins and Stearne also plays out in an atmosphere of religious, as well as military, chaos. The counties of East Anglia formed the **Eastern Association** during the Civil War, which provided a significant number of troops for the Parliamentarian war effort. Many of these troops were Puritan, and the pockets of Catholicism that still existed in counties like Norfolk were being rooted out in the mid-1640s.

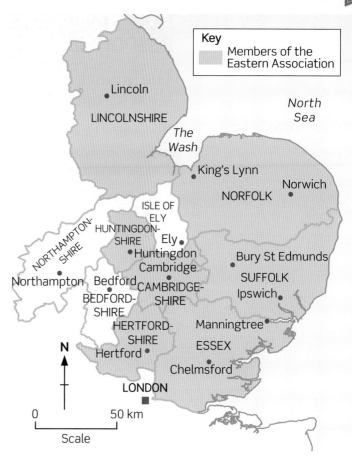

Figure 6.2 The Eastern Counties of England, 1645–47.

KEY TERM

Eastern Association
A military organisation comprising the seven county militias of Eastern England formed during the English Civil War.

1646 – Harsh winter and plague in summer

1646 – Widespread witch accusations throughout East Anglia

1648 – Stearne publishes *A Confirmation and Discovery of Witchcraft*

| 1646 | 1647 | 1648 | 1649 | 1650 |

1646 – John Gaule publishes *Select Cases of Conscience touching Witches and Witchcrafts* and begins to preach against Hopkins and Stearne

1646 – End of Civil War

1647 – Hopkins publishes *The Discovery of Witches*

1647 – Death of Hopkins

HOW FAR WERE ECONOMIC AND POLITICAL ISSUES RESPONSIBLE FOR THE EAST ANGLIAN WITCH CRAZE?

The impact of the breakdown of traditional authority and legal structures

The political context

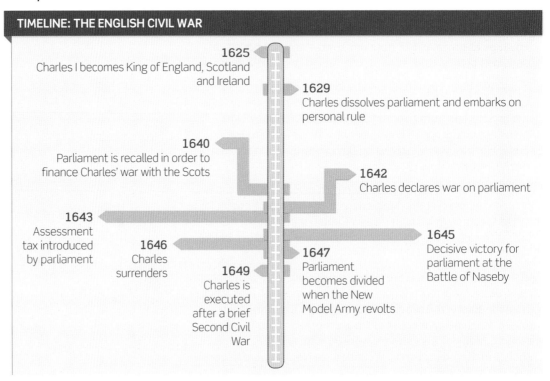

TIMELINE: THE ENGLISH CIVIL WAR

1625
Charles I becomes King of England, Scotland and Ireland

1629
Charles dissolves parliament and embarks on personal rule

1640
Parliament is recalled in order to finance Charles' war with the Scots

1642
Charles declares war on parliament

1643
Assessment tax introduced by parliament

1646
Charles surrenders

1649
Charles is executed after a brief Second Civil War

1647
Parliament becomes divided when the New Model Army revolts

1645
Decisive victory for parliament at the Battle of Naseby

In 1625, Charles I became King of England, Scotland and Ireland. He was never meant to be king, as his older brother Henry was groomed for the role and was well liked. Henry died at the age of 18, leaving the 12-year-old Charles to shoulder the burden. When Charles did become king on the death of his father, James, his stubborn and aloof personality did not help in his relations with parliament.

Although supreme power was vested in the monarch, parliament had gradually become a more important institution throughout the Tudor and early Stuart period. Its official duties included making and amending laws – with the approval of the monarch – and approving regular taxation collected on behalf of the Crown. Charles came to blows with parliament in the late 1620s, particularly over his approach to government finance and a number of failed military expeditions. In 1629, Charles dissolved parliament and ruled alone for 11 years. He recalled parliament in 1640 in order to persuade them to vote him the funds to fight a war with the Scots, who had rebelled over Charles' decision to impose the English prayer book on them.

During his 11 years of personal rule, the gentlemen who represented their counties as MPs found further cause to resent Charles. Many of the MPs were Puritan, and Charles' religious policy, which he formulated with William Laud, Archbishop of Canterbury, seemed to them to be disturbingly Catholic in appearance. Accusations of witchcraft were often not acted upon by the authorities, which goes some way to explaining why the period 1645–47 is marked by so many trials in such a short period of time. He also collected dubious taxes, the most infamous of which was Ship Money. This tax was traditionally levied on coastal counties and towns in order to provide for the fleet. Charles decided to extend the tax to the entire country, resulting in financial demands being made of the inland gentry as well as those living near the coast.

Debates between Charles and parliament continued between 1640 and 1642. In January 1642, Charles attempted to arrest five leading MPs who had acted as ringleaders in the attempts to restrict his powers, but they fled and Charles left London to raise an army in what he claimed was an act of self-defence. In August 1642, Charles raised his standard at Nottingham, signalling the start of the Civil War. The first battle at Edgehill in October 1642 is regarded as a draw, and from then what many thought would be a short-lived conflict dragged out into full-scale civil war. In 1645, parliament made a breakthrough when it assembled the **New Model Army**, with the core of its soldiers taken from the Eastern Association.

> **KEY TERM**
>
> New Model Army
> A national army made up of a number of former Parliamentary regiments. It was disciplined and well trained, and it helped parliament to gain a decisive victory at the Battle of Naseby in June 1645. After the Parliamentary victory in the Civil War, the New Model Army came to possess considerable political influence.

The impact of the breakdown of traditional authority

By 1645, East Anglia had been through three years of civil war and the county that would become the epicentre of the witch-hunt, Suffolk, served as parliament's main recruiting ground. The area saw little actual fighting, and many of the locals felt detached from the war, although they inevitably felt the effects of so many men leaving (as much as 20 percent) their villages and towns to fight. At a time when mortality rates for both adults and children were already high, further deaths from war added to a strained existence. One accused witch from Suffolk, Margery Sparham, confessed to entertaining the Devil's imps in the shape of a mole and two blackbirds. It was recorded by the court at her trial that she had been left alone and vulnerable when her husband went to fight in the war.

Across Suffolk and other Eastern counties, the dearth of men resulted in a shift in traditional power relationships. Witches discovered at Wingfield, Westhorpe and Stradbroke appeared to be connected with radical Puritan sects that believed that women could be viewed as socially, as well as spiritually, equal to men. Of course, most of the accused women in East Anglia had no connections with radical sects, and the chaos of war provided an opportunity for long-held suspicions to be brought to the surface.

In 1645, stories were reaching East Anglia about strange occurrences and omens. A Royalist woman from Lancashire was reported to have given birth to a headless baby; the body of a habitual sinner was dug up by dogs and eaten; and across the region women were beginning to drink and swear like men. With the chaos of war also came a decline in power for two of the symbols of continuity and power in the region.

- The traditional authority of the Church of England was undermined in the context of war. In areas controlled by parliament, undesirable ministers were ejected from their churches and often replaced by Puritans.

- The authority of the local gentry was also undermined as many of them left their estates to fight. Those with Royalist sympathies faced arrest and confiscation of their estates.

In the absence of traditional authority, various fears began to grow that would ultimately manifest themselves in a witch-hunt. What began as a fear of the enemy developed into a fear of 'enemies within'. Ministers in pulpits no longer preached

exclusively about the dangers associated with the Royalists and their supposed Catholic allies, but also warned about spies and on the Parliamentarian side.

SOURCE

'The world turn'd upside down', from a pamphlet produced shortly after the Civil War, shows the chaos and confusion that was thought to have taken hold. It was written by John Taylor, who describes himself as a 'well-wish to King, Parliament and Kingdom' and was published in London in 1647.

THE
World turn'd upside down:
OR,
A briefe description of the ridiculous Fashions of these distracted Times.

By T. J. a well-willer to King, Parliament and Kingdom.

London : Printed for *John Smith.* 1647.

> **ACTIVITY**
> **KNOWLEDGE CHECK**
>
> **The Civil War and the breakdown of authority**
> 1 What were the causes of the English Civil War?
>
> 2 In what ways was traditional authority undermined by war?

Legal structures in East Anglia

The assize courts were unable to function normally during the war, and justice was often meted out by local magistrates or by other individuals appointed with only limited legal experience. One Norfolk woman writing in 1645 stated that, with no kingly authority, normal laws did not apply and there could be no true justice as long as the war continued. The already fragile legal structures in East Anglia were threatened further by the later stages of the Civil War.

- Victory at Naseby in Northamptonshire in June 1645 had confirmed how powerful the New Model Army could be, and it was followed by another Parliamentarian victory in Somerset in July. A number of East Anglian gentry began returning to their estates.

- Charles' nephew and cavalry commander, Prince Rupert, advised him to renew peace negotiations, but Charles moved his forces east, towards East Anglia. It was felt that fighting in the region was now inevitable.

- In this context, the assize circuits were disrupted because it was considered too dangerous for the judges to make the journey from London.

- In July 1645, the Earl of Warwick, one of the most senior Parliamentarians, was commissioned to oversee the Essex summer assizes at Chelmsford. He possessed little legal experience, which meant he had to work closely with county magistrates Sir John Barrington, Sir Martin Lumley, Sir Henry Holcroft, Sir Henry Mildmay and William Conyers. Warwick sentenced 19 women to hang.

In Suffolk, too, the assizes were disrupted by fighting. Not long after Warwick had been appointed to oversee justice in Essex, news arrived of the latest trouble in Cambridge, where troops were being mobilised from all over East Anglia to engage Charles' forces at Huntingdon. It was decided that the assizes at Bury St Edmunds, 25 miles to the east of Cambridge, would be suspended. Prisoners already condemned were immediately executed and those awaiting trial were sent back to their cells. The commission that was established at Bury was presided over not by an assize judge, but by John Godbolt, a Serjeant-at-law (a barrister).

In this context, local fears of witchcraft were intensified and in the absence of senior judges, the witch-hunt was able to spread quickly. Mayors and town councillors were thankful for the opportunity to pay for the services of Matthew Hopkins and John Stearne because they provided what appeared to be legitimate legal knowledge and efficiency at a time when both were in short supply. Although they did not act as judges themselves, they were able to interrogate suspects and collect evidence in order to take cases to court. This resulted in an English record 42 percent conviction rate.

Despite the chaotic events of the 1640s, historians have still found it surprising that the witch-hunt became so widespread in the context of the English legal system (Extract 1).

EXTRACT 1

From William E. Burns, *Witch Hunts in Europe and America: An Encyclopedia* (2003).

The British Isles were an area of comparatively little witch-hunting activity. This is partly because of the different judicial system, the common law, which held sway in England and the varying extent of its Irish possessions in this period. The comparative insignificance of torture in the English system along with the absence of Inquisitorial trial procedure made chain-reaction hunts built on the confessions of witches much more difficult than in those areas following Roman law, such as Germany... The high degree of centralisation characteristic of the English legal system since the Middle Ages also made it virtually impossible for local magistrates to launch large-scale witch-hunts, with the exception of the time of the English Civil War in the mid-seventeenth century. The Matthew Hopkins witch-hunt, by far the largest in English history, took place in conditions of the collapse of central government authority. The county of Essex in eastern England, Hopkins's home territory, saw the most persecution of any area in England, a distinction possibly related to its high concentration of Puritans.

KEY TERMS

Ergot
A fungal disease that particularly affects rye. Eating infected food resulted in ergotism, a poisoning that caused headaches, vomiting and spasms. Some historians have blamed this poisoning for the hallucinations apparently experienced by some suspected witches.

Seed-corn
Good quality corn set aside for planting the following year.

Economic crises

As with many other witch-hunts, accusations began appearing in the context of economic crisis. Three factors worked together to encourage suspicion: poor harvests, changing land use and the impact of the Civil War itself.

Crop failure

The mid-1640s were a disastrous time for farmers. Wet summers combined with freezing winters led to regular crop failures. In 1646 for example, the summer was exceptionally wet, with disease affecting livestock and crops. The staples of wheat and rye were inedible and rotted with **ergot**. The price of meat and cheese rose dramatically, and despite the fact that Charles surrendered in that year, the price of wheat rose by 20 percent. **Seed-corn** had to be consumed in large quantities, threatening the harvest for the following year.

In October of both 1645 and 1646 – a time when people would usually be enjoying the best of the harvest – heavy rain caused crops to rot and fields to be trodden into mud. Contemporaries wrote that this was the most extreme wet weather in living memory. In a deeply religious society, this was viewed as a sign from the heavens. The many Puritan preachers in East Anglia interpreted the economic situation as a punishment from God – a sign that Charles should not be returned to the throne and he should be punished. In an air of such confusion and misery, it was easy to blame witches for people's misfortunes.

Changing land use

Changing land use in the preceding century caused resentment that also manifested itself in the witch-hunt. There is no doubt that the livelihoods of tenants and peasants had been threatened by inflation and the increased inequality that came with the enclosure of common land. As the rich were able to acquire more land to feed their cattle, the poorer residents of parishes felt shut out from any prosperity, and in the face of increased begging from the poor, the charity that was once provided by the wealthier inhabitants, such as the offering of bread and beer, was now extremely rare.

Across East Anglia, landlords who let land to tenants were increasingly tempted by the improved profits that could be made from evicting their tenants and enclosing land in order to focus on one particular agricultural product. Tenant farmers, many of whom had been settled for generations, defended their right to stay on their land with mixed success. At the same time, wealthier residents were expected to pay **poor rates** to support the poor, but some of them saw this as subsidising lifestyles that they viewed as feckless. Those that benefited from enclosure were reluctant to give to beggars, and the neighbourliness that had existed for centuries was no more. In the minds of the many wealthy Puritans of East Anglia, idleness was a sign of sinfulness.

> **KEY TERM**
>
> **Poor rates**
> A local tax levied at parish level in order to finance the support of the poor.

In the Isle of Ely, Sir Miles Sandys acted as a particularly aggressive landlord. In the 1620s he had acquired large estates and at Sutton he enclosed 4,000 acres of common land, which deprived the poor of grazing land and a source of fuel. Thirty families had even built cottages on the land that they were evicted from. The inhabitants of Sutton presented a petition to the Court of Chancery with 100 signatures to allow them to continue to use the common land, but this failed. The inhabitants began rioting in the late 1630s, and resentment of Sandys continued into the 1640s. A number of the suspected witches who faced trials at Ely in 1647 had connections with the earlier unrest over enclosure.

Even when donations were made to beggars in this divided society, donors viewed the recipients with suspicion. When the recipients were poor, older women, the better-off continued to fear that they might use magic in revenge for not receiving enough. This is not to suggest that all of the poor were viewed with suspicion, although it is easier to understand why so many from this group became embroiled in accusations as the witch craze spread.

Economic impact of the Civil War

Inflation had been an issue for many years, but since the start of the Civil War the price of livestock had increased by 12 percent and grain by 15 percent. This was primarily because of the huge resources required by the armies of both sides. Horses were regularly confiscated by soldiers as they marched through the countryside and food from the land was consumed in large quantities. While this drove up prices, wages did not increase. In 1643, parliament devised a new tax to meet the increasing cost of the war: the weekly assessment. In the counties of the Eastern Association, this was collected at a rate 12 times higher than the loathed Ship Money tax of the 1630s.

Margaret Moone, one of the first witches to be accused in the hunt from Thorpe-le-Soken, not far from Hopkins' home parish of Manningtree, is an example of someone who fell into poverty and suffered the consequences. She had been evicted from her cottage when a man offered her landlord ten shillings more than she could afford in rent per year. She fell into begging and was later blamed for the deaths of livestock and crop failures, as well as the murder of a child.

A Level Exam-Style Question Section B

How accurate is it to say that the English Civil War was the most important underlying cause of the East Anglian witch craze of 1645–47? (20 marks)

Tip
This is a question in causation which should account for other factors such as the existing economic situation and legal structures.

ACTIVITY
KNOWLEDGE CHECK

Changing legal structures and economic crises

1 How was the English legal system affected by the Civil War? How do you think this would advantage the witch-hunters?

2 Why did crop failures increase social tensions?

3 Why did the poor of East Anglia suffer in the years preceding the witch-hunt? Why did this manifest itself in witchcraft accusations?

HOW FAR WERE MATTHEW HOPKINS AND JOHN STEARNE RESPONSIBLE FOR THE EXTENT OF THE WITCH CRAZE?

Geography, numbers, class and gender of victims

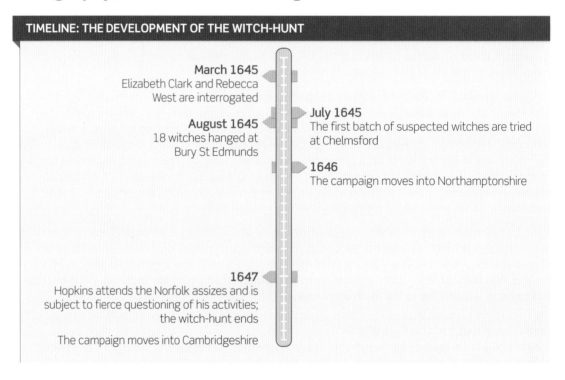

TIMELINE: THE DEVELOPMENT OF THE WITCH-HUNT

March 1645
Elizabeth Clark and Rebecca West are interrogated

July 1645
The first batch of suspected witches are tried at Chelmsford

August 1645
18 witches hanged at Bury St Edmunds

1646
The campaign moves into Northamptonshire

1647
Hopkins attends the Norfolk assizes and is subject to fierce questioning of his activities; the witch-hunt ends

The campaign moves into Cambridgeshire

As with most other witch-hunts, the majority of the accused were women (around 80 percent). It is impossible to say exactly how many were executed as a result of the hunt, but around 700 were accused or faced trial in the region at some point between 1645 and 1647. Of these, historians have estimated that around 300 to 400 were ultimately killed. The hunt began in Hopkins' home county of Essex, but soon spread to Suffolk, Norfolk, Cambridgeshire, Huntingdonshire and even into Northamptonshire and Bedfordshire. Some cases were well documented in court records, contemporary news pamphlets and in the writings of Hopkins and Stearne, but for many of the accused we only possess a name or a location.

The course of events and the geography of accusations, 1645–47
Matthew Hopkins first became concerned about witches in 1644, when he was kept awake at night by what he claimed were meetings of witches near his house in Manningtree (Source 2).

SOURCE 2

From Matthew Hopkins, *The Discovery of Witches* (1647).

The Discoverer never travelled far for it [to find witches], but in *March* 1644 he had some seven or eight of that horrible sect of Witches living in the Towne where he lived, a Towne in Essex called *Maningtree*, with divers [many] other adjacent Witches of other towns, who every six weeks in the night (being alwayes on the Friday night) had their meeting close by his house and had their severall solemne sacrifices there offered to the *Devill*, one of which this discoverer heard speaking to her *Imps* one night, and bid them goe to another Witch, who was thereupon apprehended, and searched, by women who had for many yeares knowne the Devills marks, and found to have three teats about her, which honest women have not: so upon command from the *Justice* they were to keep her from sleep two or three nights, expecting in that time to see her *familiars*, which the fourth night she called in by their severall names, and told them what shapes, a quarter of an houre before they came in, there being ten of us in the roome.

The first witches identified were all women, and from Manningtree Hopkins and Stearne began working together to identify more. In March 1645, they presented some accusations to a local magistrate named Sir Harbottle Grimston. Hopkins and Stearne did not act as judges themselves, but began to offer their services as witchfinders to parishes and towns for a fee.

EXTEND YOUR KNOWLEDGE

Sir Harbottle Grimston (c1569–1648)
The East Anglian witch craze is often associated with only Hopkins and Stearne, but a whole cast of other individuals made the hunt possible, including Sir Harbottle Grimston.

Grimston was a gentleman who lived at Bradfield Hall, just outside Manningtree. Despite being well into his seventies when the Civil War started, he continued to tour his estates, where many of the earliest accused witches lived. He was made a baronet in 1611 and entered parliament in 1614. He was a Puritan, and as an MP resisted much of Charles' policies during personal rule.

Many of the witches originally accused in March 1645 were tenants of Grimston or lived illegally on his land. Together with his fellow magistrate, Sir Thomas Bowes, he investigated witchcraft accusations in and around Manningtree, working with Hopkins and Stearne, as well as search-women (who looked for the Devil's mark) and 'watchers' who observed the suspects while they were sleep deprived. Grimston died in 1648, shortly after the end of the craze.

The first woman to be accused in Manningtree was Elizabeth Clark, an older woman with one leg and long suspected of being a witch. Four search-women inspected her body for the Devil's mark and found three teats. She was then watched for several nights by various officials and eager neighbours. According to Hopkins' account, several familiars appeared, and Clark welcomed them by referring to them by their names, which included a rabbit named Sack & Sugar and a dog-like creature named Jarmara. Elizabeth named other witches, including Rebecca West, who also admitted to suckling imps. West then turned witness for the Crown, and gained immunity from prosecution. This case gained notoriety

when it was published in an anonymous pamphlet, *A true and exact relation of the severall informations, examinations, and confessions of the late witches, arraigned and executed in the county of Essex* (Source 3).

SOURCE 3

From *A true and exact relation of the severall informations, examinations, and confessions of the late witches, arraigned and executed in the county of Essex* (1645). Rebecca West's confession was read to the court from her original interrogation records.

The Confession of Rebecca West, taken before the said Justices at Manningtree, the 21st of March, 1645:

This Examinant sayeth, that about a month since, the aforesaid Anne Leech, Elizabeth Gooding, Hellen Clark, Anne West [other accused witches], and this Examinant, met all together at the house of the aforesaid Elizabeth Clark in Manningtree, where they together spent some time in praying unto their Familiars, and every one in order went to prayers; afterwards some of them read in a book, the book being Elizabeth Clarks; and this Examinant saith, that forthwith their Familiars appeared, and every one of them made their several Propositions to those Familiars, what every one of them desired to have effected: And this Examinant saith, that first of all the said Elizabeth Clark desired of her Spirit, that Mr. Edwards might be met withal about the middle bridge, as he should come riding from Eastberyhoult in Suffolk; that his Horse might be seared, and he thrown down, and never rise again: And this Examinant saith, that the said Elizabeth Gooding desired of her Spirit, that she might be avenged on Robert Tayler's Horse, for that the said Robert suspected the said Elizabeth Gooding for the killing of an Horse of the said Robert formerly: And this examinant saith, that the said Hellen Clark desired of her Spirit, that she might be revenged on two Hogs in Misley street, (being the place where the said Hellen lived) one of the Hogs to die presently, and the other to be taken lame; and this Examinant further saith, that Anne Leech desired of her Spirit, that a Cowe might be taken lame of a mans living in Manningtree, but the name of the man this Examinant cannot remember: And this examinant further saith, that the said Anne West, this Examinants mother, desired of her Spirit, that shee might be freed from all her enemies, and have no trouble: And this Examinant saith, that she desired of her Spirit, that she might be revenged on Prudence the wife of Thomas Hart, and that the said Prudence might be taken lame on her right side. And lastly this Examinant saith, that having thus done, this Examinant, and the other five, did appoint the next meeting to be at the said Elizabeth Goodings house, and so departed all to their own houses.

A Level Exam-Style Question Section A

Read Source 3 before answering the question.

Assess the value of the source for revealing the interrogation methods of witchfinders and the role of familiar spirits in witchcraft accusations.

Explain your answer, using the source, the information given about its origin and your own knowledge about the historical context. (20 marks)

Tip
Bear in mind that this is one short extract from a pamphlet that included a large amount of detail about the case, including evidence given by Hopkins and Stearne. It was written anonymously and printed in London, suggesting that there was interest in the case outside East Anglia.

From these modest beginnings, Hopkins and Stearne took the hunt to other parishes near Manningtree, on both sides of the Essex/Suffolk border. In July, trials were held at Chelmsford for the first batch of witches, and nearly 20 were found guilty, including Elizabeth Clark.

The two witchfinders spent much of the next two years apart, investigating accusations separately across East Anglia after initially moving north into Suffolk together. Over 120 were examined in Suffolk, including an 80-year-old Royalist clergyman, John Lowes, who had antagonised his parishioners at Brandeston. He had spoken in defence of Ann Annson, who had previously been accused of witchcraft, and he included a claim that she was as much of a witch as he was. This was interpreted by his parishioners as a confession of guilt, and Hopkins subjected him to the swimming test in the moat at Framlingham Castle, where he floated. After intense interrogation, he confessed to having made a pact with the Devil and keeping several familiars, the largest of which he named Thomas. He admitted to sinking a ship off the port of Harwich, which resulted in the deaths of 14 people, and he also admitted killing cattle with witchcraft.

SOURCE
4
From John Stearne, *A Confirmation and Discovery of Witchcraft* (1648).

Thus was Parson [John] Lowes taken, who had been a Minister (as I have heard) in one Parish above forty years, in Suffolk, before he was condemned, but had been indicted... for Witchcraft, above thirty years before, and the grand Jury... who now, after he was found with the marks, in his confession, he confessed, that in pride of heart, to be equal, or rather above God, the devil took advantage of him, and he covenanted with the Devil, and sealed it with his blood, and had three Familiars or spirits, which sucked on the marks found upon his body, and did much harm, both by Sea and Land, especially by Sea, for he confessed, that he being at Landguard Fort in Suffolk, where he preached, as he walked upon the wall, or works there, he saw a great sail of Ships pass by, and that as they were sailing by, one of his three Imps; namely his yellow one, forthwith appeared to him, and asked him what he should do, and he bade it go and sink such a ship, and showed his Imp a new Ship, amongst the middle of the rest (as I remember) one that belonged to Ipswich, so he confessed the Imp went forthwith away, and he stood still, and viewed the Ships on the Sea as they were sailing and perceived that Ship immediately, to be in more trouble and danger than the rest; for he said, the water was more boisterous near that than the rest, tumbling up and down with the waves, as if water had been boiled in a pot, and soon after (he said) in a short time it sank directly down into the Sea, as he stood and viewed it, when all the rest sailed away in safety, there he confessed, he had made fourteen widows in one quarter of an hour.

After leaving Suffolk, Hopkins was invited to Yarmouth, on the Norfolk coast, where he oversaw the questioning of several arrested witches. After their charges were brought successfully, he moved on to Aldeburgh, Yoxford, Westleton and Dunwich, where he uncovered more witches and took a fee from each local council. In Norfolk 40 women were tried at the assizes of 1645.

Eight women were tried in Huntingdonshire in 1646, and the campaign moved to Northamptonshire and Cambridgeshire, where witches from the towns of Kimbolton and St Neots were sent for examination. At Kimbolton – like so many other towns visited by the witch-hunters – accusations had been made previously but never followed up by legal action. A resident of the old priory there had been in conflict with a woman notorious for swearing and cursing, and she had been suspected of killing horses, cattle, pigs and ducks. Little is known about her case other than that Hopkins was directly involved. It was around this time that Hopkins and Stearne first faced a serious setback, when a local clergyman, John Gaule, objected to their presence in his community. The role of Gaule in ending the witch-hunt is discussed later in the chapter (see page 148).

Hopkins was then offered an invitation to help identify witches in the Norfolk port of King's Lynn and the surrounding villages. Stearne, meanwhile, was busy investigating reports in Ely. In the spring of 1647, Hopkins attended the Norfolk assizes and to his surprise was subjected to hostile questioning about his activities by officials who had become suspicious. His written defence, *The Discovery of Witches*, was published in May, while Stearne was still occupied with his investigations at Ely.

There is no particular geographical pattern to the accusations, and it seems that Hopkins and Stearne simply followed the money that was available to them in communities that already harboured resentment and suspicion of the women and men at their fringes.

SOURCE

Matthew Hopkins interrogating Elizabeth Clarke and Rebecca West, printed in *The Discovery of Witches* (1647).

Gender

A study by historian Louise Jackson of the 124 confirmed suspects from Suffolk has shown that the witch trials can be interpreted as organised and deliberate violence, exclusively carried out against women. Although around 20 percent of the accused in Suffolk were men, many of these were already associated with a female accused witch. The accusations made against the women often centred on female tasks and female spaces: the home, the kitchen, the nursery, feeding, etc. Across East Anglia, poor women were involved in dairy farming, and when things went wrong in the agricultural-domestic sphere, such as cream curdling or cattle falling ill, women were especially vulnerable to being accused.

Hopkins was particularly keen to find evidence of sexual activity with (the male) Devil and the suckling of imps, actions that were more likely to be associated with women. Margaret Baytes and Good Smith, two accused witches from Suffolk, included in their confessions that they fed imps from teats.

The murders of husbands and children are regularly referred to in the trials. Susanna Stegold was found guilty of killing her husband through witchcraft after an unhappy marriage, which almost certainly involved domestic violence inflicted by him. Prissilla Collit is one of a number of women who confessed after a period of sleep deprivation to killing her children, and approximately 20 percent of accused witches were charged with harming or killing children. Jackson has also argued that the prevalence of women accused is a reflection of men's expectations of them (Extract 2).

EXTRACT

2

From Louise Jackson, 'Witches, Wives and Mothers: witchcraft persecution and women's confessions in seventeenth-century England' in *Women's History Review* (1995).

The image or stereotype of the witch had been defined as the opposite of the good or godly woman (particularly in her roles as wife and mother). The Suffolk cases contain many references to nagging wives or lewd women, infanticide and child care. These cases clearly show that the accused women, in their confessions, were judging themselves as wives and mothers – they were judging their angers, their bitterness, their fears and their failures to live up to the expectation of others.

The Suffolk women who confessed that they were witches were also confessing that they were 'bad' mothers, 'bad' wives and 'bad' neighbours. The cultural, social and psychological impact of the county-wide witch-hunt cannot be over-estimated – the knowledge that 'witches' existed and were rife at home and abroad may well have caused every woman to examine her life very closely, and some to come forward and confess. Women's insecurities about their roles as wives and mothers were being played out within the context of the witchcraft confession.

Class

It is difficult to create a useful breakdown of the class and occupations of the suspected witches, as this information is only sporadically recorded in the court records. The records of the trials at Ely, for example, record one gentleman, one weaver, one smith, one miller, one yeoman, one labourer and two husbandmen, but others are not recorded. A wide variety of backgrounds and occupations are represented, but this is by no means an exhaustive or definitive list. One way in which class can be measured in the 17th century is through literacy, and the table in Figure 6.3 shows how each person involved in the Ely trials – witches and victims – signed their names.

If they only left their mark, they were almost certainly illiterate, and therefore not from the educated yeoman, gentry or merchant classes. Figure 6.4 shows the percentage of people who only left their mark in the surviving records from the Diocese of Norwich between 1580 and 1700 in order to aid comparison. All but one (94 percent) of the Ely witches left only their mark, and as six were male and 11 were female, this figure suggests that the men were certainly from the lower labouring class. Men were more likely to be literate than women in the 17th century – even in the higher echelons of society – which makes analysis of the women's backgrounds more difficult.

	Name signed	Left mark	No signature
Witch	1	15	1
Victim	3	11	0
Searcher	0	6	12
Witness	7	4	0
Total	11	36	13

Figure 6.3 Literacy of the accused witches, victims, searchers and witnesses at Ely. From F.V.A. Valletta, *Witchcraft, Magic and Superstition in England, 1640-1670* (2000).

Occupation	% left mark
Clergy	0
Gentry	2
Yeoman	35
Tradesman	44
Husbandman	79
Servants	82
Labourers	85
Women	89

Figure 6.4 Literacy levels in the Diocese of Norwich, from surviving Diocese records, 1580–1700. Adapted from David Cressy, 'Levels of literacy in England' in *Development in the West* (1981).

It is also important to note the backgrounds of the other people involved in the witch-hunt. From the Ely records, it is clear that the searchers were all illiterate, which reflects the surviving accounts of the craze that suggest most of the searchers – both men and women – were neighbours of the accused. The victims of the witches at Ely were more likely to be literate, reflecting the fact that many accusations came about after a poor woman was denied charity from a wealthier neighbour. The witnesses were much more likely to be literate, as they were often local landowners, clergy, or even Hopkins and Stearne themselves.

> **ACTIVITY**
> **KNOWLEDGE CHECK**
>
> **The victims**
>
> 1 Why were poor women particularly vulnerable to accusations?
>
> 2 Look at the tables in Figures 6.3 and 6.4. What do they tell us about the backgrounds of the witches, victims, searchers and witnesses?

The roles and methods of Hopkins and Stearne

The roles of Hopkins and Stearne

The investigations by Hopkins and Stearne were remarkably uniform and often followed the same procedures, and the two men fulfilled what were essentially vague roles in the process. Neither of the men held any qualifications that meant they could be categorised as trained witchfinders (not an official occupation but Hopkins styled himself as one), although they were both born into the Puritan tradition. The title of 'witchfinder general' used by Hopkins was not given to him by parliament, and seems to have been an invention of his own.

Despite their lack of qualifications and experience, they became very good at their work. They were able to make assessments of suspected witches quickly and efficiently before moving on to receive their next invitation. The parishes and town councils that received them paid Hopkins and Stearne, as well as the search-women and watchers, who were essential for carrying out their work. Expenses were also paid to the men, consisting of money for horses, lodgings and food. The men carried out interrogations, sometimes alone but most often with other local magistrates or officials, and there is evidence that they occasionally testified in court, although in many cases it is impossible to say whether they were present. There is no evidence to prove they were present at the executions of the witches, although this seems unlikely as their workload was extremely great for the duration of their relatively short-lived careers.

Ultimately, Hopkins and Stearne would only stay long enough in one location to set legal proceedings in motion, leaving others to continue the cases to trial.

Methods used by the witchfinders

The methods used by both witchfinders were remarkably effective, and were concerned with uncovering the following:

- the relationship between the suspected witch and the Devil, and how they first became initiated as a witch or came into contact with the Devil

- any marks that could be associated with witchcraft

- any imps or familiars given to the witch by the Devil or by other witches

- other witches known to the accused or members of their supposed coven.

The methods themselves consisted of the following.

- Initially, Hopkins and Stearne would aim to isolate the suspect for as long as possible, in order to make them disorientated and more likely to confess. This usually took place at the suspect's home or at the home of a neighbour.

- Search-women were employed to inspect the bodies of suspects for evidence of the Devil's mark. Their evidence was often presented in court.

- A favoured method of Hopkins was 'watching', whereby a suspect would be deprived of sleep and watched by a group of people working in shifts. This method was perhaps the most successful of all, but it was also controversial. When he published his own defence of the witch-hunt shortly before his death in 1647, Hopkins insisted that sleep deprivation had been discontinued as a method, but that watching was still an essential means of detection. He claimed that if some witches continued to stay awake through the process, it was only because they were not allowing themselves to fall asleep. In his account, he failed to acknowledge that the watched suspects were bound to a hard stool by their hands and feet.

- Other torture, although rarely mentioned in the official records, undoubtedly took place. The confessions of the Suffolk witches recorded by Stearne and the magistrates indicate that suspects had not only been starved of sleep but had also been subject to intimidation and physical violence. A woman from the village of Wattisham explained to a magistrate that she had received injuries to her forehead when one of her imps hurled her out of her chair while she was being watched by her interrogators. It is more likely that after days of sleep deprivation she was confused, possibly suffering from hallucinations. The magistrate was never able to ascertain precisely how she received her injuries.

- 'Walking' was another method utilised by the witchfinders, and was often used in conjunction with watching. Forcing the suspect to walk around a room constantly meant that they were more likely to stay awake and became more exhausted and willing to confess. Hopkins defends his use of walking in Source 6.

- Finally, the swimming test could be used. As we have seen, this was used on John Lowes in Suffolk, and it was seen as a cheap and persuasive method of proving guilt. It had an air of legitimacy because it had already been approved by King James I in *Daemonologie*. One of the suspected women of St Neots was subjected to this test when she was thrown off a bridge into a river by a mob. An innocent man volunteered to follow her into the water as a control, and she floated, signalling her guilt. Magistrates were often sceptical about the test, and her case was not immediately committed to trial. Instead, a party went to her house and carried out a search of her body, where no teats were found. Her fate is unknown, but John Stearne continued to seek witnesses against her.

SOURCE

6 From Matthew Hopkins, *The Discovery of Witches* (1647). In this extract, Hopkins defends the use of 'walking' as a method in discovering witches.

It was in the same beginning of this discovery, and the meaning of walking of them at the highest extent of cruelty, was only they to walke about themselves the night they were watched, only to keepe them waking: and the reason was this, when they did lye or sit in a chaire, if they did offer to crouch downe, then the watchers were only to desire them to sit up and walke about, for indeed when they be suffered so to crouch, immediately comes their Familiars into the room and scareth the watchers, and heartneth on the Witch, though contrary to the true meaning of the same instructions, diverse have been by rusticall People, (they hearing them confess to be Witches) mis-used, spoiled, and abused, diverse whereof have suffered for the same, but could never be proved against this Discoverer to have a hand in it, or consent to it; and hath likewise been un-used by him and others, ever since the time they were kept from sleepe.

ACTIVITY
KNOWLEDGE CHECK

The methods of Hopkins and Stearne

1 What were the roles of Hopkins and Stearne in bringing suspected witches to trial?

2 Which of the witchfinders' methods do you think was most successful in extracting confessions? Explain your answer.

3 Why did Hopkins and Stearne only need to spend a limited amount of time in each place?

The reasons for Hopkins' and Stearne's influence and power

Hopkins

Matthew Hopkins was ideally suited for his self-declared role of witchfinder general, as the son of a Puritan clergyman, James Hopkins, and from good social standing. Very little is known about the life of Matthew Hopkins, apart from the events of 1645–47 and the circumstances of his death. He was likely born around 1620, meaning he was probably around 25 when he began his career as a witch-hunter and no older than 28 when he died. His father had been minister at Great Wenham in Suffolk, and died in 1634, when Hopkins was in his early teens. His father was liked and respected by his congregation, and raised his children in the strictest ways of godliness.

Hopkins had two older brothers, so from an early age he was well aware that he would never inherit the family estate, and would instead have to pursue a career in trade, law or in the clergy. It is not known which of these professions he set his sights on in the early 1640s, but he came into some inheritance and was able to establish himself as a gentleman in Manningtree. Historian Malcolm Gaskill has suggested that as an outsider newly arrived in the town, Hopkins was in an ideal position to investigate the memories and myths of Manningtree from an objective perspective, and locals may have sought him out as someone who could make a neutral judgement on suspected witches.

There is evidence that contemporaries came to believe that parliament (or its representative) had appointed Hopkins as their agent with an official commission to discover witches. In such dangerous times, there is no doubt that he and Stearne would have required letters of safe-passage from a high power in order to avoid being apprehended by either side. Many of their activities were conducted after they had received written invitations, and their journey mirrored that of William Dowsing, the Parliamentarian soldier who had been appointed 'Iconoclast General', tasked with seeking out statues and idols associated with Catholicism. He travelled throughout East Anglia in 1643–44, and it may be that Hopkins and Stearne had official backing to follow up his work in seeking out evil and superstition. Either way, Dowsing's journey mapped areas that would be receptive to their work and areas where they were likely to encounter resistance.

Despite the potential for official backing, the title 'Witchfinder General' was first used only on the cover of Hopkins' work, *The Discovery of Witches*, published in 1647, and may have been an invention of his publisher. It seems most likely that Hopkins was able to possess such considerable influence and power because he was in the right place at the right time. Here was a young man, a Puritan with an enthusiasm for tackling evil, who presented himself as a saviour at a time when East Anglia was riddled with economic and political crisis.

Stearne

Even less is known about the life of John Stearne. We do know that he was older than Hopkins, and was in his mid-30s during the craze. He grew up in rural Suffolk, and was married to Agnes Cawston. They had a daughter, Anne, who was baptised in 1644 and Stearne must have spent much time away from his young family while he was involved in witchfinding. He was also a Puritan, and we know from his only surviving written account that he had a good working knowledge of Scripture. He lived significantly longer than Hopkins and died in 1670.

Although Hopkins is most often referred to as the senior partner in the operation, it was Stearne who first received a warrant to search suspected witches from the Manningtree magistrates Sir Harbottle Grimston and Sir Thomas Bowes. It seems that Hopkins then volunteered to assist him. It is not known why Stearne was in Manningtree in 1645, but he did maintain a house there so it would be logical to conclude that he was engaged in business of some sort. Stearne was passionate about witchfinding from the outset, and suggested at the beginning of the hunt that the elderly Elizabeth Clark be subjected to the swimming test, although this was probably blocked by the magistrates.

Malcolm Gaskill has suggested that Hopkins and Stearne did not believe themselves to have significant power, and instead acted as facilitators who simply assisted accusers and gave them the confidence to pursue suspects (Extract 3).

EXTRACT

3 From Malcolm Gaskill, *Witchfinders: A Seventeenth-Century English Tragedy* (2006).

Hopkins and Stearne were not commanders-in-chief of the witch-hunt: they were catalysts who gave accusers confidence by confirming their suspicions and beliefs. In their books they were emphatic that *they* had never accused anyone of anything: they went only to places where they were invited, and applied their expertise to suspects identified by the inhabitants. There was truth in this. It was for the searchers and watchers appointed by their own parishes to decide whether there were grounds to prosecute, and for victims and their allies to choose whether to go to law. Thereafter the progress of a prosecution depended on the consideration of a godly magistrate (and sometimes a minister), and even then proceedings might still be thwarted by a grand jury, after that by a trial jury under the guidance of a judge. Even if a suspect were convicted and condemned, according to Scripture and the statute of King James I it was no more than he or she deserved. They were witchfinders and proud of it but cunning folk, searchers, watchers and witnesses – likewise justices, jurors and judges – were witchfinders as well.

ACTIVITY
KNOWLEDGE CHECK

The influence of Hopkins and Stearne

1 Why do you think Hopkins and Stearne were able to become so influential? Did they possess any qualities that made them ideally suited to witch-hunting?

2 How could it be argued that Hopkins' and Stearne's success was due to their being in the right place at the right time?

A Level Exam-Style Question Section B

'The unique political and economic situation in East Anglia accounts for the extent of witch persecutions in the years 1645–47.'

How far do you agree with this explanation of the East Anglian witch craze of 1645–47? (20 marks)

Tip
The roles of Hopkins and Stearne should be balanced against the factors given in the question.

WHY DID THE WITCH CRAZE COME TO AN END IN 1647?

The growing cost

Every aspect of the witch-hunt resulted in various costs, including the following.

- Imprisonment was a vast expense, at around three pence, per prisoner, per day. The witches imprisoned at Ipswich, for example, cost up to £50 to keep while they waited for their date at the assize court. The jailer at Ipswich complained that he was suffering financially because money collected to keep the suspects was never enough.

- Feeding prisoners became an issue as more and more were detained on charges of witchcraft. At Bury St Edmunds, an officer was appointed specifically to collect bread-money for the witches detained in the gaol. Those who had enjoyed watching the executions of John Lowes and the other Suffolk witches now had to pay for the privilege.

- The assizes themselves were also expensive. A sheriff was required to find funds and accommodation for the judges, as well as providing horses, heat and food for the officers, administrators and the witchfinders themselves. The meat list for one assize court included beef, veal, lamb, duck, pike, carp and salmon. The judge at the 1645 trial at Bury St Edmunds, John Godbold, sent an invoice for a staggering £130 to cover his and his assistant's costs.

- Executions themselves carried a huge cost. One of the witches executed at Yarmouth, Mary Lakeland, was burned for murdering her husband, at a cost three times higher than it would have been to hang her. Over £3 was spent on her execution alone. In Suffolk, churchwardens and overseers of the poor were instructed to collect a new levy to pay for the searching and trying of witches.

- Finally, the fees demanded by Hopkins and Stearne became controversial. They inevitably had to stay in inns, and the upkeep of horses and the paying of search-women and watchers also incurred expense. Hopkins complained that he and his assistants would have to travel many miles to investigate a case and would be paid just 20 shillings (around a month's wages for a labourer).

Hopkins and Stearne were eager to claim that their services were good value for money, as Sources 7 and 8 show, and they continued to maintain that they took just 20 shillings for each visit. Official records show that the fees paid to the witchfinders were considerably higher than this, however. Hopkins helped to convict seven witches at Aldeburgh, and in February 1646, the corporation treasurer settled his accounts. Together with his search-woman, Mary Phillips, he accumulated a bill of £6 over two visits. The gaoler received £2, while a local innkeeper was paid £15 for supplying food and drink during the trial. A carpenter was paid £1 for erecting the gallows and the executioner 11 shillings. In total, the witch-hunt cost Aldeburgh more than £40. This constituted one-seventh of the town's entire annual budget, and a special tax was raised to pay for the investigations.

SOURCE

From Matthew Hopkins, *The Discovery of Witches* (1647). The following dialogue is based on genuine questions Hopkins was asked at the Norfolk assizes.

Query:

All that the witch-finder doth is to fleece the country of their money, and therefore rides and goes to towns to have employment, and promiseth them fair promises, and it may be doth nothing for it, and possesseth many men that they have so many wizards and so many witches in their town, and so heartens them on to entertain him.

Answer:

You do him a great deal of wrong in every of these particulars. For, first,

1. He never went to any town or place, but they rode, writ, or sent often for him, and were (for ought he knew) glad of him.

2. He is a man that doth disclaim that ever he detected a witch, or said, Thou art a witch; only after her trial by search, and their own confessions, he as others may judge.

3. Lastly, judge how he fleeceth the Country, and enriches himself, by considering the vast sum he takes of every town, he demands but 20 shillings a town, & doth sometimes ride 20 miles for that, & hath no more for all his charges thither and back again (& it may be stays a week there) and find there 3 or 4 witches, or if it be but one, cheap enough, and this is the great sum he takes to maintain his company with 3 horses.

SOURCE

8   From John Stearne, *A Confirmation and Discovery of Witchcraft* (1648).

Now whosoever thou be that thinks I ever made such gain of the way, or favoured any, and persecuted others, or took bribes, I call God to witness, that considering the charge of going to several places, and Assizes, and Gaol-deliveries, and the time I expended thereabouts, I never, one time with another, got so much as I did by my Calling and Practice, towards the maintenance of my family.

And as for taking any money or other thing, by way of bribe or gift, I never did, to the value of one penny, neither one way nor other, but what I openly took the view of the Townsmen where I came; and that in many places I never received penny as yet, nor any am like, notwithstanding I have hands for satisfaction, except I should sue; but many rather fall upon me for what has been received: but I hope such suits will be disannulled, and that where I have been out moneys for Towns in charges and otherwise, such course will be taken, that I may be satisfied and paid with reason. And in truth, concerning him who is dead [Hopkins], who likewise was an agent in the business, for my part, I never knew that he either unjustly favoured any, or received bribes, or used such extremity as was reported of him; only at first, before he or I ever went, many Towns used extremity of themselves, which after was laid against us.

But to my knowledge, we have been both much injured in words, and he since his death: but I am certain (notwithstanding whatsoever has been said of him) he died peaceably at Manningtree, after a long sickness of a Consumption, as many of his generation had done before him, without any trouble of conscience for what he had done, as was falsely reported of him. And though many of these things may seem very strange, and hardly to be believed, yet this is the very truth; and that he was the son of a godly Minister, and therefore without doubt within the Covenant. Therefore let no man take upon him either to speak or write more than he knows to be the truth; for this I am able to manifest and prove to be truth. And so I leave myself to the censure of the world, yet desire it might be left to the Almighty, who knows the secrets of all hearts: For, blessed are they that do his commandments.

At the end of 1647, John Stearne's witch-hunt was over and his partner Hopkins was dead (probably of tuberculosis). He was able to return home to his wife, who was expecting their second child, but he must have known that the brief golden age of East Anglian witch-hunting was over. Judges and juries were now reluctant to convict suspects, and across the region – but particularly in Suffolk – the cost of keeping and prosecuting witches was simply too high to warrant further investigations. Critics of both the cost and the nature of the hunt began making their voices heard, and with funds still required to finance the war effort, witch-hunting was viewed as an unnecessary luxury.

A number of debts owed to Stearne for his work were never called in, suggesting that he was aware of the futility of pursuing them. Lawsuits had been filed against him to overturn wrongful convictions, and there is also evidence that he was taken to court in order to recover fees.

ACTIVITY
KNOWLEDGE CHECK

The growing cost
Why were town and parish authorities more reluctant to pay Hopkins and Stearne for their services in 1646 and 1647?

The re-establishment of traditional authority

As the cost of witch-hunting spiralled, an element of traditional authority was returned to East Anglia. The majority of fighting ceased when Charles surrendered to the Scots at Newark in May 1646, and East Anglia was safe enough to receive the assize judges more regularly. By late summer, more and more suspected witches were beginning to be acquitted.

Although parliament maintained control of the country, many Royalist gentry were able to return to their estates in East Anglia, and began to punish their tenants and servants if they had been involved in fighting for parliament. Even clergy who had been accused of being Royalist sympathisers were beginning to take up new livings across the region. The Puritan-dominated pursuit of witches was now being disturbed by the previously established authorities.

SOURCE

This woodcut from an anonymous pamphlet entitled *Dogs Elegy, or Ruperts Tears for the late defeat given him at Marston Moor, where his beloved dog, named Boy was killed by a valiant soldier* presents Prince Rupert's dog as a witch's familiar that was reputedly killed with a silver bullet. The association between Royalism and witchcraft had never been clearer.

The end of the Civil War meant some relief to the suffering of the population, although harvests would continue to be poor for the next few years. It is in this context that acquittals became more likely, and the authorities in towns and parishes were not as fearful as they had been, and were not in need of scapegoats as they had been previously. Two cases towards the end of 1646 signified that traditional authority had been restored in East Anglia and that Hopkins' and Stearne's days as witchfinders were numbered.

- First, Hopkins visited King's Lynn on 24 September to give evidence against nine accused witches he had interrogated. The judge at this trial was Miles Corbett, who had found a number of witches guilty at Yarmouth the previous year. In an effort to signal their authority, the mayor and aldermen of the town were in attendance, as well as the JPs. All prisoners – eight women and one man – pleaded not guilty, and after evidence given by Hopkins, searchers and watchers, the jury retired to consider their verdict. Seven of the suspects were acquitted and two were convicted. Hopkins was given £2 for his testimony and departed from the town promptly.

- The second case occurred two days later, when three witches were tried at the assize court at Ely. Again, the judge, John Godbold, had experience of witchcraft trials, as he had acted as special commissioner at Bury St Edmunds the previous summer. All three women were acquitted, possibly at the direction of Godbold.

At the Norfolk assizes of 1647, which tried several of Hopkins' and Stearne's cases, the presiding judges were given a list of questions compiled by a number of leading gentry who had taken issue with aspects of the witch-hunt. These questions were influenced by the scepticism presented by John Gaule in his book (discussed on page 148). We know what most of the questions were because they were repeated as queries Hopkins responded to in his *Discovery of Witches*, and Hopkins must have been increasingly desperate to defend his reputation as he made it clear that this work was based on his answers in court and it was addressed to the assize judges of Norfolk. The questions and statements made to Hopkins included the following.

- Was Hopkins himself a witch, because he had a great knowledge of sorcery?

- Did Hopkins meet with the Devil and receive the Devil's Book, which included a list of all the witches in England?

- Where did Hopkins acquire his skills?

- Why are so many people condemned for having strange marks on their bodies, when most of these marks can be explained naturally?

- If the Devil is a spirit, how can he or his familiars desire to suck the blood of witches?

- Both watching and walking are unreasonable methods of investigation, and will make people say anything.

- The swimming test is not allowed by law, so why did Hopkins insist on using it?

- Believing that witches and the Devil have the power to kill and maim is blasphemous because God has the power to place limits on the Devil and believing in witches suggests a lack of faith in God's power.

The questions were clearly well prepared and critical, and according to Hopkins' book, he had an answer for each of them, although we will never know if he was able to answer so eloquently in court.

ACTIVITY
KNOWLEDGE CHECK

The re-establishment of traditional authority

1 Create a flow chart or storyboard to explain the movements of Hopkins and Stearne in 1647. Did any of their actions encourage resentment against witch-hunting?

2 Why did the end of the Civil War result in a renewed scepticism of witch-hunting in East Anglia?

The role of John Gaule

The work of Hopkins and Stearne came to the attention of John Gaule, the minister of Great Staughton, in mid-1646. His parish lay between St Neots and Kimbolton, where a number of suspected witches had been investigated. Gaule was well aware that his parishioners were increasingly blaming witches for their misfortunes, and he believed instead that their own sins were to blame. He had heard about the recent confessions at Huntingdon, and visited one of the detained suspects to hear her account of what had happened to her. The visit does not seem to have convinced him that the witchfinders were doing noble work.

Gaule published his criticisms of the witchfinders in his *Select Cases of Conscience touching Witches and Witchcrafts* in 1646. Here, Gaule made a number of key points.

- He affirmed the existence of witches and noted his approval of witch-hunting, but criticised the methods of Hopkins and Stearne.

- He pleaded for common sense and restraint in following up accusations of witchcraft, and stressed that witchfinding should be carried out in a meticulous and cautious way.

- He even alleged that the craze for witchfinding was becoming idolatrous. He complained that people in East Anglia were praising the witchfinders more than they praised God, Christ and the Bible.

SOURCE 10

From John Gaule, *Select Cases of Conscience touching Witches and Witchcrafts* (1646).

Having taken the suspected Witch, shee is placed in the middle of a room upon a stool, or Table, crosse legg'd, or in some other uneasie posture, to which if she submits not, she is then bound with cords, there is she watched & kept without meat or sleep for the space of 24 hours. For (they say) within that time they shall see her Impe come and suck; a little hole is likewise made in the door for the Impe to come in at: and lest it might come in some lesse discernible shape, they that watch are taught to be ever & anon sweeping the room, and if they see any spiders or flyes, to kill them. And if they cannot kill them, then they may be sure they are her Impes.

Gaule seems to have had some communication with the witchfinders, and in his publication he criticised the process of watching witches after it had been explained to him (Source 10). In his publication, Gaule also reprinted a letter from Hopkins to an anonymous parishioner of Gaule's, known only as 'M.N.', stating that he would not visit Great Staughton without a better welcome (Source 11).

SOURCE 11

A letter from Matthew Hopkins to 'M.N.', reprinted in John Gaule, *Select Cases of Conscience touching Witches and Witchcrafts* (1646).

My service to your Worship presented, I have this day received a Letter – to come to a Towne called Great Staughton to search for evill disposed persons called Witches (though I heare your Minister [Gaule] is far against us through ignorance). I intend to come (God willing) the sooner to heare his singular Judgement on behalf of such parties; I have known a Minister in Suffolke preach as much against their discovery in a Pulpit, and forc'd to recant it (by the Committee) in the same place. I much marvaile such evill Members should have any (much more any of the Clergy who should daily preach Terrour to convince such Offenders) stand up to take their parts against such as are Complainant for the King, and sufferers themselves with their Families and Estates.

KEY TERMS

Conservative
Someone who is averse to change and holds traditional values.

Episcopacy
The hierarchy of bishops that controlled the Church of England.

From his writings, it is clear that Gaule was a **conservative**. He noted privately his anger that the **episcopacy** had been eroded and replaced with independent churches during the Civil War, and how churches were being used as stables, and stables used as churches. He was particularly aggrieved, therefore, that the witchfinders had assumed authority where in reality they had none.

As well as his writings, Gaule launched a campaign of preaching in Great Staughton against the witchfinders. As well as interviewing imprisoned witches, he spoke to his parishioners about their views on the craze. In one sermon, he asked his congregation to consider how unlikely it was that every witch that had been convicted had a genuine connection with the Devil. He told his audience that even confessions should not be taken at face value, and that the evaluation of evidence should only be carried out by magistrates, and not by private individuals calling themselves witchfinders.

Although Gaule's attacks on the witchfinders may not have gained much support initially, his work helped to convince the authorities, and especially judges, that the witch-hunt was no longer necessary as traditional authority was re-established and the costs of the investigations spiralled ever further.

ACTIVITY
KNOWLEDGE CHECK

John Gaule

Were Gaule's opinions on the witchfinders revolutionary? Explain your answer.

Conclusion: Why was the craze so widespread?

Although the witch-hunt lasted only two years, the intensity of the persecutions was unique in England. As with all historical events, a number of factors working in unison help to explain why the craze took hold so quickly and why Hopkins and Stearne were welcomed by communities before ultimately being rejected by them.

- It was a time of extreme economic hardship, as problems of poor weather and inflation combined with the effects of the Civil War. As harvests became less fruitful and soldiers required more food and supplies, people began to seek scapegoats. Those who were better off began to resent the increased begging of those at the bottom of society. Even at the end of the Civil War, the economic situation had not improved much, but as East Anglia returned to more effective central control, it was more difficult to pursue legal cases against witches.

- There was a breakdown of the traditional authority that was usually exercised by the Crown, gentry and clergy. Across East Anglia, clergy that were sympathetic to the Royalist cause were removed from their livings and were replaced with Puritans. The connection made by Puritans between Royalists, Catholics, superstition and witchcraft meant that those who had long been suspected of sorcery were now targeted.

- The craze would not have become as widespread as it did without the breakdown of the traditional legal system. There were isolated accusations against witches in the 1620s and 30s, but they rarely went to trial, and when they did other suspects were generally not interrogated. The assize courts, seen as more incorruptible and staffed by more experienced judges than local magistrates, were interrupted and it was difficult for assize judges to keep to their usual timetables. This meant that men like Hopkins and Stearne, as well as local magistrates such as Sir Harbottle Grimston and Sir Thomas Bowes, could wield significant power over cases of witchcraft with minimal accountability. When the traditional legal system was restored at the end of the war, there was less need for men like Hopkins and Stearne.

- There is no doubt that Hopkins and Stearne played a significant role in beginning the craze and ensuring it became widespread. The fact that the leading critic of the witchfinders, John Gaule, singled out Hopkins for blame suggests that his personal role was great. The fact that the end of the persecutions coincides with Hopkins' death in August 1647 also emphasises his personal role. The techniques used in interrogations were almost exclusively associated with Hopkins and Stearne, and the success of searching, sleep deprivation, walking and swimming can be associated with them. After Hopkins' death, Stearne played a significant role in initiating further persecutions, despite the growing pressure from critics and the courts to end the witch-hunt.

Questions and answers

Questions that historians ask vary depending on what they think is important. It is the questions that interest us that define the history that is written. These questions change with time and place. Different historians will also come up with different answers to the same questions, depending on their perspectives and methods of interpretation, as well as the evidence they use.

Work in groups of between three and six. Read the information in the tables below about the three historians and the key events in the East Anglian witch craze. Then answer the following questions.

Three historians who had different areas of interest:

Thomas Macaulay	Christopher Hill	Sir Charles Firth
A political historian who lived in the 19th century. He was interested in the idea that great men shape history.	An economic and political historian who lived in the 20th century. He was interested in the role of the lower classes and the economy and how they contributed to historical change.	A military historian who lived in the late 19th and early 20th centuries. He was very interested in the minute detail of history including how armies were organised and what tactics they used.

Some key events in the East Anglian witch craze:

Matthew Hopkins first hears about witches in his home town of Manningtree.	The first witch, Elizabeth Clark, is interrogated.	John Stearne is first given a warrant to investigate witchcraft.
80-year-old clergyman John Lowes is executed after defending a suspected witch.	John Gaule begins to preach and write against the witchfinders.	The Civil War ends, restoring some traditional authority in East Anglia.
Matthew Hopkins dies.	The inexperienced Earl of Warwick acts as a judge at the Essex assizes.	A succession of wet summers results in poor harvests.

1. Which of the events would have been of most interest to each historian? Explain your answer.

2. Each take the role of one historian and devise a question that would interest them about each of the events.

3. Discuss each event in turn. Present the questions that have been devised for each historian and offer some ideas about how they would have answered them.

4. For each event, decide as a group which question is the most interesting and worthwhile of the three.

Answer the following questions in pairs.

5. Identify the different ways that each historian would approach writing an account of the beginning of the witch craze in East Anglia.

6. In what ways would Macaulay and Hill differ in their explanations of the significance of the craze? What would be the focus of their arguments?

Answer the following questions individually.

7. All three historians may produce very different accounts and explanations of the same piece of history. Of the three historians, whose account would you prefer to read first? Explain your answer.

8. Do the differences in these accounts mean that one is more valid than the others?

9. Explain why different historical explanations are written by different historians.

10. Explain why different explanations of the same event can be equally valid.

ACTIVITY
SUMMARY

The beginning and end of the East Anglia witch craze

1 Create two pieces of writing, based on the opinions of contemporaries at the start and end of the witch-hunt.

   a) The first should be a speech made by a Puritan clergyman to his congregation at the start of the craze in 1645. It should outline how the craze came about and why you feel your parishioners should support Hopkins and Stearne in their work.

   b) The second should be a letter written by the critic John Gaule to the MPs assembled at Westminster in 1647. You should argue that the witch-hunt should be stopped immediately and explain why you feel Hopkins and Stearne are no longer required by the people of East Anglia.

2 Create a list of reasons why the craze became so widespread and a list of reasons why it went into decline so quickly. Choose one reason on each list that you feel is the most significant and explain why you have chosen it.

WIDER READING

Gaskill, M. *Witchfinders*, Murray (2005). Both comprehensive and accessible, and provides context to the craze, as well as detailed coverage of the journeys of Hopkins and Stearne.

Hopkins, M. *The Discovery of Witches* (1647). A relatively short piece but provides justification for Hopkins' actions. Can be found on www.gutenberg.org.

Pavlac, B. *Witch Hunts in the Western World*, Greenwood (2010). Provides a concise summary of the entire case.

Stearne, J. *A Confirmation and Discovery of Witchcraft* (1648). Longer than Hopkins' work and less accessible, but provides an overview in Stearne's own words of the entire witch-hunt. Can be found on www.archive.org.

3.7 Cotton Mather and the Salem witch-hunt, 1692–93

KEY QUESTIONS

- How far were social, economic and political issues responsible for the Salem witch-hunt?
- To what extent did accusations lead to a widespread witch-hunt?
- Why did the witch-hunt come to an end?

INTRODUCTION

Colonial witch-hunts

At the same time as witch-hunting was flourishing in Britain, the British Empire began its rise. Although the British conquered lands in Africa and Asia, and witchcraft beliefs were widespread in these areas, it is in North America that the greatest fear of witches was to be found. In the early 17th century, two British colonies emerged on the east coast: in Virginia, where the first British settlement was created at Jamestown in 1607, and in Massachusetts to the north, first settled in 1620.

The two colonies followed different religious traditions.

- In Virginia, and later in the colony of Maryland (founded in 1632), Catholic refugees were welcomed, and the colonies became a haven for those that followed **high church** traditions.

- The first settlers to arrive at Massachusetts on the *Mayflower* in 1620 were Puritans, and when they established the Massachusetts Bay Colony in 1629, it was established on Puritan principles. Like the Puritans involved in the East Anglian witch-hunt of 1645–47, they were particularly mindful that the Devil was ever-present and attempting to entice people into becoming witches.

The Puritans of Massachusetts were more militant than those in England, and while asserting their own religious liberties, they refused to tolerate people of other religious denominations. Every aspect of life in Massachusetts followed strict religious principles, and the clergy were highly respected. Preachers spoke out against the use of magic, and offered prayers, fasting and deeper religious devotion as solutions. As was the case in Europe, colonists worried about acts of *maleficium* that caused harm, but there was confusion between this and the diabolical pact.

The first official witch to be executed in the colonies was Alice Young, who was hanged in 1647 in Connecticut. Twenty-seven more were hanged before the Salem trials of 1692, but many more were subject to whipping, fines or exile.

KEY TERM

High church
A tradition within the Church of England that emphasised ritual, the authority of bishops, sacraments and much continuity with Catholic practices.

1688 – Glorious Revolution in England weakens authorities in the North American colonies

1689 – Cotton Mather publishes work on witchcraft and demonic possession

| 1685 | 1686 | 1687 | 1688 | 1689 | 1690 | 1691 |

1686–89 – Massachusetts is incorporated into the Dominion of New England

1689 – Governor Edmund Andros is arrested during the Boston Revolt

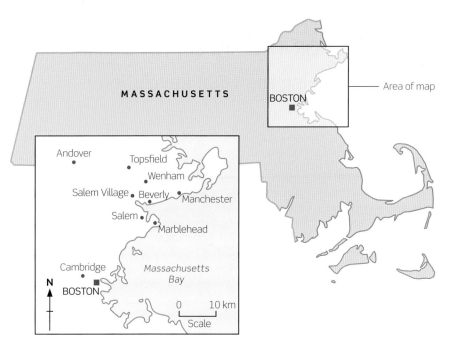

Figure 7.1 The location of Salem within the Massachusetts Bay Colony. Note that many of the accusers came from Salem Village, three hours' walk from Salem town itself.

The importance of Salem

Salem is the most famous, most studied and most deadly of all British colonial witch-hunts. Twenty people lost their lives as a result of the hunt, but before 1692, witch-hunting was not common in New England. Only around 100 cases had been heard in the previous 50 years, and only about 25 percent of these had resulted in executions. In the majority of these cases, the suspected witch was someone who was already the subject of resentment from their neighbours, but in Salem anyone could be accused. The hunt at Salem went out of control in the same way that events in East Anglia, Bamberg and North Berwick had in the preceding century.

More than 200 people were accused of practising witchcraft at Salem and 20 were killed as a result. The craze has been intensely studied and many historians agree that it came about as a result of fear and scapegoating, but became particularly widespread because the events were acted out in a relatively small, isolated community. Because the community was so isolated, the people had a heightened sense of fear – particularly of the Devil – and when one woman, Tituba, confessed to practising magic, panic and hysteria ensued. Tensions between older settlers and newcomers, and between wealthier and poorer residents, fuelled the craze further.

1692 – Salem witch-hunt begins when a number of girls suffer symptoms of possession

1692 – The majority of witch trials take place

1697 – Judge Samuel Sewall apologises for his role in the witch-hunt

| 1692 | 1693 | 1694 | 1695 | 1696 | 1697 | 1698 |

1693 – Governor Phips issues a general pardon

HOW FAR WERE SOCIAL, ECONOMIC AND POLITICAL ISSUES RESPONSIBLE FOR THE SALEM WITCH-HUNT?

Weakened authority following the 1688 Revolution

Massachusetts Bay Colony government: 1630–85

The first settlers to arrive in Salem set sail from England in April 1630. One of the earliest voyages included Governor John Winthrop and nearly 800 colonists. Winthrop carried with him a colonial charter stating that the colony was a possession of the Crown. The 1630s were a difficult time for England's Puritans, as Charles I and his Archbishop of Canterbury, William Laud, were pursuing high church policies and punishing radicals in the **Star Chamber**. Perhaps 10,000 Puritans migrated to Massachusetts between 1630 and 1642.

The colony's economy became stronger in the 1640s and 50s, and increasingly successful trade in fur and lumber, as well as a flourishing fishing industry, led to the growth of a merchant class. Despite the progress that had been made, the government of Massachusetts was still dominated by Puritans, and the colony became resistant to Charles II's (1660–85) attempts to allow the Church of England to become established. Puritanism was central to government and society in places like Salem, and residents were required to pay taxes to the church although it was not compulsory to be a member. Members of the Puritan church were given the exclusive right to vote for local officials, and non-Puritans could be banished from the colony for spreading dissent.

Charles II was concerned with extending royal influence over his colonies by centralising control in the hands of the royal court, and Massachusetts became the most resistant of all colonies. Attempts were made by Charles to revoke the royal charter in 1678 and 1681 and consolidate all New England colonies into one in order to centralise control, but as a result of resistance from the Puritan authorities, the charter was not formally annulled until 1684.

The reign of James II and governorship of Sir Edmund Andros

Charles II died in 1685 and was succeeded by his Catholic brother, James II. From 1686, James was able to administer all of the New England colonies as the Dominion of New England, which was governed by Sir Edmund Andros. Although he had experience as a soldier and had acted as bailiff of Guernsey, his high church tendencies and unwillingness to include well-established local Puritans on his council made him unpopular.

EXTEND YOUR KNOWLEDGE

Dominion of New England
James II was apprehensive about the amount of independence the New England colonies had received, and was also concerned about the military threat posed by the French and the native tribes that came into regular conflict with English settlers. All the New England colonies, which included Massachusetts, Plymouth Colony, Rhode Island, Connecticut and New Hampshire, were consolidated in 1686 under the control of a single governor as the Dominion of New England.

For the English, the unification of the northern colonies was viewed as a sensible measure, but it was viewed with resentment by many of the Puritan settlers. It is no surprise that the Dominion experienced little success, and when the colonists saw an opportunity to end it after the Glorious Revolution, they wasted no time.

A number of Andros' policies contributed to his fall and the subsequent lack of authority after the Glorious Revolution of 1688.

- He attempted to fulfil the late Charles II's wish for Church of England services to be delivered in Puritan churches. Many of the Puritans of Massachusetts suspected him not only of high church Anglicanism, but of having Catholic sympathies.

- He introduced new taxes, particularly focusing on import and export duties. Since Massachusetts had no previous tax laws, this created severe resentment, but was necessary as the colony was becoming a drain on the English Exchequer.

- All landownership titles issued under the now defunct Massachusetts Bay Colony were declared void, and the Puritan landowners were required to pay fees in order to challenge and take back ownership. Much of the money collected through these fees was required to pay for fortifications against the increased Indian attacks that blighted Salem.

- Finally, he restricted the number of town meetings that could be held, as these were often sources of discontent.

The Glorious Revolution

In April 1687, James II issued a Declaration of Indulgence in England, suspending the existing penal laws against Catholics. This unpopular move was followed by him dissolving parliament in the summer and thus increasing opposition from the political establishment. After seven bishops refused to read another Declaration of Indulgence in May 1688, their acquittal after they were arrested was met with public rejoicing. Seven leading figures from the political nation, terrified at the prospect of a Catholic heir after James' wife finally fell pregnant, sent an invitation to William of Orange to bring a force against James.

William arrived, and in December 1688, James fled the country. A Convention Parliament was established in January 1689, and it declared that William would rule jointly with his wife, Mary, the Protestant daughter of James. They were presented with a Declaration of Rights, which affirmed a number of constitutional principles, such as the prohibition of unparliamentary taxation and the need for regular parliaments. Pressure from William ensured that a Toleration Act was passed in May 1689, granting many Protestant groups, but not Catholics, religious freedom.

Meanwhile, James attempted to amass a force in Ireland in order to take back the throne, which led to William leading an army against him at the Battle of the Boyne in 1690, which resulted in victory for William's forces.

Impact of the Revolution on Massachusetts

News of the Revolution reached Massachusetts in April 1689, and the colonists of Boston – who already felt immense resentment against James and his agents – revolted against Governor Andros. The revolt began with a number of clandestine meetings of leading Puritans in Boston, and when a messenger arrived with news of the Glorious Revolution in England, Andros had him arrested, although the news spread quickly regardless. In the meantime, a militia from Massachusetts assembled by Andros mutinied in fear that they were being used in a **popish plot**.

KEY TERM

Popish plot
A conspiracy to replace the Protestant authorities with Catholics.

The rebels were led by a father and son, Increase and Cotton Mather, who were both well-known ministers. Increase Mather's predominant role in Puritan Massachusetts meant that he was ideally suited to lead negotiations in England over a new charter, and he spent the years 1688–92 in London advocating on behalf of the colony. Between 1689 and 1692, one of Mather's allies, Simon Bradstreet, acted as governor. When Mather returned to Massachusetts in May 1692 with a new governor, Sir William Phips, the Salem witch-hunt had already begun.

On 18 April 1689, rebellious militia companies began arresting officials in and around Boston and surrounded Andros' residence at Fort Mary. The rebels declared that they were supporters of William of Orange and had no choice but to act in the face of the rumoured popish plot by Andros, who was originally appointed by James II. Andros attempted to flee by boat, but was captured and taken into custody. He was eventually sent to England to face trial, although he later became colonial governor of Virginia.

The various colonies within the Dominion were able to restore their own charters, but Massachusetts was a more difficult issue to settle. It was governed immediately after the revolt by a council comprising Andros' former agents, as well as former leaders of the colony and some high-profile Puritans. Eventually, in October 1691, Massachusetts was given a new charter and was now known as the Province of Massachusetts Bay.

King William was fearful that Massachusetts could once again fall into religious rule, and so enforced the following.

- Voting eligibility was now based on property ownership rather than religious denomination.

- All officials were to be appointed by the Crown rather than elected.

- The governor could block any laws passed by the council.

In this context, it is easy to see why the residents of Salem felt their way of life had been disturbed by outside forces, and the revolt that had removed their apparently oppressive governor, Edmund Andros, had resulted in few changes. With less representation from local Puritan leaders, problems and disputes in the community could not be settled as easily and there was a lack of legal authority. As things started to go wrong, the majority-Puritan population saw the Devil at work.

ACTIVITY
KNOWLEDGE CHECK

The impact of revolution and revolt

1 Why was Sir Edmund Andros resented by the people of Massachusetts? Why did he cause the revolt of 1689?

2 Why did the Glorious Revolution in England cause problems in New England?

3 Why did weakened authority make a witch-hunt more likely?

Indian threats and economic crisis

Indian threats

Until the mid-1980s, historians generally discounted Indian attacks as a primary cause of the witch craze, but more recently it has been given credibility by historians such as James Kences and Mary Beth Norton. Indian attacks had been a reality since the earliest days of European settlement in North America, but towards the end of the century they intensified, especially in Massachusetts. King Philip's War, often referred to as the First Indian War, took place between 1675 and 1678, and devastated towns across Massachusetts, Connecticut, Rhode Island and Maine. One-tenth of all military-age men were killed and in Salem, the constant threat of attack caused residents to become wary.

After the overthrow of Andros, colonial defences were weakened and fewer troops were available for service. Attacks became more common, and colonists were regularly killed. The young girls who gave evidence at the trials would certainly have been affected by their friends and neighbours becoming victims of such attacks. A number of outsiders who had survived Indian attacks moved to Salem in the years preceding the witch-hunt. The Salem trials coincide with King William's War, which is also referred to as the Second Indian War. This was part of the wider Nine Years' War (1688–97) that William of Orange was fighting against France. Both sides made alliances with Indian tribes.

In the Puritan mindset, the Indians were Devil-worshippers who were doing everything they could to prevent a godly society from being created. They were also the allies of the hated French and Spanish, and in contemporary accounts they are treated as subhuman and in need of extermination. A number of historians have suggested that one of the instigators of the craze, the healer and accused witch Tituba, was Indian. Recent theories advanced by historians have placed emphasis on the role of fear of Indian attacks, which fostered a deep-seated paranoia concerning God's willingness to allow the Devil's agents in the form of the Indians to punish Puritan settlers.

EXTRACT

1 From Mary Beth Norton, *In the Devil's Snare: The Salem Witchcraft Crisis of 1692* (2002).

The Lord, in short, was simultaneously punishing New England in two different ways – through the Second Indian War on the northeastern frontier and through the operations of witchcraft in Essex County [where Salem was located]. As the evidence... demonstrated, the assaults from the visible and invisible worlds became closely entwined in New Englanders' minds. Those connections permeated the witchcraft examinations and trials, as revealed by repeated spectral sightings of the "black man," whom the afflicted described as resembling an Indian; and in the threats that the witches and the devil – just as the Wabanakis [tribe] had – would "tear to pieces" or "knock in the head" those who opposed them.

Joshua Scottow's "Narrative of the Planting of the Massachusetts Colony," written shortly after the end of the witchcraft crisis, also tied the two themes inextricably together. Scottow, a longtime resident... who had earlier referred to several Wabanaki sachems [leaders] as "Satan's Emissaries," presented the Wabanakis' attacks and those of the witches as related phenomena, both instigated by God.

The contemporary Joshua Scottow presents his belief in a link between witches and the Indian threat in Source 1.

SOURCE

From Joshua Scottow, *Narrative of the Planting of the Massachusetts Colony* (1694). Scottow was a Puritan merchant who had served as a captain in the First Indian War.

The Lord seeth the Land-Defiling and Desolating sins amongst us: what Witchcrafts, and what other abominations are in the midst of us, we have just cause both to lay ourselves down in the Dust, and with indignation to bear all witness justly due against them, and all our Pagan walking in... abominable wickedness, by which Gods Name is Blasphemed among us; for which as the Lord vomited out these Natives, to make room for us, so he now hath vomited us out, to make room for them; in this War he hath Ruined and Destroyed a whole Shire, and in a manner Depopulated a whole Province; in which Desolation, two Churches gathered according to Gospel Order are extinguished: One of them about Fifty years standing, which was one of the first attacks upon us, having there been made the greatest Slaughter, Captivity, and Plunder; the Town remaineth, but the Churches Candlestick was removed: the other Church not of much lesser standing, where its said, not above Four Males left of their Society, the rest Dead, Slaughtered, or Captivated.

These wicked Cannibals, who are Gods Sword, and have been so for many years together, and when the end will be none of our Prophets have told us: we mention not the other circumstances relating to that Province & Shire; it's said there have been Killed & Captivated, a 1000, besides about 140 Slain the other day: but leave it to such whose Lot it will be to draw it up, our Pequod and Narraganset Wars lasted about three years, whose Narrative is faithfully Published by two persons of Worth, to the Honour of God, King, and Country: It's thought no English Pen will hardly Undertake this.

Economic crisis

The First Indian War left the economy of Massachusetts virtually ruined, with half of New England's towns attacked and the important Massachusetts settlement of Springfield entirely burnt to the ground. However, a population growth rate of three percent per year and the establishment of new towns meant that the settlers' livelihoods were not completely destroyed. In the 1680s, however, the colonists asked for military assistance from England, and this contributed to a rise in their tax burden under Sir Edmund Andros.

A series of Navigation Acts passed by the English parliament also hampered the economic fortunes of the colony. The first was passed in 1651, with other modified versions issued in 1660, 1662 and 1673. According to the original Act, goods imported to England and its territories had to be carried on English ships. This was designed to remove the Dutch monopoly on freight trade across northern Europe and North America. It also required that all crews of English ships had to be at least half English by nationality. Historian Christopher Hill has argued that the Act was important because it represented the victory of a *national* trading interest over the separate interests of the various private trading companies and fleets based in the colonies.

SOURCE

From the Navigation Act, October 1651.

No goods or commodities whatsoever of the growth, production or manufacture of Asia, Africa or America, or of any part thereof; or of any islands belonging to them, or which are described or laid down in the usual maps or cards of those places, as well of the English plantations as others, shall be imported or brought into this Commonwealth of England, or into Ireland, or any other lands, islands, plantations, or territories to this Commonwealth belonging, or in their possession, in any other ship or ships, vessel or vessels whatsoever, but only in such as do truly and without fraud belong only to the people of this Commonwealth, or the plantations thereof.

Further Acts stipulated that goods being transported from the colonies to any destination had to travel to England first. Massachusetts possessed a strong fleet that had a reasonable amount of independence, and when captains of the fleet ignored the demands of the Acts, they were reprimanded and this rebellious behaviour helps to explain why Charles II and James II attempted to centralise control over the colony. The Acts effectively reduced the amount of money and resources that flowed into Massachusetts because instead they were directed towards England. It became virtually impossible to ship grain to England as a result of the Acts, and many farmers in and around Salem had to diversify. The Dutch traditionally offered the best shipping rates for fish caught out of Salem, and with the use of Dutch ships now illegal, fishermen were forced to pay higher fees to transport their produce to England.

ACTIVITY

KNOWLEDGE CHECK

Indian threats and economic crisis

1 Why has it been argued that the Indian threat helped to cause the witch craze?

2 What economic problems existed in late 17th-century Massachusetts? Why do you think these contributed to a heightened sense of fear?

Social tensions

Religion

For most of its existence, Salem and the wider community of Massachusetts had been governed as a **theocracy** and religion was at the heart of everyday life. The Puritans who had settled here saw themselves as God's chosen people, and as they had in England, they were concerned with seeking signs of God's approval and the presence of the Devil at all junctures in life.

The Scientific Revolution was largely ignored by the Puritan authorities in Massachusetts, and they preferred to interpret crop failures, fires, illnesses and hallucinations as the work of the Devil. Anyone who did not conform to the Puritan ideal was viewed with suspicion. This included non-English European settlers, Indians, beggars and, especially, women.

As with virtually all other witch-hunts, the majority of accused were women. In the eyes of Salem Puritans, women were inferior to men, and preachers reinforced this idea in their sermons. In the Bible, Eve had been tempted to eat the forbidden fruit of knowledge in the Garden of Eden and this set a precedent for women to be easily tempted by the Devil.

Class

Social tensions emerged in the two major settlements in the area, located at Salem Town and Salem Village to the north-west. Together, they made up a community of more than 600 people. The majority of accusers came from Salem Village, which was largely agricultural and made up of well-established and staunch Puritans. Those who lived in the area closest to the main Ipswich Road and Salem Town itself were likely to have more contact with the outside world and were less reliant on agriculture, as well as being less driven by religious belief. Many of these families established themselves as merchants in the decades before the witch craze, and it is easy to see how jealousies could drive accusations at a time when harvests were poor. This view has been put forward by historians Paul Boyer and Stephen Nissenbaum in their influential study, *Salem Possessed: The Social Origins of Witchcraft* (1974).

Attempts had been made by residents of Salem Village to gain independence from Salem Town, but as the Town relied on the agricultural produce of the Village, this was fiercely resisted by the authorities in the Town. According to Boyer and Nissenbaum, the conflict between the two groups was based on differing visions of how communities should be run. The more old-fashioned, agrarian-based, Puritan group to the north-west were concerned with public goodwill, whereas the emerging merchants were concerned with private interests.

One of the most prominent families in Salem Village were the Putnams, who were heavily involved in the accusations. They were also leaders of the movement towards separation, and were opposed in this by the Porters, who were the richest family in Salem. The Porter family had a number of business interests in Salem Town and wider New England. The family made an attempt to put an end to the witch craze once it had started, but many of their allies soon found themselves under suspicion.

The historian Benjamin C. Ray has challenged the view that there were underlying social tensions based on proximity to Salem Town (Extract 2). He argues instead that social tensions are more difficult to assess, and that accusers and accused actually came from a wider geographical area than first thought.

KEY TERM

Theocracy
A system of government in which God is held to be supreme ruler and clergy are involved in the day-to-day running of the state.

EXTRACT

2 From Benjamin C. Ray, 'The Geography of Witchcraft Accusations in 1692 Salem Village' in *William and Mary Quarterly* (2008).

Geographic analysis of the accusations in the village shows there was no significant villagewide east-west division between accusers and accused in 1692. Nor was there an east-west divide between households of different economic status. Equally important, eastern village leaders were not opposed to the village's attempts to gain independence from Salem Town.

Social tensions

1 What impact did the theocratic government have on society in Salem?

2 What evidence exists to suggest that Salem was divided sharply along class lines?

TO WHAT EXTENT DID ACCUSATIONS LEAD TO A WIDESPREAD WITCH-HUNT?

The influence of Cotton Mather

Mather's background

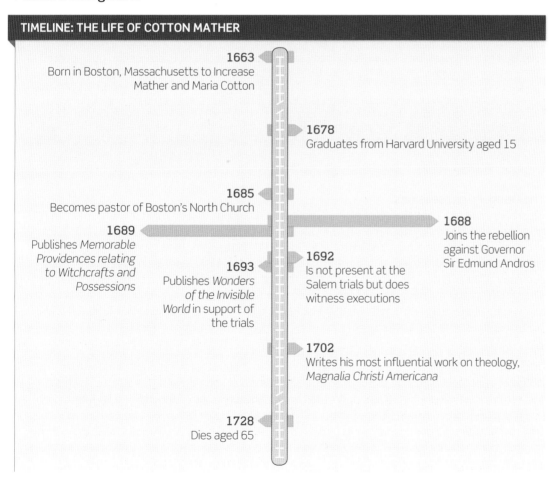

TIMELINE: THE LIFE OF COTTON MATHER

1663 Born in Boston, Massachusetts to Increase Mather and Maria Cotton

1678 Graduates from Harvard University aged 15

1685 Becomes pastor of Boston's North Church

1688 Joins the rebellion against Governor Sir Edmund Andros

1689 Publishes *Memorable Providences relating to Witchcrafts and Possessions*

1692 Is not present at the Salem trials but does witness executions

1693 Publishes *Wonders of the Invisible World* in support of the trials

1702 Writes his most influential work on theology, *Magnalia Christi Americana*

1728 Dies aged 65

Cotton Mather (1663–1728) and his father, Increase Mather, were two of the most senior Puritan clergymen in Massachusetts. Cotton was particularly convincing when it came to preaching about the danger of witches, and he was able to relay real-life examples of his own contact with witches and those who had been bewitched.

Cotton was a third-generation colonist, as his father had been born in Massachusetts and his grandfather, Richard Mather, who was also a minister, migrated to New England in the 1630s from England. His grandfather on his mother's side was John Cotton, a well-respected minister who, as a Puritan, had fled to New England under pressure from the Anglican authorities in England. Mather graduated from Harvard at the age of 15 and joined the ranks of the clergy almost immediately.

His comprehensive religious training enabled him to write extensively and he became an authority on Puritanism in the colonies. He wrote over 400 books, and by the time of the Salem trials, he had already preached widely and had published a number of works on witchcraft.

The publication of *Memorable Providences relating to Witchcrafts and Possessions*

Published in 1689, Mather's *Memorable Providences relating to Witchcrafts and Possessions* acted as an inspiration and a guide to those who conducted the Salem hunt and subsequent trials. It contained two sections:

- an extensive account of the so-called Goodwin possessions, which would serve to influence the possessions at Salem

- a sermon delivered by Mather and reprinted, warning against the presence of witches and offering advice on how to detect them.

SOURCE

3

From Cotton Mather, *Memorable Providences relating to Witchcrafts and Possessions* (1689).

Go tell Mankind, that there are Devils and Witches; and that tho those night-birds least appear where the Day-light of the Gospel comes, yet New England has had Examples of their Existence and Operation; and that not only the Wigwams of Indians, where the pagan Powaws often raise their masters, in the shapes of Bears and Snakes and Fires, but the House of Christians, where our God has had his constant Worship, have undergone the Annoyance of Evil spirits. Go tell the world, What Prays can do beyond all Devils and Witches, and What it is that these Monsters love to do; and through the Demons in the Audience of several standers-by threatned much disgrace to thy Author, if he let thee come abroad, yet venture That, and in this way seek a just Revenge on Them for the Disturbance they have given to such as have called on the Name of God.

The Goodwin possessions

Before the hunt at Salem, the story of the Goodwin possessions told by Mather was particularly powerful. John Goodwin was a mason from Boston, and Mather recalls that he and his wife had six children, and the entire family was extremely devoted to Puritanism. In the summer of 1688, the eldest Goodwin child, 13-year-old Martha, had accused the family laundress of the theft of some bed linen. Mather notes that he was convinced the linen was somehow used to practise witchcraft. The laundress was the daughter of Mary Glover, who Mather calls 'an ignorant and scandalous old woman in the neighbourhood'. Mather also notes that before he died, even her husband had complained that she was a witch.

Mary Glover was a typical outsider. She only spoke Gaelic and was a Catholic, which must have made life in Puritan Massachusetts very difficult. Mather claims that when confronted with her daughter's apparent theft, she swore at Martha Goodwin and soon the girl was afflicted by fits. Mather then dedicates a significant part of his book to descriptions of fits suffered by Martha, one of her sisters and two brothers. A doctor, Thomas Oakes, was called, and he concluded that only witchcraft could be to blame for the fits. His justification for this conclusion was that all of the children were afflicted by pains in the same parts of their bodies at the same times, even though they were not kept in the same rooms. Source 4 is typical of Mather's descriptions of possession.

SOURCE 4

From Cotton Mather, *Memorable Providences relating to Witchcrafts and Possessions* (1689).

The variety of their tortures increased continually; and tho about Nine or Ten at Night they always had a Release from their miseries, and ate and slept all night for the most part indifferently well, yet in the day time they were handled with so many sorts of Ails, that it would require of us almost as much time to Relate them all, as it did of them to Endure them. Sometimes they would be Deaf, sometimes Dumb, and sometimes Blind, and often, all this at once. One while their Tongues would be drawn down their Throats; another-while they would be pull'd out upon their Chins, to a prodigious length. They would have their Mouths opened unto such a Wideness, that their Jaws went out of joint; and anon they would clap together again with a Force like that of a strong Spring-Lock. The same would happen to their Shoulder-Blades, and their Elbows, and Hand-wrists, and several of their joints. They would at times lie in a benumbed condition and be drawn together as those that are tied Neck and Heels;' and presently be stretched out, yea, drawn Backwards, to such a degree that it was fear'd the very skin of their Bellies would have crack'd. They would make most piteous out-cries, that they were cut with Knives, and struck with Blows that they could not bear. Their Necks would be broken, so that their Neck-bone would seem dissolved unto them that felt after it; and yet on the sudden, it would become, again so stiff that there was no stirring of their Heads; yea, their Heads would be twisted almost round; and if main Force at any time obstructed a dangerous motion which they seem'd to be upon, they would roar exceedingly.

SOURCE 5

The title page of Mather's *Memorable Providences relating to Witchcrafts and Possessions* (1689). This influential work contained an account of the Goodwin possessions, which some historians have interpreted as the inspiration for the Salem accusations.

MEMORABLE PROVIDENCES,
Relating to
WITCHCRAFTS
And POSSESSIONS.

A Faithful Account of many Wonderful and Surprising Things, that have befallen several Bewitched and Possessed Persons in New-England. Particularly, A NARRATIVE of the marvellous Trouble and Releef Experienced by a pious Family in Boston, very lately ,and sadly molested with EVIL SPIRITS.
Whereunto is added,
A Discourse delivered unto a Congregation in Boston, on the Occasion of that Illustrious Providence.
As also
A Discourse delivered unto the same Congregation; on the occasion of an horrible Self-Murder Committed in the Town.
With an *Appendix,* in vindication of a Chapter in a late Book of Remarkable Providences, from the Calumnies of a Quaker at Pen-silvania.

Written By Cotton Mather, Minister of the Gospel.

And Recommended by the Ministers of Boston and Charleston

Printed at Boston in N. England by R. P. 1689. Sold by Joseph Brunning, at his Shop at the Corner of the Prison-Lane next the Exchange.

Mary Glover was arrested, and a search of her house revealed she had been making dolls out of rags and stuffing them with goat hair. She admitted to using the dolls in witchcraft, and when one was given to her in court, the Goodwin children, who were present at the trial, fell into fits and screamed out in pain. Mary Glover was unable to recite the Lord's Prayer correctly – it was believed that witches were unable to do this – and she ultimately confessed to being in league with the Devil.

As with a number of other suspected witches, Mather interviewed her in person, although he admitted to finding the encounter with Glover difficult because he had to rely on an interpreter. He failed to rid her of the Devil and convert her to Puritanism, and she was given an execution date of 16 November 1688, although she told Mather that this would not end the children's misery. After she was hanged, the children's fits continued. Mather took Martha Goodwin into his home in order to exorcise her, but her fits once again resumed before eventually stopping again. Ultimately, all of the Goodwin children appeared to be cured.

During Mather's interview with Glover before her death, she apparently named other witches who had assisted her in bewitching the children. Mather never released their names because he believed that women who made a pact with the Devil were inclined to lie. It is clear, however, that the pattern of accusations and symptoms experienced by the children bore a resemblance to those found at Salem in 1692. Through the Salem trials, Mather preached that the evidence of a witch should never be used to charge another suspect because the Devil may have been attempting to incriminate innocent people.

ACTIVITY
KNOWLEDGE CHECK

Cotton Mather

1 Why was Mather well respected in Massachusetts society?

2 In what ways did his preaching and writing affect the hunt at Salem?

3 Read Source 4 (on page 161). In what ways does Mather attempt to cause shock and alarm amongst his readers?

Who instigated the hunt?

Samuel Parris

The hunt began in the winter of 1691–92 in the household of Samuel Parris (1653–1720), the Puritan minister of Salem. Parris was born in London but migrated to Boston where he attended Harvard University and after a career as a plantation owner moved to Salem to enter the ministry. He followed three other ministers who had failed to impress the congregation, and took over a year to make the decision himself after being invited to take up the ministry by the people of Salem. During this year he attempted to increase his salary and benefits, such as free firewood and exclusive ownership of the minister's house. He immediately faced problems with his congregation, and as an outsider he found it difficult to settle their disputes. Shortly before the witch-hunt began, the town refused to pay his wages after he purchased unnecessary items for the Puritan meeting house, such as gold candlesticks, further strengthening the town's animosity towards him.

Parris's preaching also had an impact on widening the divisions that already existed in Salem. Shortly before his own daughter and niece reported being bewitched, Parris delivered a sermon that claimed the church was under siege by the Devil, who was being assisted by wicked men in the community. There is no doubt that the wicked men he referred to were his opponents in Salem.

Some historians have come to view Parris as self-centred and deceptive and his role and motivation for instigating the trials has never been fully understood. All of the initial accusations involved people in Parris' household: his daughter, her cousin and his slave, Tituba. He also acted as a key witness at the trials.

The role of children

During the winter of 1691, Samuel Parris's nine-year-old daughter, Elizabeth, and her 11-year-old cousin, Abigail Williams, began to experiment with fortune telling. They were curious to know what would happen to them in the future, and were particularly interested in finding out the social status of their future husbands. To do this they used a device known as a 'venus glass', which consisted of an egg white placed in water in which shapes and figures could be seen and interpreted. They began to share their findings with other young girls in Salem. It was later reported that on one occasion, the venus glass revealed the shape of a coffin, after which the supernatural events began.

In January 1692, Elizabeth Parris started to lose concentration and her father concluded that she had become preoccupied. She would forget prayers and would bark like a dog when her father confronted her. On hearing certain prayers she would scream loudly and at one point hurled a Bible across a room. Her father believed that continued prayer would cure this behaviour, but his efforts were not rewarded. Her symptoms continued, and she began to have fits and be afflicted by problems with her limbs.

Abigail Williams also began to exhibit strange behaviour, and the local doctor, William Griggs, was called to assess the girls. He decided that witchcraft was to blame and recommended prayer and fasting as a cure. As godly Puritans, the Parris family had already been doing this, and it seemed to be having little impact as more girls began to exhibit symptoms of possession.

Other children involved in the accusations included the following.

- Ann Putnam was the eldest child of Thomas and Ann. The Putnam family were one of the most influential in Salem Village and were instrumental in the spreading of accusations. Twelve-year-old Ann Jr. was friends with Elizabeth Parris and Abigail Williams, and in March 1692 claimed she was possessed and began showing similar symptoms. Along with the other girls, Ann played a leading role in the prosecution at the trials, and her name is mentioned over 400 times in the court documents. Interestingly, she apologised for the part she played in the craze in 1706, claiming she was deceived by the Devil when she made her accusations.

- Mary Walcott was 18 years old and, although she was not among the most notorious of the accusers, her role was significant. She was one of the first to suffer fits, and her aunt, Mary Sibley, decided to use counter-magic against some of the suspects, especially Tituba (discussed on page 164). Walcott's father Joseph married Deliverance Putnam after the death of his first wife, making him brother-in-law of Thomas Putnam, the father of Ann. Walcott remained calm throughout much of the episode, in contrast to Putnam, and sat quietly knitting through much of the trial proceedings. She did occasionally, however, show signs of possession.

- Nineteen-year-old Mercy Lewis accused a total of eight people and gave evidence against them. Her parents were killed in an Indian attack, which was possibly witnessed by Mercy herself, and she was sent to live as a servant with Reverend George Burroughs (who would later be executed at the Salem trials after her evidence). She was also sent to the household of Thomas Putnam before the trials, where she became friends with Ann Jr. and Mary Walcott.

- Elizabeth Hubbard was 17 years old at the beginning of the craze, and she acted as one of the leading accusers. Less is known about her than the other girls, but it is known that she went to Salem to live with her great-aunt, Rachel Hubbard Griggs, and William Griggs, the town doctor. Despite being a relative, Elizabeth worked as a servant in the household. By the end of the trials, she had testified against 29 people, 17 of whom were arrested. Of those, 13 were hanged (out of a total of 19 who were hanged in total) and two died in jail. Like the other girls, she would have fits in the courtroom, and she would often fall into trances, unable to speak.

The children were called as witnesses at the trials, and their evidence was central to many of the individual cases (Source 6). Because Elizabeth Parris, Abigail Williams and Ann Putnam were too young to testify, their accusations were endorsed by adults, including Ann's father. In court, the girls' performances became notorious, as they would collapse to the ground and scream in agony when they saw the accused.

SOURCE

6 From Increase Mather, *A Further Account of the Trials of the New-England Witches* (1693).

There were three Girls from 9 to 12 Years of Age, each of them, or thereabouts. Elizabeth Parris, Abigail Williams, and Ann Putman; these were most of them at Goodwife C.'s [Martha Corey's] Examination, and did vehemently Accuse her in the Assembly of Afflicting them, by Biting, Pinching, Strangling, etc.

Ann Putman did there affirm, that one day when Lieutenant Fuller was at Prayer at her Father's House, she saw the shape of Goodwife C. and she thought Goodwife N. [Rebecca Nurse] Praying at the same time to the Devil; she was not sure it was Goodwife N. she thought it was; but very sure she saw the shape of Goodwife C. The said C. said, they were poor distracted Children, and no heed to be given to what they said. Mr. Hathorne and Mr. Noyes replied, It was the Judgment of all that were present, they were Bewitched, and only she the Accused Person said, they were Distracted.

It was observed several times, that if she did but bite her under lip in time of Examination, the Persons afflicted were bitten on their Arms and Wrists, and produced the Marks before the Magistrates, Ministers, and others. And being watched for that, if she did but Pinch her Fingers, or Grasp one Hand hard in another, they were Pinched, and produced the Marks before the Magistrates, and Spectators. After that, it was observed, that if she did but lean her Breast against the Seat in the Meeting-House, (being the Bar at which she stood), they were afflicted. Particularly Mrs. Pope complained of grievous Torment in her Bowels, as if they were torn out. She vehemently accused the said C. as the Instrument.

The afflicted Persons asked her, why she did not go to the Company of Witches which were before the Meeting-House Mustering? Did she not hear the Drum beat? They accused her of having Familiarity with the Devil, in the time of Examination, in the shape of a Black Man whispering in her Ear; they affirmed, that her Yellow Bird sucked betwixt her Fingers in the Assembly; and Order being given to see if there were any sign, the Girl that saw it, said, it was too late now; she had removed a Pin, and put it on her Head; which was found there sticking upright.

A Level Exam-Style Question Section A

Read Source 6 before you answer this question.

Assess the value of the source for revealing the role of children and the use of evidence in the late 17th-century witch trials.

Explain your answer, using the source, the information given about its origin and your own knowledge about the historical context. (20 marks)

Tip

Take note of both the author and the date it was written. What was the position of Increase Mather? What is the significance of the source being produced in 1693?

The motivations of the children

For many years, historians presented the children as selfish frauds who pursued their accusations out of spite. More recently, historians have concluded that the girls were more likely to have been bored and frustrated with their stifled upbringing in Puritan New England. In the case of Ann Putnam and probably others, her parents played an important role in providing her with names. Historians have offered the following explanations.

- Bernard Rosenthal has suggested that the girls may have been experiencing psychological disorders.

- The Victorian historian Charles Upham offered a mixture of explanations: hallucinations, naivety and excitement on the part of the girls.

- Carol Karlsen has suggested that the accusations were a response to the girls' own insecurities. Mercy Lewis, for example, had experienced a traumatic childhood and lived in poor economic circumstances. For her, the accusations were a form of escapism.

- Mary Beth Norton has drawn attention to the role of Indian attacks. Many of the girls had been directly or indirectly affected by attacks, which traumatised them.

ACTIVITY
KNOWLEDGE CHECK

Samuel Parris and the role of children

1 In what ways did Samuel Parris encourage the witch-hunt?

2 Do the afflicted girls appear to have anything in common? Does this help to explain why they became accusers?

Tituba

Together with her husband, John Indian, Tituba worked as a household servant, or possibly a slave, of the Parrises. She first became embroiled in the witch-hunt when Mary Sibley, the aunt of Mary Walcott, approached her and John asking them to make a witch's cake in order to counter the possessions. This cake, which included the urine of the afflicted children, was fed to the Parris family dog. The dog was then supposed to sniff out any witches that had bewitched the girls. This did not work, and the fits that the girls were suffering only became worse. Samuel Parris became suspicious and filed charges against Tituba, triggering the witch-hunt.

Historians have debated the origins of Tituba and her husband and it seems they were of mixed Caribbean and African heritage, and it is known that Tituba was purchased in Barbados. It is likely that Mary Sibley turned to them for magical assistance because they brought magical practices with them from the West Indies. It is likely that Tituba played a role in looking after Elizabeth and the other children, and it has been suggested that the stories she told them from her homeland were tinged with tales of demonic possession and **Voodoo**. This may have played an important part in forming the fantasies of the young girls.

According to surviving accounts, Tituba confessed quickly to a pact with the Devil and named other witches. She recalled that the Devil was a white man dressed in black, who made her sign his book. She also claimed that she had flown through the air using a pole and that the other witches changed into animals.

Despite the emphasis placed by historians on Tituba's role in influencing the girls, there is no mention in the court documents of her teaching the practice of fortune telling to the girls. The technique they used was already common in New England, and was viewed by Puritans as a devilish practice. Interestingly, Tituba also said that she was beaten by Samuel Parris and she was forced to confess to witchcraft.

KEY TERM

Voodoo
A religion of West African origin practised in the Caribbean. It is based on a belief in multiple gods, ancestor worship and magic.

Tituba and the Children.

Figure 7.2 No contemporary images exist of the original victims, which has given rise to depictions of them as ugly, deformed and frail women. This image, showing Tituba performing acts of sorcery for Elizabeth Parris and Abigail Williams, in the kitchen of the Parris household, is taken from *A Popular History of the United States* by William Cullen Bryant (1878).

ACTIVITY
KNOWLEDGE CHECK

Tituba

1 What was Tituba's role in sparking the hunt?

2 Why did Samuel Parris become suspicious of her?

3 How important was her role? Would the hunt have happened without her?

The nature of the victims

As with most other witch-hunts, the majority of victims were women. Around 20 percent of victims were men. Like the men caught up in the East Anglian witch craze, many of these had connections to accused women before they became involved themselves.

The first three witches to be accused give some indication of the typical nature of the victims. They were Tituba (discussed previously), Sarah Good and Sarah Osborne.

- Sarah Good was a social outcast, and was also accused of hurting children. She was 40 years old, and although she originally came from a well-off family, she was destitute after making poor investments and not marrying into money. Her entire family were homeless, and at the beginning of the hunt they had resorted to wandering the streets begging. At her trial, even her own husband and daughter testified against her, although her sentence was delayed due to pregnancy. She denied being a witch at first, and accused Sarah Osborne of afflicting the girls.

- Sarah Osborne was a well-established widow with a relatively high social standing, but her behaviour fell short of what was expected in Salem society. She lived openly with an unmarried, Irish **indentured servant** named Alexander Osborne and she attempted to remove the children she had with her deceased husband from her inheritance.

These first three accused witches were all outcasts, or from the margins of society. In such a godly society, their low social standing was easily associated with the Devil. Other accused witches included the following.

- Bridget Bishop has been presented as a woman with an independent mind, who possessed all the qualities disliked by Puritans. She was an innkeeper and wore clothes that Puritans disapproved of, and ran an establishment where drinking and gambling took place. She was the first to be tried and executed.

- Reverend George Burroughs was the only Puritan minister executed at the trials. As one of the three ministers who served in quick succession before the arrival of Samuel Parris, Burroughs became involved in local conflicts, and borrowed money from the Putnam family that he was unable to pay back.

- Another woman of independent mind was Martha Carrier, who is revealed in the court documents to be unsubmissive and of contentious spirit. She had been accused two years earlier of causing a smallpox epidemic through witchcraft.

- Rebecca Nurse was an older and well-respected member of the community. Many of her friends and neighbours wrote petitions claiming her to be innocent, but the testimony of the girls was too convincing. She was initially found not guilty, but after the jury was asked to reconsider, they found her guilty. She was given a pardon by Governor Phips, but men from Salem persuaded him to change his mind and she was executed on 19 July 1692.

- Susannah Martin was a 67-year-old widow. She was also accused by the original girls as well as 15 of her neighbours, although she maintained her innocence until the end. Like Martha Carrier, she had a previous history of witchcraft accusations against her. The historian Carol Karlsen has suggested that she was targeted because she represented a threat to the orderly transmission of property in Salem, as she was in an ongoing court dispute over her father's will. He had died in 1688 leaving two daughters, a granddaughter and a second wife to share in his estate. Susannah and her sister only received a small portion, while the majority of the estate passed to her father's second wife, who died shortly afterwards. She in turn left the majority of the estate to the father's granddaughter, excluding Susannah once again. All of Susannah's appeals were unsuccessful.

KEY TERM

Indentured servant
Someone contracted to work for another person without pay for a fixed period of time in exchange for free passage to their new country. When the fixed period had ended, they were freed. Most labourers in 17th-century New England arrived as indentured servants.

ACTIVITY
KNOWLEDGE CHECK

The nature of the victims
Create a table to assess the nature of the victims you have encountered so far. Include the headings 'name', 'social status', 'accusations'.

The trials and executions

The trials

A day after the arrests of the first three suspects, a meeting was called at the village meeting house, where the possessed girls gave evidence against the women. This initial meeting, and the rest of the trials, were defined by their use of **spectral evidence**, which was apparently very convincing at first. The girls claimed that the witches forced them to sign the Devil's Book, suckled familiars and caused the fits that had afflicted them.

KEY TERM

Spectral evidence
Evidenced based on testimony that claimed the accused or their spirit appeared in dreams and visions.

Figure 7.3 In this illustration from an 1876 American history book, Mary Walcott is shown giving evidence while one of the afflicted girls falls to the floor in a fit. The use of spectral evidence was accepted by the court and was key to securing so many convictions.

More suspects were soon named, including more respectable figures in the community such as Reverend George Burroughs and Rebecca Nurse. As more people became accused, some of them began to confess. Abigail Hobbs and her stepmother, Deliverance Hobbs, confessed to attending a meeting where a number of named witches plotted to bewitch all of Salem Village. At the Salem trials a confession actually improved the chances of a suspect, as more than 50 of those who confessed were ultimately freed.

The number of accused came to 165, although only 39 ended up facing serious charges. The recently appointed Governor William Phips established a **Court of Oyer and Terminer** in May to officially hear the cases. At the trials, the girls continued to shriek, wail and shout when the accused gave testimony. Half-hearted searches for the Devil's mark were also carried out and were used as evidence. One of the judges resigned within a month when he became suspicious about the legitimacy of the proceedings. Bizarrely, he was replaced with a prosecuting lawyer.

KEY TERM

Court of Oyer and Terminer
A specially convened court established to investigate a predetermined matter. It roughly translates from Anglo-French as 'to hear and determine'.

Convictions were easily made for a number of reasons.

- Spectral evidence was accepted by the court.
- The accused were allowed few resources to mount a defence.
- Petitions by neighbours testifying to the good character of the accused were generally ignored.
- Long-standing and existing gossip from Salem Village was accepted as evidence.

The executions

Bridget Bishop was the first to be hanged on 10 June 1692, followed by Rebecca Nurse and Sarah Good on 19 July. Giles Corey, who refused to say anything at all, even declining to enter a plea, was tortured by pressing on 16 September. He was laid on a wooden platform while another large wooden piece was placed on his chest. Stones were added which slowly weighed him down and suffocated him. His wife and daughter were hanged on 22 September.

The Reverend George Burroughs prayed and recited the Lord's Prayer at the gallows on 19 August, but it was not enough to save him. He was hanged with several others. By 22 September, 19 had been hanged and one tortured to death, but the hunt would soon be over.

> **ACTIVITY**
> **KNOWLEDGE CHECK**
>
> **The trials and executions**
>
> 1 Why do you think the authorities were prepared to accept spectral evidence and the testimonies of young children?
>
> 2 Look at Figure 7.3. What do you think the impact of spectral evidence would have been in the court room?

A Level Exam-Style Question Section B

'The role of children as witnesses was essential in ensuring the Salem witch craze became widespread.'

How far do you agree with this statement? (20 marks)

Tip

As well as including evidence from the sections on children, the victims and the trials themselves, think about the contextual background to the witch-hunt and how this created an environment well suited to the trials.

WHY DID THE WITCH-HUNT COME TO AN END?

The roles of Cotton Mather's father and Governor Phips

Increase Mather

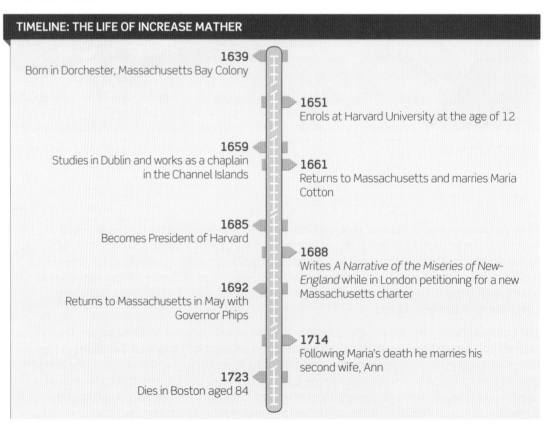

TIMELINE: THE LIFE OF INCREASE MATHER

1639 Born in Dorchester, Massachusetts Bay Colony

1651 Enrols at Harvard University at the age of 12

1659 Studies in Dublin and works as a chaplain in the Channel Islands

1661 Returns to Massachusetts and marries Maria Cotton

1685 Becomes President of Harvard

1688 Writes *A Narrative of the Miseries of New-England* while in London petitioning for a new Massachusetts charter

1692 Returns to Massachusetts in May with Governor Phips

1714 Following Maria's death he marries his second wife, Ann

1723 Dies in Boston aged 84

In September 1692, the list of the accused was still growing, despite the number of executions that had taken place. Governor Phips' wife was now implicated, as well as Reverend Samuel Willard, who had previous documented cases of possession that he had come across.

Increase Mather, Cotton Mather's father, was a well-respected Puritan minister and president of Harvard University. He published his sceptical work *Cases of Conscience Concerning Evil Spirits Persecuting Men* in September 1692. While not rejecting the notion of witchcraft, Mather used his extensive knowledge of scripture and knowledge of recent history to argue that genuine cases of witchcraft were rare, and much of the evidence used at the trials was dubious (Source 7).

SOURCE 7

From Increase Mather, *Cases of Conscience Concerning Evil Spirits Persecuting Men* (1692).

The Devil may appear indeed in the Form of Dead Persons, but that he cannot represent such as are living... And that evil Angels have sometimes appeared in the likeness of living absent persons is a thing abundantly confirmed by History... I could mention dismal Instances of Innocent Blood which has been shed by means of the Lies of some confessing Witches.

Have we not known some that have bitterly censured [criticised] all that have been complained of by bewitched Persons, saying it was impossible they should not be Guilty, soon upon which themselves or some near Relations of theirs, have to the lasting Infamy of their Families been accused after the same Manner, and personated by the Devil? [This] should make all men to be careful how they join with Satan in Condemning the Innocent.

As well as his writing, Mather made a number of sermons that were supportive of the trials themselves, but deeply critical of the use of spectral evidence. As Mather had such a wide following and was well respected across Massachusetts, godly Puritans began to heed his warnings and the number of accusations started to slow down dramatically.

Governor Phips

Increase Mather's scepticism about the use of spectral evidence led him to start discussions with a number of influential officials in Massachusetts, including Governor William Phips.

Phips was born in Maine in 1651 to a moderately prosperous family of fur and weapons traders. He became a sea captain and treasure hunter, travelling to London in 1683 to seek funding to investigate the wrecks of sunken Spanish ships in the Caribbean. After he was successful in this endeavour, he gained royal favour, and was knighted by James II in 1687 at the age of 36. He returned to Boston where he met Increase and Cotton Mather and briefly acted as Provost Marshal General for New England.

He was baptised in Cotton Mather's church in 1689 and began to take religion much more seriously than before. Some historians have suggested that his sudden conversion may have been to gain favour with the influential Mather family. Either way, he was deeply influenced by their interest in witchcraft around this time. From London, he worked with Increase Mather to renew the

SOURCE 8

In 1692 Increase Mather published *Cases of Conscience concerning Evil Spirits Persecuting Men*. In it, he emphasised the importance of fair trials and the dangers of miscarriages of justice.

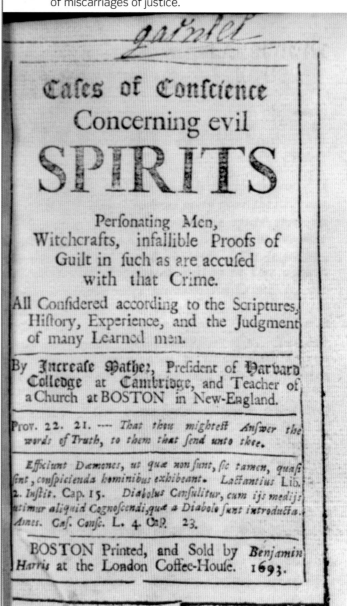

Massachusetts Bay Colony charter and Mather used his influence to place Phips in the post of Governor under the new charter.

Mather and Phips only returned to Massachusetts when the craze had already started, and there is no doubt that Phips supported the accusations wholeheartedly at first, ordering the prisoners to be put in chains and creating the Court of Oyer and Terminer.

Phips was quick to appoint William Stoughton, his lieutenant-governor, as chief judge at the trials, and Phips may well have viewed this as a mistake in hindsight. Stoughton was unrelenting in his pursuit of witches and took the lead in demanding that spectral evidence be heard. It is clear that Phips' relationship with Increase Mather influenced his decision to close down the court, and his attempt to give a reprieve to Rebecca Nurse demonstrates his softening position.

After weeks of careful consideration, Phips closed down the Court of Oyer and Terminer on 26 October 1692 and released those who were still under investigation. As was common in both England and the colonies, those who had spent time in jail still had to find the money to cover their fees, and one woman, Margaret Jacobs, had to wait in prison until another citizen paid them. Tituba's life, as well as that of her husband John Indian, was spared but she remained a slave and was sold to a new master.

A letter dated 12 October 1692 demonstrates Phips' own opinion of the trials (Source 9).

SOURCE 9

From a letter from Governor William Phips to an unknown recipient in England, 12 October 1692.

When I first arrived I found this province miserably harassed with a most Horrible witchcraft or Possession of Devils which had broke in upon several Townes, some score of poor people were taken with preternatural torments some scalded with brimstone some had pins stuck in their flesh others hurried into the fire and water and some dragged out of their houses and carried over the tops of trees and hills for many Miles together...

There were many committed to prison upon suspicion of Witchcraft before my arrival. The loud cries and clamours of the friends of the afflicted people with the advice of the Deputy Governor and many others prevailed with me to give a Commission of Oyer and Terminer for discovering what witchcraft might be at the bottom or whether it were not a possession..

When the Court came to sit at Salem... they convicted more than twenty persons of being guilty of witchcraft, some of the convicted were such as confessed their Guilt... I was almost the whole time of the proceeding abroad in the service of Their Majesties in the Eastern part of the Country and depending upon the Judgement of the Court as to the right method of proceeding in cases of Witchcraft but when I came home I found many persons in a strange ferment of dissatisfaction which was increased by some hot Spirits that blew up the flame, but on enquiring into the matter I found that the name and shape of several persons who were doubtless innocent and to my certain knowledge of good reputation for which cause I have now forbidden the committing of any more that shall be accused without unavoidable necessity, and those that have been committed I would shelter from any Proceedings against them wherein there may be the least suspicion of any wrong to be done unto the Innocent. I would also wait for any particular directions or commands if their Majesties please to give me any for the fuller ordering of this perplexing affair.

I have also put a stop to the printing of any discourse one way or the other, that may increase the needless disputes of people upon this occasion, because I saw a likelihood of kindling an inextinguishable flame if I should admit any public and open Contests...

I hereby declare that as soon as I came from fighting against their Majesties Enemies and understood what danger some of their innocent subjects might be exposed to, if the evidence of the afflicted persons only did prevail either to the committing or trying of any of them, I did before any application was made unto me about it put a stop to the proceedings of the court and they are now stopped till their Majesties pleasure be known. Sir I beg pardon for giving you all this trouble, the reason is because I know my enemies are seeking to turn it all upon me and I take this liberty because I depend upon your friendship, and desire you will please to give a true understanding of the matter.

ACTIVITY
KNOWLEDGE CHECK

Increase Mather and Governor Phips

1 What was the role of Increase Mather in ending the craze?

2 Why do you think Governor Phips changed his attitude towards suspected witches?

3 Read Source 9. According to this source, why has Governor Phips put an end to the investigations into witchcraft? Are there any other motivations he may have had that are not mentioned in the text?

The general pardon

Although he had encouraged Cotton Mather to write *Wonders of the Invisible World*, an account of the trials in late 1692, in 1693 Phips issued a general pardon, officially excusing eight people whom Stoughton had condemned to die in the latest round of trials. In January, a new Superior Court of Judicature had been established in Salem, led again by William Stoughton. Although Stoughton had not changed his view of witches and spectral evidence, the political pressure on him to avoid convictions was immense and Phips ordered him to discount spectral evidence. The first five prisoners to face trial had been held since the first wave of accusations and were found not guilty. Charges were dismissed against more prisoners, but three were found guilty. Phips pardoned these three shortly after Stoughton had signed their death warrants. The court sat again at the end of the month, finding five people not guilty. The court met for a final time in May 1693, where five people: Susannah Post, Mary Bridges, Eunice Frye, William Barker and Mary Barker were found not guilty. This sudden rush to find defendants innocent was probably directed, or at least heavily influenced, by Governor Phips.

EXTEND YOUR KNOWLEDGE

William Stoughton (1631–1701)

William Stoughton is remembered in history as an unforgiving religious zealot who would stop at nothing to secure convictions. In reality, many historians have blamed Governor Phips for the extent of the trial because he allowed Stoughton to act with minimal interference.

A native of Massachusetts, Stoughton studied at Harvard and in England, and like most other people involved in the trials, he was a godly Puritan. He served the Massachusetts government for many years, and was even involved in Sir Edmund Andros' unpopular administration.

As well as being appointed Lieutenant Governor by William Phips, Stoughton was made chief justice of the colonial courts, a role he would retain for the rest of his life. His extensive powers meant that he could act as both a judge and prosecutor at the Salem trials. Although other judges and important figures such as Increase Mather were suspicious of the use of spectral evidence, Stoughton was absolutely convinced of its usefulness.

Unlike many of the other magistrates involved in the trials, he refused to admit to any mistakes. He became acting governor of Massachusetts Bay in 1694 and died in 1701.

Phips was particularly critical of Stoughton's role, and in a letter to King William in February 1693, he criticised him for allowing the craze to develop so extensively. Phips also defended himself in the letter, and claimed that he only set up the court under pressure from leading religious figures in Boston.

In 1695, the government in London repealed a law passed by the Massachusetts legislature in 1692 that enabled swift prosecutions for witchcraft. In January 1697, one of the judges involved in the trials, Samuel Sewall, officially apologised to Massachusetts officials and asked for forgiveness. Many of the girls who had acted as chief accusers slowly began to apologise as they grew older and realised the error of their ways. In 1711, compensation was paid to the families of the victims.

ACTIVITY
KNOWLEDGE CHECK

The general pardon

1 Why do you think it took so long for Phips to issue a general pardon?

2 Why were the final accused witches found not guilty?

A Level Exam-Style Question Section B

To what extent was the weakened authority of the Massachusetts government after the Glorious Revolution the main cause of the Salem witch trials? (20 marks)

Tip

You should dedicate a significant section of the essay to the impact of the breakdown of authority after the 1688 Revolution, and compare to the other underlying social, economic and political factors.

Conclusion: Why did the craze become so widespread?

Although the events at Salem took place over a few months, they became widespread very quickly and more than 200 people were accused. Historians have put forward a number of reasons to explain why this was the case.

- Salem, and Massachusetts more generally, was a deeply Puritan society. Fear of the Devil and witches was part of everyday life. Dangers could be found everywhere in New England, which had only recently been settled, and witchcraft and magic helped people to explain what was going on around them.

- The dangers associated with the Indian threat also played a significant role in heightening the sense of fear that would result in a witch craze. Many of the girls who made the original accusations had been personally affected by Indian attacks.

- The role of Elizabeth Parris, Abigail Williams, Ann Putnam and the other girls meant that the court had a large number of witnesses prepared to testify against suspects. They were apparently convincing, and may have gained at least some of their awareness and knowledge from the slave, Tituba.

- Social divisions in Salem meant that resentment and jealousy was part of daily life. The fact that the majority of accusers came from the less wealthy, more agricultural and more Puritan Salem Village is telling. Many of the accused were either social outcasts or resided in the more prosperous part of Salem.

- The role of individuals is crucial in explaining the extent of the hunt, and Cotton Mather was the most outspoken supporter of witch-hunting in the years before the Salem trials. He came from a respected family of ministers and thousands of people heard his sermons in the months before the trials.

- William Stoughton's acceptance of spectral evidence meant that evidence that would be viewed as dubious by most courts was fully accepted and relied upon. When individuals such as Increase Mather and Governor Phips began to question the use of this evidence, there is no way the trials would have been able to continue.

ACTIVITY
SUMMARY

Accusers and accused

1 Create a table to assess (a) the motivations of accusers and (b) the nature of the victims.

   a) Under the heading 'the motivations of the accusers', find as many names of accusers as possible and write down as much information as you can about their background and role in the trials. You could make use of wider reading to find the information.

   b) Under the heading 'the nature of the victims', find as much information as possible about the names of the victims, their backgrounds and their status in Salem society.

2 Based on your findings, answer the following questions.

   a) What do the accusers have in common?

   b) What are the most important factors that motivated the accusers? Think of at least three.

   c) What do the victims have in common?

   d) What factors made it more likely for a person to be accused?

   e) If the community of Salem was in England rather than America, do you think the witch-hunt would have happened? Explain your answer.

THINKING HISTORICALLY   Cause and consequence (7c)

The value of historical explanations

Historical explanations derive from the historian who is investigating the past. Differences in explanations are usually about what the historians think is significant. Historians bring their own attitudes and perspectives to historical questions and see history in the light of these. It is therefore perfectly acceptable to have very different explanations of the same historical phenomenon. The way we judge historical accounts is by looking at how well argued they are and how well evidence has been deployed to support the argument.

Look at the approaches to the causes of witch crazes in the table below. Then answer the questions that follow.

Different approaches to the causes of witch crazes		
Approach A	**Approach B**	**Approach C**
Witch crazes are caused by decisions taken by politicians and officials, such as the passing of the Witchcraft Act or the writing of King James' *Daemonologie*. Witch crazes are imposed from the top by great men. Ordinary people then fall into line and do whatever they are told.	Witch crazes are mass movements of similar people with similar ideas and attitudes. The small aspects of commonality all add up together to create a witch craze.	Witch crazes within communities of people who share a common religion are inevitable. Events in history point us to this fact. Events are caused from the 'bottom up'.

Work in small groups. (You will need an even number of groups in the class.)

1 In your groups, devise a brief explanation (200–300 words) of why the Salem witch craze took place. Your explanation should match one of the approaches above. Present your explanation to another group, who will decide on two things.

   a) Which of the approaches is each explanation trying to demonstrate?

   b) Considering the structure and the quality of the argument and use of evidence, which is the best of the three explanations?

2 If you choose a 'best' explanation, should you discount the other two? Explain your answer.

WIDER READING

Boyer, P. and Nissenbaum, S. *Salem Possessed: The Social Origins of Witchcraft*, Harvard (1974). Provides considerable detail on the social and economic context of the witch-hunt.

Norton, M.B. *In the Devil's Snare: The Salem Witchcraft Crisis of 1692*, Knopf (2002). An up-to-date analysis of all aspects of the trials.

Pavlac, B.A. *Witch Hunts in the Western World*, Nebraska (2010). Includes a concise section on the Salem hunt and colonial hunts more generally.

Preparing for your A Level Paper 3 exam

Advance planning

Draw up a timetable for your revision and try to keep to it. Spend longer on topics which you have found difficult, and revise them several times. Aim to be confident about all aspects of your Paper 3 work, because this will ensure that you have a choice of questions in Sections B and C.

Paper 3 overview

Paper 3	Time: 2 hours 15 minutes	
Section A	Answer 1 compulsory question for the option studied, assessing source analysis and evaluation skills.	20 marks
Section B	Answer 1 question from a choice of 2 on an aspect in depth for the option studied.	20 marks
Section C	Answer 1 question from a choice of 2 on an aspect in breadth for the option studied.	20 marks
	Total marks =	60 marks

Section A questions

There is no choice of question in Section A. You will be referred to a source of about 350 words long, printed in a Sources Booklet. The source will be a primary source or one that is contemporary to the period you have studied, and will relate to one of the key topics in the Aspect of Depth. You will be expected to analyse and evaluate the source in its historical context. The question will ask you to assess the value of the source for revealing something specific about the period, and will expect you to explain your answer, using the source, the information given about its origin and your own knowledge about the historical context.

Section B questions

You will have a choice of one from two questions in Section B. They will aim to assess your understanding of one or more of the key topics in the Aspect of Depth you have studied. Questions may relate to a single, momentous year, but will normally cover longer periods. You will be required to write an essay evaluating an aspect of the period. You may be asked about change and continuity, similarity and difference, consequences, significance or causation, or you may be given a quotation and asked to explain how far you agree with it. All questions will require you to reach a substantiated judgement.

Section C questions

You will have a choice of one from two questions in Section C. Questions will relate to the themes of the Aspects of Breadth you have studied, and will aim to assess your understanding of change over time. They will cover a period of not fewer than 100 years and will relate either to the factors that brought about change, or the extent of change over the period, or patterns of change as demonstrated by turning points.

Use of time

- Do not write solidly for 45 minutes on each question. For Section B and C answers you should spend a few minutes working out what the question is asking you to do, and drawing up a plan of your answer. This is especially important for Section C answers, which cover an extended period of time.
- For Section A it is essential that you have a clear understanding of the content of the source and its historical context. Pay particular attention to the provenance: was the author in a position to know what he or she was writing about? Read it carefully and underline important points. You might decide to spend up to ten minutes reading the source and drawing up your plan, and 35 minutes writing your answer.

Preparing for your A Level exams

Paper 3: A Level sample answer with comments

Section A

These questions require you to analyse and evaluate source material with respect to its historical context.
For these questions remember to:

- look at the evidence given in the source and consider how the source could be used in differing ways to provide historical understanding
- use your knowledge of the historical context to discuss any limitations the source may have
- use your historical understanding to evaluate the source, considering how much weight you would give to its argument
- come to a judgement on the overall value of the source in respect to the question.

Study Source 3 (Chapter 6, page 137) before you answer this question.

Assess the value of the source for revealing the methods used by witch-hunters and common perceptions of witches' covens in the 17th century.

Explain your answer, using the source, the information given about its origin and your own knowledge about the historical context. (20 marks)

Average student answer

The source is from a pamphlet published to report on the witch trials in East Anglia in 1645. It was published in the same year as the trial of Rebecca West but the author is unknown. There was a wide interest in the East Anglian witch trials and because it was published in London, the source demonstrates this. The trials were taking place in the middle of the English Civil War, and both London and East Anglia were important centres for recruiting Parliamentarian soldiers. This may explain why the source was printed in London, because most Londoners would sympathise with Matthew Hopkins' quest to rid the country of witches, who were associated with Catholicism and the Royalists. Prince Rupert, the nephew of Charles I, had a pet poodle that parliament presented as a witches' familiar, which shows how passionately parliament and their sympathisers were about ridding the country of witches.

The source recounts the examination of Rebecca West, and it says that she and other accused witches met in the house of Elizabeth Clark, and also that they prayed to their familiars. It seems to show that Rebecca West was admitting all the charges against her, including that the witches used their familiars to cause harm to other people. Elizabeth Clark made her spirit cause harm to a Mr Edwards, who was 'thrown down' off his horse to 'never rise again'.

The typical nature of a witches' coven is built upon when Rebecca West confesses that Elizabeth Gooding used her familiar spirit to damage Robert Tayler's horse, and Hellen Clark killed and caused harm to some hogs. The fact that covens often consisted of several generations of the same family is shown because Anne West, Rebecca's mother, is mentioned. She used her familiar spirit to free her from her enemies and the witches agreed a time and a place for another meeting.

> This is a weak opening paragraph because although it provides some context about the witch-hunt and the Civil War it does not focus on the specific question. The comment on the nature of the source is assertion. There is some specific development regarding the fact that it was printed in London, but this is not linked adequately to the issues raised in the question.

> The points in these paragraphs show a general understanding of the evidence given by Rebecca West. It would benefit from more specific references to the text and some awareness of the context which made these women vulnerable to prosecution.

176

Rebecca West and her associates were always likely to be suspected of witchcraft. They were outsiders who had long-standing feuds with their neighbours. The first woman to be accused by Matthew Hopkins and John Stearne was Elizabeth Clark, an elderly woman with one leg. Like all of the women suspected in East Anglia, she was searched for the Devil's mark, and so were Anne and Rebecca West. These women were also deprived of sleep and watched for several nights. Some of the women appeared to have familiars, but these were more likely to be innocent pets. Rebecca West was originally named by Elizabeth Clark, but she gained immunity from prosecution when she agreed to be a witness for the court.

> The context of the source is covered in this paragraph, but is not related to either of the two issues in the question. It would be useful to relate the information in this paragraph to the source itself.

Overall the source is of great value in providing evidence of the methods and perceptions of witch-hunting in the mid-17th century. It makes clear that witches were interrogated in order to extract confessions, and that the confession of one witch would often lead to many others being accused and dragged into the legal process. The presence of familiars is also discussed in the source, and this would have been at the forefront of people's minds when investigating cases of witchcraft. The source is reliable as it does not appear to be written by someone who was directly involved in the trials, and it was published in London suggesting that there was a great interest in the hunt outside East Anglia.

> Some judgement but needs more specific development to provide substance. The point about reliability is weak and is based on assumptions.

Verdict

This is an average answer because:

- it shows a basic understanding of the source material and identifies some key points, which could be explained and illustrated more clearly
- it shows some knowledge of context but this could be developed

- it has some evaluation of the source material but this tends towards assertion and would benefit from specific development
- there is some overall judgement but it needs more development to make it substantial.

Use the feedback on this essay to rewrite it, making as many improvements as you can.

Paper 3: A Level sample answer with comments

Section A

These questions require you to analyse and evaluate source material with respect to its historical context.
For these questions remember to:

- look at the evidence given in the source and consider how the source could be used in differing ways to provide historical understanding
- use your knowledge of the historical context to discuss any limitations the source may have
- use your historical understanding to evaluate the source, considering how much weight you would give to its argument
- come to a judgement on the overall value of the source in respect to the question.

Study Source 3 (Chapter 6, page 137) before you answer this question.

Assess the value of the source for revealing the methods used by witch-hunters and common perceptions of witches' covens in the 17th century.

Explain your answer, using the source, the information given about its origin and your own knowledge about the historical context. (20 marks)

Strong student answer

The source was produced in the midst of the greatest witch-hunt ever to take place in England. While the country was being ravaged by civil war, Matthew Hopkins and John Stearne were able to take advantage of both existing and new fears in Essex and Suffolk. The confession of Rebecca West featured in the source was a breakthrough for the witchfinders, who were then able to expand their scope and influence into Norfolk, Cambridgeshire and beyond.

The social, political and religious context is essential to fully understand the source. East Anglia was a hotbed of Puritanism and ideally suited to witch-hunting. A number of Catholic gentry had also been based there who went to fight for the king. With the county coming under immense pressure as a result of the war, with ten percent of men killed fighting, traditional legal structures were interrupted. As well as this, the price of wheat increased by 20 percent, enclosure of land and new taxes required to pay for the war effort enhanced existing pressures and people looked for others to blame for their misfortunes. The common perception of a witch as a poor outcast (usually female) was emphasised more than ever in the East Anglian witch-hunt, and women such as Rebecca West were easy targets for angry neighbours. The pamphlet that featured her confession was distributed widely and published in London, which suggests that there was a great interest in the hunt in other parts of the country. Indeed, it is highly likely that parliament sanctioned the hunt, as they had sanctioned William Dowsing to act as 'Iconoclast General' in 1643.

The source reveals much regarding the methods used by witchfinders, and gives a number of subtle indications of popular attitudes towards witches' covens. It is likely that the transcript found in the source is from the original court records, and West begins by immediately naming other witches. It should be noted that West became a witness for the Crown, and therefore she was likely to be rewarded or treated more leniently in exchange for an elaborate confession that named many other witches. They are described as spending 'some time in praying unto their Familiars'. It was a common belief in the 17th century that witches met in groups – usually of 13 – and that they would consult with familiar spirits. Elizabeth Clark, who is mentioned in the source, was known as a ringleader and she was inspected by four search-women. In Hopkins' own account, he records that Clark possessed a number of familiars. Matthew Hopkins took a

A focused opening that provides some important context, illustrated with specific evidence. The awareness of the political and religious context of the Civil War is particularly strong.

This paragraph tackles the key issue of witches' covens and relates the source material to their own contextual knowledge of popular attitudes towards witchcraft.

particular interest in finding evidence of familiars, and the practice of 'watching' was a regular feature of his investigations. The mention of the group continuing to 'read in a book' is also of note, as witches were known to sign the Devil's Book, often as part of an initiation pact.

In terms of the methods used by witch-hunters, a number of inferences can be made from the source. Extracting confessions was the most crucial way Hopkins and Stearne could secure convictions, and West's evidence was invaluable at a number of trials. West also names her own mother as a witch, when the source states 'this Examinant further saith, that the said Anne West, this Examinants mother, desired of her Spirit, that shee might be freed from all her enemies'. The witch-hunters were also concerned with finding evidence that familiars had been responsible for causing harm, and this is mentioned a number of times. It is mentioned that West used her familiar to cause harm to the wife of Thomas Hart, and the witch-hunters would regularly use evidence of people who had been mysteriously lamed in order to secure convictions for witchcraft. Hopkins and Stearne separated shortly after the interrogations of Rebecca West and the other women she named, and it was usual for them to spend only a short time in each parish. Once they had secured confessions such as West's that could be used in court, they moved on in order to collect more money from other suspicious neighbours. The first batch of 20 witches, which included the women mentioned by West, were executed in Chelmsford in July 1645.

> This section provides more context and explains and illustrates the methods used by the witchfinders, as required in the question.

Overall, it is clear that common perceptions of witchcraft were reflected in court proceedings, as the witchfinders were concerned with the discovery of covens and familiars. However, the need for torture and to secure confessions is also highlighted in the source. The 20 witches executed at Chelmsford may not have been convicted if Rebecca West did not confess. What is missing from the source is any tangible evidence of torture, although it is well known that this was involved in securing convictions. Dubious methods such as the swimming test were also used by Hopkins, and 'watching' and 'walking' were used and accepted by the courts as legitimate methods of investigation.

> A balanced conclusion which explains the significance of the source in showing both the methods and popular perceptions of witches.

The source is very valuable, providing a specific example of a detailed confession from the East Anglian trials. The fear present in the population is evident, as well as the bitterness that was felt by neighbours who had suspected these women for a long time, in some cases decades.

Verdict

This is a strong answer because:

- it identifies and illustrates the key points in the source

- it deploys some effective own knowledge to develop these points and provide context
- it reaches a clear and substantiated conclusion.

Paper 3: A Level sample answer with comments

Section B

These questions require you to show your understanding of a period in depth. They will ask you about a quite specific period of time and require you to make a substantiated judgement about a specific aspect you have studied.

For these questions remember to:

- organise your essay and communicate it in a manner that is clear and comprehensible
- use historical knowledge to analyse and evaluate the key aspect of the question
- make a balanced argument that weighs up differing opinions
- make a substantiated overall judgement on the question.

To what extent was the North Berwick witch-hunt in the years 1590–91 influenced by events in Denmark? (20 marks)

Average student answer

The North Berwick witch trials were incredibly influential. They caused the king, James VI, to become increasingly suspicious of witches and in 1597 he published *Daemonologie*. They also influenced the wider Scottish panic that spread to counties such as Stirlingshire in the late 1590s. The later hunt also came at a time of widespread plague and a poor harvest, conditions noted by historians as ideal for witch-hunts. It also seems that a 'general commission' was established after the North Berwick hunt in order to investigate cases of witchcraft further. In 1595, authorities in Edinburgh tortured Alison Balfour for two days and her son and daughter were both tortured. She was executed despite the fact that she recanted her original confession and the case goes some way to explaining why the Privy Council began to wind down the number of investigations they approved.

Witch-hunting in Denmark influenced events in Scotland for a number of reasons. Denmark had a strong tradition of witch-hunting, although they did not believe in the satanic pact and torture was not officially used. It went through a Protestant Reformation like Scotland, and there was strong anti-Catholic feeling behind many accusations. Peter Palladius was a clergyman who strongly encouraged witch-hunting and by 1590 there had been a number of recent cases. When James wanted to meet his bride, Anne of Denmark, he suggested that she travel to Scotland but her journey was delayed three times by storms. James then intended to send the Earl of Bothwell to collect her, but was told by the Treasury that he should collect her in person to save money. When he did attempt to travel to Denmark, he was delayed by storms and had a difficult journey. This is when witchcraft was first suggested as an explanation for the events. The North Berwick witches eventually admitted to raising storms to sink Anne's ship and use demons to board the ship and pull it under the water.

James VI of Scotland had a personal belief in witches. He wrote a book on witch-hunting in 1597 called *Daemonologie*. In it, he attempted to prove that witches and necromancers have a close association with the Devil, and that a number of methods can be used to discover witches. He advocated searching for the Devil's mark, as well as the swimming test. He also recommended the use of fasting and prayer to cure cases of possession, and mentioned the particular vulnerability of women to the temptations of the Devil. He personally interrogated a number of the suspected witches at North Berwick, and probably approved of their torture. James became particularly convinced by the reality of witchcraft when one of the accused witches, Agnes Sampson, took him aside and repeated the exact words that had passed between him and Anne on their wedding night.

This is a weak opening paragraph because it concentrates on the impact of the North Berwick witch-hunt rather than the causes and does not introduce the factors that will be discussed in the essay, especially the impact of events in Denmark.

This paragraph is too descriptive and vague, and does not explicitly state why events in Denmark caused the North Berwick hunt to become extensive.

This paragraph includes an adequate discussion of James' role, but fails to evaluate this against any other factors, leading to a descriptive approach. The discussion of the contents of *Daemonologie* is irrelevant because the book was published years after the 1590–91 hunt.

The trials became extensive because of the weaknesses of monarchy. Historically, Scotland had been home to a number of rival clans who regularly came into conflict with each other, and James himself had a number of rivals. The Earl of Bothwell was one of these, and he was caught up in the witch-hunt himself. There were few judges able to assist James in his duties, and local hunts could easily spiral out of control. Suspicious neighbours had little to stop them if they wanted to pursue convictions and although the Privy Council was supposed to approve the use of torture, it was regularly used without their permission.

> Although this is a relevant paragraph, it is too brief to gain significant credit and does not use enough specific evidence from the North Berwick hunt.

Scottish society was very patriarchal and women were viewed with suspicion by the authorities. Like most countries, the majority of people accused of witchcraft were women, and the children of accused witches would suffer the same reputation as their parents. These children were referred to as 'witch's get' and would be viewed with suspicion throughout their lives. Women who were antisocial or caused their neighbours distress were often labelled as witches. Women who practised folk magic and healing were also likely to be accused. Scotland was also poor and in the 16th century was liable to experience poor harvests and plague.

> A general discussion about witchcraft in Scotland that is not specific to the North Berwick hunt or the demands of the question.

In conclusion, events in Denmark were crucial in explaining why the witch-hunt became extensive. Danish witch-hunting was less extensive than Scottish, but when James arrived in Denmark he soon realised that the only explanation for his misfortunes at sea was witchcraft. The entire case centred on the storms that affected his and Anne's ships, and if it was not for his voyage it is likely that no trials would have taken place and no one would have been executed.

> This conclusion is focused solely on events in Denmark, and no effort is made to evaluate this factor against any others discussed in the essay.

Verdict

This is an average answer because:

- it doesn't sustain focus on the specific question
- it deploys some accurate knowledge, but this is not used to best advantage

- it makes a judgement, but it lacks the illustration and explanation to be substantiated.

Use the feedback on this essay to rewrite it, making as many improvements as you can.

Paper 3: A Level sample answer with comments

Section B

These questions require you to show your understanding of a period in depth. They will ask you about a quite specific period of time and require you to make a substantiated judgement about a specific aspect you have studied.

For these questions remember to:

- organise your essay and communicate it in a manner that is clear and comprehensible
- use historical knowledge to analyse and evaluate the key aspect of the question
- make a balanced argument that weighs up differing opinions
- make a substantiated overall judgement on the question.

To what extent was the North Berwick witch-hunt in the years 1590–91 influenced by events in Denmark? (20 marks)

Strong student answer

The North Berwick witch-hunt took place against a backdrop of superstition, a weak monarchy and natural disasters. The central accusation in the hunt was that storms were conjured up by witches to prevent James VI and his new wife, Anne of Denmark, from travelling to Scotland after their marriage. Scotland already had an established tradition of witch-hunting, with an execution rate of 54 percent in all 16th- and 17th-century trials. Witch-hunting in Denmark, however, arrived relatively late. Suspected witches had more state protection than in Scotland, and in 1547 an Act was passed to ensure fair trials. Unlike Scotland, torture was not allowed, and the concept of the satanic pact was rarely mentioned. Despite the relative lack of desire to hunt witches among the Danish authorities, there had been a number of high-profile witch-hunts in the years leading up to the North Berwick panic, and there is no doubt that James was influenced by events in Denmark. Other factors that explain the extent of the North Berwick hunt should also be considered, such as the impact of Gilly Duncan's confession and wider views of women in Scotland, the personal role of James VI and the relatively weak royal and judicial systems.

This is a focused introduction providing context that is illustrated with specific detail. The factors that are going to be discussed are also introduced.

Denmark is linked to the North Berwick trials for two reasons. Firstly, a coven of witches was apparently discovered around the time of James' visit to his new bride, and secondly, James' visit itself convinced him that witches were working against him. Denmark had experienced a Protestant Reformation similar to the one Scotland had been through, and high-profile clergy such as Peter Palladius were known for encouraging witch-hunting. Palladius reported that 52 witches were killed in a single hunt. The most tangible link between Scottish and Danish witch-hunting, however, is the case of Anna Koldings. She was suspected in 1590 of interfering with the voyage of Anne and James. She gave up the names of five accomplices, one of whom was the wife of the mayor of Copenhagen. All of the suspects confessed to raising a storm to sink Anne's ship and send demons on board. Before Koldings and her accomplices were accused, the Danish finance minister was accused of negligence. He quickly placed the blame on one of Koldings' associates, which suggests the women were merely scapegoats.

This is an excellent assessment of the factor given in the question (the Danish connection). The impact of both Danish witch-hunting and James' voyage are discussed, and a counter-argument is provided to suggest that this factor may not be crucially important.

James' voyage itself was also influential. Anne of Denmark attempted to set sail for Scotland three times in 1589 and 1590, but storms prevented her from travelling. When James finally arrived to collect her, the outward and return journeys were both beset by problems with the weather. As well as this, there is little evidence to suggest James was interested in witchcraft before 1590, and it has been suggested by historians that James' meeting with a theologian, Niels Hemmingsen, in Denmark, may have encouraged his belief in witchcraft. However, because Danish beliefs rarely focused on the satanic pact, this argument is limited.

There can be no doubt that the witch-hunt would not have been as widespread if James did not take a personal interest in witches, and it can be argued that the storms he experienced in Denmark simply added to his existing state of superstition. As monarch, he was in a position to pursue accusations personally, as well as order a general commission to investigate witchcraft in Scotland as late as 1597. He viewed himself as an intellectual, and he was concerned with gaining as much knowledge as he could. Although it was published at the end of the wider Scottish witch-hunt, his book, *Daemonologie*, demonstrates his passion for witch-hunting. Some historians have argued, however, that his role in the panic is overstated, and that from 1592 he was content to pass much of the responsibility for dealing with cases on to other people.

> The alternative factor of James' role is put forward convincingly and is linked to the Danish connection.

Another important factor behind the North Berwick witch-hunt is the lack of strong central control and a strong legal system. The monarchy was relatively weak and Scotland had a long history of royal and clan rivalry. The fact that the Earl of Bothwell was so closely associated with events demonstrates just how volatile and vulnerable the monarchy was, as Bothwell was noted to be a rival to the throne. Scotland had a simpler system of government than England, with fewer royal agents at the monarch's disposal. Panic was able to spread quickly in this context. Torture could only be used officially with the consent of the Privy Council, but because the monarchy had limited resources, local magistrates were able to use harsh methods. The judicial system, which included the use of majority verdicts in jury trials, meant that convictions were more likely. There is no doubt that this factor is important, but it must be noted that the trials took place not outside of royal control, but with the consent of the king. His personal role, therefore, and his experience in Denmark, remains crucial.

> This factor is weighed up against the previous factors discussed.

Witch trials could not take place without confessions and the first, made at North Berwick by Gilly Duncan, set the tone for the entire hunt. She was noted for her healing abilities, and although she was neither old nor isolated, she was soon under suspicion from her employer, David Seaton. If it was not for Seaton's zeal, she may have never confessed. She was tortured with thumb-screws and with cords around her head, methods which were almost certainly not approved by the government. When she eventually confessed, she named a number of other people, such as Agnes Sampson and John Fian.

> Although not as strong as the previous paragraphs, this is an adequate counter-argument to the assumption that the trials were influenced only by events in Denmark.

Scotland was relatively poor, and in this context, the idea that the Devil was able to offer eternal riches would have been well received by some. Scotland was also a deeply patriarchal society, and antisocial women were quick to be labelled as witches.

In conclusion, it is clear that a number of factors contributed to the North Berwick witch-hunt becoming extensive in its scope, but it is unlikely that it would have gained momentum without the personal intervention of James VI. He personally interrogated suspects and strongly believed that they had been responsible for his personal misfortunes. It is also clear that his journey to Denmark and the witch-hunt that took place there encouraged him in his endeavours. However, Scottish society was already well suited for such a hunt taking place because the legal system and government were relatively weak.

> This is a sound conclusion that weighs up the various factors discussed in the essay and comes to a substantiated conclusion.

Verdict

This is a strong answer because:

- it identifies a range of key factors and links them into an argument
- it deploys some sound factual knowledge to illustrate and develop the points being made
- it examines both sides of the argument and argues a judgement.

Paper 3: A Level sample answer with comments

Section C

These questions require you to show your understanding of a subject over a considerable period of time. They will ask you to assess a long-term historical topic and its development over a period of at least 100 years, and they require you to make a substantiated judgement in relation to the question.

For these questions remember to:

- organise your essay and communicate it in a manner that is clear and comprehensible
- use historical knowledge to analyse and evaluate the key aspect of the question covering the entire period
- make a balanced argument that weighs up differing opinions
- make a substantiated overall judgement on the question.

How far do you agree that the publication of Reginald Scot's The Discoverie of Witchcraft *(1584) was the key turning point in belief in the power of witchcraft in the years c1580–c1750? (20 marks)*

Average student answer

Between 1580 and 1750, attitudes to witchcraft changed enormously. The belief that witches had entered into a pact with the Devil began to be questioned and in 1712 Jane Wenham was famously acquitted. At her trial, the judge stated that he could not hear evidence that she had been seen travelling through the sky because there was no law against flying. In 1736 the Witchcraft Act was repealed. Along the way, many sceptical cases became notorious and a number of sceptical works were published.

Reginald Scot was a member of the Family of Love, a radical sect that rejected many traditional Protestant and Catholic practices such as infant baptism. Their core belief was that nature controlled all events on Earth day-to-day rather than God. This group's particular dislike for the Catholic Church makes Scot's passion for rooting out frauds and superstition more understandable. In his book he criticised conjuring and magic tricks, which he associated with Catholics. He is also highly critical of the Catholic Inquisition for using false evidence to prosecute suspected witches.

Other than Scot, there were a number of other influential authors who wrote about witchcraft. One of these was Samuel Harsnett. Harsnett had been personally involved in the Boy of Burton case of 1596–97, where Thomas Darling had faked having fits and being possessed. Darling claimed that his fits became worse when passages of the New Testament were read out to him, confirming a doctor's suspicions that he had been bewitched. Alice Goodridge and Elizabeth Wright were identified as witches and Alice was arrested. The exorcist John Darrell became involved and apparently helped to heal Darling and another man, William Somers. Darling, Somers and Darrell were all ordered to London where they were examined by the Bishop of London and Samuel Harsnett, and Harsnett became suspicious. Harsnett then wrote a pamphlet where he revealed the fraud. He claimed that John Darrell called into question the reliability of witnesses, which is something that all guilty men do according to Harsnett. He also accused Darrell of being blasphemous due to the type of songs he played as an amateur musician. Other sceptical writers included Thomas Ady, John Webster and Balthasar Bekker, who were all influenced by Reginald Scot in some way.

> This is a weak opening paragraph which shows some address to the general topic but not to the specific question. In particular, there is no reference to Scot who is the central figure in the debate that the question is designed to provoke.

> This paragraph focuses on Scot and discusses his influences, but does not tackle the question directly. There is no analysis of the role of his book as a key turning point. There is some reference to the content of his book, but this is too brief.

> Although relevant, this section is quite descriptive and although it includes accurate factual detail, it is not linked to the demands of the question. There is far too much detail given to the Boy of Burton and Harsnett and the other sceptics are glossed over.

Other cases influenced popular opinion and encouraged people to become sceptical of witchcraft. Edmund Robinson started the Pendle Swindle in 1634. Robinson was ten years old and claimed that he was looking for plums one evening when he was approached by two dogs. One of the dogs turned into the wife of a local man that he knew and the other turned into a boy. He then reported that the boy turned into a white horse and he was forced to ride with the woman to a house where he witnessed a gathering of witches. The case was reported to the local magistrates and Robinson led them to a number of churches where he identified witches. A report of the case was sent by one of the judges to the Privy Council in London, and it was discovered that Robinson and his father were probably making false accusations. The women they accused were also sent to London and inspected by William Harvey and the king himself, Charles I. They were found to have no unnatural marks on their bodies. After the case ended Edmund Robinson worked with his father and uncle as a witchfinder. He would enter local churches and identify witches in the congregation. This may have made the family money. The boy eventually admitted that his father forced him to tell his original story, as he was motivated by revenge against one of the suspected witches, Frances Dickinson because they had entered into a dispute over the sale of a cow.

> This paragraph is far too descriptive and only discusses one sceptical case. It makes no links to the demands of the question and does not weigh this case up against Scot's work or the other sceptical publications.

The last witch to be executed in England was Alice Molland in 1684, and Jane Wenham was famously placed on trial in 1712. This was an important turning point because the case was not taken seriously and she was acquitted. She had a long-standing reputation as a wise-woman and she was supposed to have bewitched a farmer's daughter and Anne Thorne, a servant to a local clergyman. She confessed to practising magic but the judge at her trial was sceptical. There were a number of judges towards the end of the period who acquitted accused witches and this goes some way to explain why prosecutions became rare.

> A promising start with accurate factual material, but this paragraph does not directly address the question. Sceptical judges are mentioned but there are no specific examples given.

Overall there is no doubt that attitudes to witchcraft change significantly between 1580 and 1750. There were setbacks along the way, but Scot's beliefs still rang true at the end of the period. Many individuals and factors played a role, but there is no doubt that Scot's work set the trend for others and made the most significant contribution to the repealing of legislation.

> There is a judgement, but it is not substantiated and is largely assertion.

Verdict

This is an average answer because:

- there is some attempt to address to the topic in general but there is insufficient analysis regarding the specific question
- there is some deployment of own knowledge, including the sceptical works, but it is not wide ranging

- there is some coverage across the whole time period, but it needs more specific illustration and explanation
- there is a judgement, but it is not substantiated.

Use the feedback on this essay to rewrite it, making as many improvements as you can.

Paper 3: A Level sample answer with comments

Section C

These questions require you to show your understanding of a subject over a considerable period of time. They will ask you to assess a long-term historical topic and its development over a period of at least 100 years, and they require you to make a substantiated judgement in relation to the question.

For these questions remember to:

- organise your essay and communicate it in a manner that is clear and comprehensible
- use historical knowledge to analyse and evaluate the key aspect of the question covering the entire period
- make a balanced argument that weighs up differing opinions
- make a substantiated overall judgement on the question.

How far do you agree that the publication of Reginald Scot's The Discoverie of Witchcraft *(1584) was the key turning point in belief in the power of witchcraft in the years c1580–c1750? (20 marks)*

Strong student response

There is no question that Scot's *The Discoverie of Witchcraft* had a significant impact on attitudes towards witchcraft, and although it was not well received by everyone in intellectual circles at first, events over the next 150 years would certainly prove that his assertions about witchcraft were accurate. The fact that the Witchcraft Act was not modified until 1736, however, shows that changing attitudes were gradual, and a number of other sceptical publications, such as Thomas Ady's *A Candle in the Dark* and later John Webster's *The Displaying of Supposed Witchcraft* (1677) and Balthasar Bekker's *The Enchanted World* (1691) were perhaps more influential. As well as these publications, a number of key turning points contributed towards changing attitudes, such as the fraudulent cases of John Darrell and the Demon Drummer of Tedworth. Finally, judicial pressure ensured that convictions for witchcraft became rare from the late 17th century, with Sir John Holt playing a particularly vital role.

There is no doubt that Reginald Scot is an important figure in the development of sceptical beliefs towards witchcraft. *The Discoverie of Witchcraft* is recognised as the first major work of English scepticism, and he was greatly influenced by the Dutch physician Johan Weyer, who also held a sceptical view. As a member of the Family of Love, Scot despised the Catholic Church and his critical view of witchcraft was influenced by this. Scot disapproved of the Chelmsford witch trials that had taken place shortly before he published his work. Although Scot ultimately believed in witches, he disapproved of the methods used at Chelmsford. The 1582 hunt there was driven by Brian Darcy, who favoured harsh continental-style punishments.

Scot is an important figure because of his rationalist approach. In his work, he argued that many people who appeared to be possessed were in fact suffering from delusions, and he doubted that witches were able to use supernatural methods to cause harm. Instead, he argued, they inflicted pain through natural means such as the use of poison. He dedicated a significant portion of his book to criticising magic tricks, which he categorises with the sacraments of the Catholic Church. The Catholic Church is also blamed for the cruelty of the Inquisition. It could be argued that with such anti-Catholic feeling present in late 16th-century England, most people were not ready to accept Scot's interpretation and were happy to associate Catholicism with witchcraft. James VI ordered all copies of Scot's book to be burned.

As well as Scot, there were a number of other important authors who influenced changing beliefs in magic and witchcraft. Samuel Harsnett, for example, was suspicious of the so-called 'Boy of Burton' case and in particular the exorcist John Darrell. In 1599 he wrote *A Discovery*

This is a focused introduction which identifies the significance of Scot's work, but also introduces a number of other issues relevant to the question.

The points in these paragraphs are effectively supported. They demonstrate extensive knowledge of Scot's book, and also include a brief discussion of the drawbacks to his work in order to provide a counter-argument.

of the Fraudulent Practises of John Darrel, where, like Scot, he criticised the Catholic Church for focusing too much on rituals and superstition. His work is also highly critical of Darrell's methods. A pamphlet war was started by Harsnett, and he gained support in Puritan circles. However, Harsnett's view was still a minority opinion.

> Other sceptical works are used to compare with Scot's, and they are placed in context and relevant links between them are made clear.

Other sceptical works included Thomas Ady's *A Candle in the Dark*, which used the Bible to discount contemporary beliefs in witches and also mentions magicians and conjurors, as well as John Webster's *The Displaying of Supposed Witchcraft*, which claimed that although witches did exist, they were not able to command supernatural powers. In 1691, Balthasar Bekker published *The Enchanted World*. This work gained more attention than many other sceptical publications, and whereas Scot relied on rumours and stories, Bekker approached his work in a more reasoned way. He used this reason to argue that it is impossible for the Devil to influence events on Earth because he is forever banished to hell. Although Bekker had no particularly new ideas to put forward, his book sold 4,000 copies in its first two months, and it has been argued by historians that his influence coincided with a general change in the intellectual climate.

A number of fraudulent cases influenced the sceptical writers, including the Pendle Swindle in 1634. A young boy, Edmund Robinson, was discovered to have lied about witnessing a meeting of witches. The Demon Drummer of Tedworth case (1662) also became infamous. The apparent haunting initially became nationally famous, and Joseph Glanvill, a member of the Royal Society, claimed to have witnessed supernatural events at Tedworth. Both Webster and Bekker later criticised Glanvill's account.

> A limited paragraph that discusses fraudulent cases. Although not as strong as earlier sections, it provides sound evidence and a relevant argument.

Finally, scepticism from judicial circles ensured that attitudes towards witchcraft changed. Sir George Mackenzie, a Scottish judge, defended a suspected witch in court and spent much of the 1670s and 80s attempting to convince other legal professionals that approaches to witchcraft cases encouraged miscarriages of justice. Sir John Holt, Lord Chief Justice from 1689, acquitted every witch that was presented to him, sometimes in the face of determined opposition. Despite Holt's efforts, his immediate predecessor, Matthew Hale, was willing to accept dubious evidence in cases of witchcraft, and it would be decades before the Witchcraft Act was modified.

> A final factor, that of judicial scepticism, includes specific examples and is relevant to the overall argument.

Jane Wenham, who was famously found guilty of witchcraft and then acquitted in 1712, also benefited from a sceptical judge, Sir John Powell. Powell discounted evidence in Wenham's trial from witnesses who said they had witnessed her flying, and even endeavoured to secure a royal pardon.

In conclusion, the work of Reginald Scot clearly set the tone for further scepticism regarding magic and witchcraft. Although his work was not vastly popular in his lifetime, other authors essentially followed his lead and offered little in the way of new arguments. With a changing intellectual climate and an increase in fraudulent cases, later authors such as John Webster and Balthasar Bekker received more attention. It was only when the judicial climate changed, however, that real action could be taken, and this only took place towards the end of the period, when Sir John Holt was at the height of his powers. On balance, Scot's work may not be the key turning point in the period, but without it the intellectual framework that would eventually lead to the end of witchcraft legislation would have been very different.

> The concluding paragraph emphasises overall development and makes clear the contribution of the factor cited in the question. It then comes to a supported conclusion.

Verdict

This is a strong answer because:

- it addresses the stated factor and illustrates and explains its significance
- it identifies a sound range of other factors with some effective illustration
- it develops an overall argument and comes to a supported judgement.

Index

Acknowledgements

The authors and publisher would like to thank the following individuals and organisations for permission to reproduce photographs and text in this book.

Photographs

(Key: b-bottom; c-centre; l-left; r-right; t-top)

akg-images Ltd: British Library 102; **Alamy Images:** AF Archive 130, Art Directors and TRIP 99, Classic Image 53, Interfoto 8, 26, 90, 113, 118, 122, 127, Lebrecht Music and Arts Photo Library 39, National Geographic Image Collection 6, North Wind Picture Archives 161, 165, Pictorial Press Ltd 41, 47, 133, World History Archive 139, 167; **Bridgeman Art Library Ltd:** Private Collection 97; **Library of Congress, Prints and Photographs Division:** 169; **Mary Evans Picture Library:** 12; **TopFoto:** British Library Board 19; **Wellcome Library, London:** 28, 34, 56

Cover image: Corbis: Bettmann

All other images © Pearson Education

Figures

Figure 3.3 data from The Survey of Scottish Witchcraft, www.shca.ed.ac.uk/Research/witches/ © University of Edinburgh; Figure 4.3 adapted from *The Trials of the Lancashire Witches*, 4th ed., Hendon Publishing Co. Ltd (Peel, E. and Southern, P.1994) p.174, Appendix 3 © Edgar Peel and Pat Southern 1969, 1972, 1985, 1994. Figure 5.2 from Frost Witches: The Spark of the Bamberg Witch Craze, *Oglethorpe Journal of Undergraduate Research (OJUR)*, Vol. 2, Issue 1, Article 3, p.16 (Palframan, J. R. 2013), http://digitalcommons.kennesaw.edu/ojur/vol2/iss1/3; Figure 6.3 from *Witchcraft, Magic and Superstition in England, 1640–70*, Ashgate Publishing (Valletta, F.V.A. 2000) p.171 © Frederick Valletta 2000 (Source of data: CUL, MSS E/12, Ely assize files); Figure 6.4 adapted from *Literacy and Social Development in the West: A reader*, Cambridge University Press (Graff, H. J. (ed.) 1981), Ch. 6 Levels of Literacy in England 1530–1730 by David Cressy, p.108, Table 6.1.

Text

Source 1 p.10 from *The Malleus Maleficarum of Heinrich Kramer and James Sprenger* (1486) (Lovelace, W. and Rice, C. (transcribed by)) Part II, Question I, Chapter II, http://www.malleusmaleficarum.org/downloads/MalleusAcrobat.pdf; Source 4 p.14 from *A true report of the strange torments of Thomas Darling, a boy of thirteene years of age, that was possessed of the Devil, with his horrible fittes and terrible Apparitions by him uttered at Burton upon Trent in the County of Stafford, and of his marvellous deliverance* (Darling, T. (attrib.) 1597) http://faculty.history.wisc.edu/sommerville/367/J.D.%20Wonderful.htm#coppice; Source 6 p. 17, Extract 3 p.100 and Source 7 p.100 from *The Trials of the Lancashire Witches*, 4th ed., Hendon Publishing Co. Ltd (Peel, E. and Southern, P.1994) pp.97, 40, 42 © Edgar Peel and Pat Southern 1969, 1972, 1985, 1994; Extract 1 p.22 from *A Popular History of Witchcraft* (Routledge Library Editions: Witchcraft), Routledge (Summers, M. 2011) p.231; Extract 2 p.23 from Hole, Christina. *Witchcraft in England* (1977). Reproduced with kind permission of B.T. Batsford, part of Pavilion Books Company Limited.; Extract 3 p.24 from *Witch Hunts in the Western World*, Greenwood Press, an imprint of ABC-CLIO, LLC (Pavlac, B.A. 2009) p.145 Copyright © 2009 by Brian A. Pavlac Republished with permission of Greenwood Publishing Group, Inc. in the format Republish in a book via Copyright Clearance Center, permission conveyed through Copyright Clearance Center, Inc. ; Extract 4 p.26 and Extract 2 p.113 ©

Bengt Ankerloo, Stuart Clark and William Monter, 2002, Witchcraft and Magic in Europe: Volume 4: The Period of the Witch Trials, The Athlone Press, an imprint of Bloomsbury Publishing Plc; Source 11 p.31 and Source 12 p.32 from *A Candle in the Dark* (Ady, T. 1656) pp.6–7, Cornell University Library Witchcraft Collection; Source 14 and Source 15 p.35 from Balthasar Bekker, *The Enchanted World* (1691) and Source 1 p.67 from *Newes from Scotland* (1591) from *Witchcraft in Europe, 1100–1700*, University of Pennsylvania Press, Inc (Kors, A. and Peters, E. 1972) pp.372–3, 374, 224 Reprinted with permission of the University of Pennsylvania Press.; Source 3 p.44 from *Johannes Kepler Gesammelte Werke* (M. Caspar et al. (eds) 1937) Vol. 3: *Astronomia Nova*, pp.177–8, Translated from the German by J.V. Field (MacTutor History of Mathematics archive, School of Mathematics and Statistics, University of St Andrews, Scotland, http://www-history.mcs.st-and.ac.uk/Quotations/Kepler.html); Source 5 p.47 republished with permission of University of California Press from *Dialogue Concerning the Two Chief World Systems, Ptolemaic and Copernican* 2nd rev. ed., Galilei, G. (author), Drake, S. (translator) 1963 permission conveyed through Copyright Clearance Center, Inc.; Extract 1 p.48 from *Galileo: Decisive Innovator*, Cambridge University Press (Sharratt, M. 1996) Preface (pp.xi, xii); Extract 2 p.50 from Henry, J., *The Scientific Revolution and the Origins of Modern Science*, 2008, Palgrave Macmillan reproduced with permission of Palgrave Macmillan; Source 6 p.52 and Source 7 p.53 from *Novum Organum* (Bacon, F. 1620) Preface, xcv, http://www.constitution.org/bacon/nov_org.htm; Source 10 p.57 from The Royal Society, https://royalsociety.org/about-us/history/royal-charters/; Source 3 p.58 from The Royal Society and the Decline of Magic, *Notes and Records of the Royal Society of London*, Vol. 65, No. 2 pp.103–119 (Hunter, M. 2011) by permission of the Royal Society; Source 2 p.71 and Extract 3 p.81 from *The Demonology of King James I: Includes the Original Text of Daemonologie and News from Scotland* by Donald Tyson, copyright 2011 Llewellyn Publications, 2143 Wooddale Drive, Woodbury, MN55125. All rights reserved, used by permission; Extract 1 p.80 from The 'Devil' of North Berwick, *The Scottish Historical Review*, Vol. 15, No. 60, p.318 (Murray, M. 1918); Extract 2 p.81 from *Witchcraft and Black Magic*, Dover Publications Inc. (Summers, M. 1946) p.90, Reprint edition (1 Feb. 2000); Source 1 p.89, Extract 1 p.92 and Extract 2 p.94 from *The Lancashire Witches: Histories and Stories*, Manchester University Press (Poole, R. (ed.) 2002) pp.76–7, Chapter 5 'Witchcraft, economy and society in the forest of Pendle', Swain, J., p.28, Chapter 2 'Potts, plots and politics: James I's Daemonologie and The Wonderfull Discoverie of Witches', Pumfrey, S., pp.80, 81, Chapter 5 'Witchcraft, economy and society in the forest of Pendle', Swain, J.; Extract 1 p.113 from Hugh Trevor-Roper, *The Crisis of the Seventeenth Century: Religion, the Reformation and Social Change*, Chapter 3 The European Witch-Craze of the Sixteenth and Seventeenth Centuries, Section IV, (Indianapolis: Liberty Fund, 2001). 11/10/2015 <http://oll.libertyfund.org/titles/719>; Source 2 p.115 Republished with permission of Routledge from *Witchcraft in Continental Europe: New Perspectives on Witchcraft, Magic, and Demonology*, Routledge (Levack, B. P. 2013) Chapter 'Godly States': confessional conflict and witch-hunting in early modern Germany by R. Walinski-Kiehl, (book first published in 2002), in the format Republish in a book via Copyright Clearance Center permission conveyed through Copyright Clearance Center, Inc.; Source 3 p.117, and Source 10 p.125 adapted from *Reformation and the German Territorial State: Upper Franconia, 1300–1630*, University of Rochester Press (Bradford Smith, W. 2008) pp.276, 179; Source 5 p.119, Source 6 p.120, Source 7 p.120 from *Translations and Reprints from the Original Sources of European History*, Vol III, No. 4, University of Pennsylvania History Department (Burr, G. L. 1896) The Witch-Persecutions, pp.23–28; Source 8 p.121 from Witches' Confessions: Stereotypical Structure and Local Colour – The Case of the Prince-Bishopric of Bamberg, *Southern Humanities Review*, Vol. XXIV, No. 4 Fall, pp.303–4 (Sebald, H. 1990), Copyright 1990 by Auburn University; Source 11 p.126 from The petition of Barbara Schwarz, 20 September 1630, translated by Steven Banks; Extract 1 p.134 from *Witch Hunts in Europe and America: An Encyclopedia* Greenwood Publishing Group (Burns, W. E. 2003) pp.208–209, republished with permission of Greenwood Publishing Group in the format Republish in a book via Copyright Clearance Center, permission conveyed through Copyright Clearance Center, Inc.; Source 3 p.137 adapted from *A true and exact relation of the severall informations, examinations, and confessions of the late witches, arraigned and executed in the county of Essex* (1645) http://www.witchtrials.co.uk/trial.html, thanks to Steve Hulford, www.witchtrials.co.uk; Source 4 p.138 and Source 8 p.145 from *A Confirmation and Discovery of Witchcraft* (Stearne, J. 1648) http://www.witchtrials.co.uk/stearne.html; Transcribed into Modern English by Steve Hulford 2005©, thanks to Steve Hulford, www.witchtrials.co.uk; Extract 2 p.140 from Witches, Wives and Mothers: witchcraft persecution and women's confessions in seventeenth-century England, *Women's History Review*, Vol 4 (1), pp.63–83 (quote pp.80–81) (Jackson, L. 1995), Taylor & Francis, reprinted by permission of the publisher (Taylor & Francis Ltd, http://www.tandfonline.com); Extract 3 p.143 from *Witchfinders: A Seventeenth-Century*

English Tragedy, John Murray (Gaskill, M. 2006) pp.273–4, Copyright © 2005 Malcolm Gaskill, reproduced by permission of John Murray, a division of Hodder and Stoughton Limited.; Source 10 and Source 11 on p.148 from *Select Cases of Conscience touching Witches and Witchcrafts* (Gaule, J. 1646), Courtesy of The Norris Museum; Extract 1 p.156 from *In The Devil's Snare: The Salem Witchcraft Crisis of 1692* by Mary Beth Norton, copyright © 2002 by Mary Beth Norton. Used by permission of Alfred A. Knopf, an imprint of the Knopf Doubleday Publishing Group, a division of Penguin Random House LLC. All rights reserved. 'Any third party use of this material, outside of this publication, is prohibited. Interested parties must apply directly to Penguin Random House LLC for permission.'; Source 1 p.157 from *Narrative of the Planting of the Massachusetts Colony* (Scottow, J. 1694) pp.39–40, http://digitalcommons.unl.edu/scottow/4/; DigitalCommons@University of Nebraska–Lincoln, transcribed and edited by Paul Royster; Extract 2 p.159 from The Geography of Witchcraft Accusations in 1692 Salem Village, *William and Mary Quarterly*, 3rd series, Vol. LXV, No. 3, July, p.453 (Ray, B. C. 2008); Source 3 p.160 and Source 4 p.161 from *Memorable Providences relating to Witchcraft and Possessions* (Mather, C. 1689) http://law2.umkc.edu/faculty/projects/ftrials/salem/asa_math.htm; Doug Linder, Professor of Law (Seminar in Famous Trials). © 1995–2011; Source 9 p.170 from *A letter from Governor William Phips to an unknown recipient in England, 12 October 1692* (1692) http://law2.umkc.edu/faculty/projects/ftrials/salem/asa_lett.htm; Doug Linder, Professor of Law (Seminar in Famous Trials). © 1995–2011.